41 Belgrave Squ [illegible] ACSAB since 1956, became so well known in local government that 'Belgrave Square' became almost the collective noun for LACSAB and the negotiating bodies. Visitors were surprised that tough negotiations were held in such elegant surroundings in a building that, in turn, was the home of one of Queen Victoria's sons, an Archbishop of York, a First Lord of the Admiralty, a Marquis (and in turn his three wives) and a Baronet Member of Parliament. In 1911, No. 41 was lent to the Archduke Charles of Austria-Hungary when, as heir apparent to the eleven nation Empire, he arrived in Britain to attend the coronation of King George V. Charles was the nephew of the direct heir, Archduke Franz Ferdinand whose violent death at Sarajevo was to spark off a world war.

The house was built in 1831 on land that had previously been little more than swamp and marsh. Most of the area now known as Belgravia had passed into the possession of the Grosvenor family in 1656 when the daughter of Alexander Davies Esq of Ebury Farm married Sir Thomas Grosvenor the ancestor of the Duke of Westminster. The long lease on No. 41 was purchased by LACSAB in 1956 for the princely sum of £43,625 and at a rent fixed at £400 per annum until the year 2043.

ACKNOWLEDGEMENTS

A History of the Local Authorities Conditions of Service Advisory Board. First published in Great Britain in 1991 by Centurion Press Limited, 52 George Street, London W1H 5RF.

Photo Credits

Paul Popper Ltd – pages 29, 37, 38, 44, 45
Network – pages 22, 54, 56, 66, 78, 91, 101, 145, 153, 156, 184, 186, 193
Format – pages 60, 131, 132, 172
The Press Association – pages 46, 73, 109
Photo Co-op – pages 123, 141, 164, 180, 183

British Library Cataloguing Publication Data

Kelly, Geoffrey
A History of LACSAB: Industrial Relations in Local Government

1. Great Britain. Local Government. Personnel. Industrial Relations.
I. Title
331. 04132080941

ISBN 0-948500-50-0

Typeset by Senator Graphics, London.

Printed and bound in Great Britain by
Centurion Press Limited, 52 George Street, London W1H 5RF.

CENTURION

The Local Authorities' Employers Organisation

A HISTORY OF THE LOCAL AUTHORITIES' CONDITIONS OF SERVICE ADVISORY BOARD 1947 to 1991

Industrial Relations in Local Government

By Geoff Kelly

FOREWORD

I have for many years felt that the history, work, successes and disappointments of LACSAB should be recorded in one document.

My 30 years' association with the Board as customer, professional colleague, employee and finally Secretary, has enabled me to see at first hand the pivotal role that the organisation has played in the development of personnel management and industrial relations in local government and to appreciate the breadth and importance of its work.

Although a limited company (retaining its formal title of the Local Authorities' Conditions of Service Advisory Board) the Board has always been firmly rooted in local government and has operated as one of its 'Associations'. In recent years it adopted the title of the Local Authorities' Employers' Organisation - a much better description of its role and responsibilities. As a major employer local government holds an important place in the economic life of the country and its personnel and industrial relations policies have to be set in that context. Some measure of the scope and complexity of LACSAB's activities can be grasped by the fact that the industrial relations system covers 24 separate negotiating bodies involving 400 employer seats filled by representatives of 30 separate organisations who meet 40 trade unions to negotiate pay and conditions for some 2 million employees of 500 local authorities.

When it became clear that a phase of LACSAB's history would be coming to an end with the merger with the Local Government Training Board from 1 April 1991 it seemed to me even more appropriate to produce this brief history.

All I had to do was to set the ball in motion and decide who should be asked to write the book and to publish it. In both cases the choice was an easy one.

Geoffrey Kelly had recently retired after 23 years of distinguished service to LACSAB during which he had served under three Secretaries and had worked in most of our negotiating areas. I knew he could be counted upon to produce a professional, honest and accurate account of LACSAB's activities.

I had first met David Evans, now the Managing Director of Centurion Press, in 1963 when he was a junior representative of another publishing company and I was a relatively junior officer at LACSAB. Despite his subsequent success, David has handled much of LACSAB's printing work ever since and has maintained an interest in the organisation which has gone beyond any normal business relationship.

I am most grateful to both of them for making this book possible.

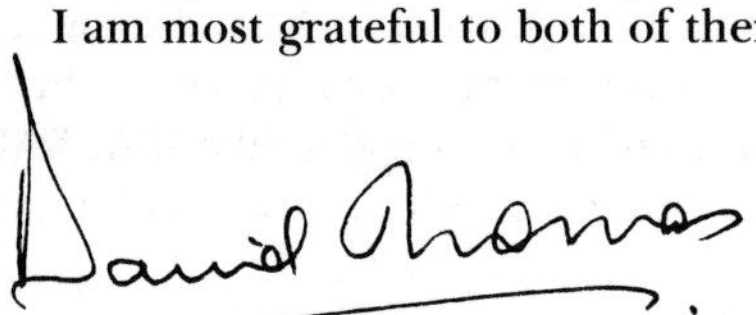

David Thomas
Secretary

PREFACE

LACSAB was a fascinating - dare I say unique? - outfit to work for, so when David Thomas, the LACSAB Secretary, asked me shortly before I retired to write a history of the organisation I readily agreed. The normal pressures of work at LACSAB meant that I got little done before I left and so this has mostly been done in my first few months of retirement.

David and I both had in mind a shorter book than what is now before you. The more I grappled with it, the more I believed that a much shorter version would be little more than a catalogue of events: dry bones without any life breathed into them. A meaningful record of what has happened at LACSAB over its forty or so years must give a flavour of the many negotiating issues of the day - not only the exciting topics which captured the headlines, but also the routine grind through which much was achieved quietly with a minimum of fuss.

So I have tried to identify the main issues dealt with by the LACSAB Board and also the principal negotiations conducted. To give some idea of the typical work of LACSAB I have sought to show the continuous thread of negotiations for the major negotiating bodies together with a few of the more special issues of other groups.

A difficult problem has been how best to marshal the material. To give a year by year account of everything going on across the spectrum of LACSAB activities would destroy any thread of continuity in the separate spheres. To deal with each negotiating group separately would mask the extent of co-ordination achieved by LACSAB and how one negotiation impacted on others. So I have endeavoured to reflect both continuity and co-ordination by breaking the LACSAB story into nine periods, not of even size, but using natural breaks as they occurred. I have first outlined the political and economic context for each period before recording the main LACSAB events as this often had a profound influence on the direction and shape of what LACSAB had to do. The manual worker group naturally came first in the record of negotiations on account of being one of the original three groups on the creation of LACSAB and because so often they became the pacesetters for many pay rounds. I have tried wherever possible to describe negotiations on pay before moving on to non-pay issues: but life at LACSAB was never that simple, and I could not be dogmatic on this when pay and non-pay issues were inextricably interwoven.

I have been greatly helped as the LACSAB house journals - News Summary, Local Government Manpower and Local Government Employment - have provided a contemporaneous public account of what has happened at LACSAB and at the same time put this in the setting of the economic and political life of the time. So these have been my major source except for the first five years before they were published. This has mercifully meant that I did not have to pore endlessly over the billions of words which have poured forth from Belgrave Square in the form of agenda, minutes, circulars, etc. I have however studied all the minutes of the LACSAB Board, some selected papers of specific negotiating groups and certain other sources, such as NALGO's histories – "White Collar Union" and "Path to Maturity", as well as "Wages and Employment Policy, 1936-1985" by Russell Jones. And of course I have also relied on my memory of all that took place during my 23 years' stint at Belgrave Square.

It is not surprising that on occasion the LACSAB journals have been rather coy in the way they have recorded events: for example, they could hardly be expected to expose the full extent of successful industrial action at the time, or to be too explicit about the more extravagant settlements which would arouse most envy – but the truth usually emerges eventually at a safe interval.

Readers may notice that I have written at greater length about more recent years and wonder whether this is due to my own greater knowledge and interest in latter events. That certainly was not my intention: it does I believe reflect the wider breadth of activities and complexities of modern times, such as the teachers' and manual workers' marathons of the 1980s.

In typical LACSAB style there is little reference in this account of events to the personalities involved – whether they be LACSAB officers, elected members or trade union officials. I think this is right and properly accepts the continuing emphasis at LACSAB on the corporate image and collective responsibility, as well as recognising the sustained effort of many loyal people behind the scenes. In any event it would now be hazardous and well-nigh impossible to rewrite the stories of yesteryear in terms of the personalities concerned. To balance this to some extent I have included brief pen pictures of some of the main players at the end of each chapter.

All smiles at the last LACSAB Reception held in 1990. Left to right: David Thomas (Secretary), John Toft (Vice-Chairman), Sir John Lovill (Chairman 1977 to 1983), Sid Dennett (Chairman 1989 to 1990) and Tony Prendergast (Chairman 1983 to 1989)

As I have largely used material from LACSAB's own journals there has seemed no point in indulging in multitudinous cross-references which can be distracting. Where appropriate I have acknowledged sources in the text.

I have been obliged to use acronyms liberally if only to save a lot of space! I have tried to spare a thought for the reader puzzled by much trade jargon by a propitious sprinkling of full titles. In addition I have incorporated a glossary of acronyms and abbreviations in the index at the back of this book.

I sincerely hope that the outcome in the following pages is not only seen as an authentic account of the activities of LACSAB from 1947 to 1991, but that it also proves to be of considerable interest and benefit to readers from a variety of backgrounds, such as those involved in personnel management and industrial relations in local government as well as students of industrial relations. For I reckon that this shows what an immense and sustained influence this one national employers organisation has had on the events of post-second world war Britain, especially in its own sphere of industrial relations and as a national organisation of local government. Many readers more steeped in the climate of the last decade will find it most difficult to appreciate the continuous vacillations, twists and turns of central government policies (irrespective of political colour) in the larger portion of LACSAB's history before the 1980s.

One matter of great regret to me is that what was intended as a history of one period of a living organisation has turned out to be its story from beginning to end as the proposals to merge LACSAB into a new Local Government Management Board come to fruition by March 1991.

I apologise in advance for any errors or omissions which I may have inadvertently perpetrated. I am especially conscious that it has not been possible to mention individually many of the stalwarts who have served LACSAB well over the years.

My special thanks go to David Thomas for his great encouragement and help throughout; to many LACSAB colleagues past and present for their help in providing the data on which I have relied; to David Evans and Michael Card for their kind guidance in the word processing/printing stages; and, last but not least, to my wife, Pat, for her forbearance and support as I spent much time in my first months of retirement concentrating on this book.

Geoff Kelly

J.H. Whitley in 1906, who was later to become the Speaker of the House of Commons from 1921 and 1928 and who was the father of 'Whitleyism'.

The 1906 election address of J. H. Whitley, parliamentary candidate for Halifax.

A Message to the Electors.

The long looked for Election at last is near at hand!

Be ready, by work and vote to strike a crushing blow at the attempted revival of Protection and Food Taxes.

The forces of Reaction are always strong.

Let the ranks of Progress be united & alert to give the power that alone can overcome all obstacles!

Then the year 1906 may mark a great and sound advance along the road of good government and Social Reform.

J.H. Whitley

1 ESTABLISHMENT AND ORIGINS

The Local Authorities' Conditions of Service Advisory Board (LACSAB) was established on 27th November 1947 arising from a proposal in 1946 by the local authority associations and the London County Council (LCC) to form a joint secretarial and information bureau. At that stage there were only three negotiating bodies which would come within the scope of the new Board –

- The National Joint Council for Local Authorities' Administrative, Professional, Technical and Clerical Services
- The National Joint Industrial Council for Local Authorities' Non-Trading Services (Manual Workers)
- The National Joint Council for County Council Roadmen

Until then there had been an employers' joint management committee co-ordinating staffing and accommodation issues on behalf of the employers' sides of these three negotiating bodies.

The constitution of the new Board provided that its functions were to co-ordinate the activities of the employers' sides of local authority wage negotiating bodies; to provide a joint secretariat; to maintain liaison with other employers; and to obtain and disseminate information on conditions of service.

Appointments of chairman and vice-chairman were delayed until the second meeting on 10th December 1948 when Sir George Mowbray, Bart. County Councils Association (CCA) was appointed chairman and Colonel S.P. Dawson, APT&C employers, as vice-chairman. Edward Bishop, who was already employers' secretary of the three negotiating bodies, was appointed as first LACSAB Secretary on secondment from the North Western provincial employers – and with a free flat provided in the London office at 37 Upper Grosvenor Street. Also included in the first permanent staff appointments made was H.G.(Harry) Rae from NALGO as Assistant Secretary.

The establishment of LACSAB in 1947 occurred as national collective bargaining was becoming widely recognised in local government after a chequered history of national "Whitleyism" (see footnote) since 1919. Until 1943 national employers' sides consisted only of representatives from provincial employers' sides: their recommendations were accepted neither by the local authority associations nor by the majority of local authorities. So, for example, the National APT&C Council was "national" in name only, with only 553 out of 1,530 local authorities (including but 3 out of 62 county councils) members of provincial councils and thus even indirectly represented on it. The other two-thirds remained outside, refusing to acknowledge their existence or to surrender

[FOOTNOTE. Sir Horace Wilson, Secretary of the Whitley Committee which reported on industrial relations in 1917 commented on the principles of 'whitleyism' at a LACSAB function in October 1957. Whitleyism was based on the belief that the cause of harmony in industry, and even in local government, was served by the creation of a body representative of both sides to discuss matters of common concern. Even when it was impracticable to say "Yes", it was at least all the more necessary to have machinery for saying "No". A copy of Whitley's election address of 1906 is included in the illustrations.]

the freedom they had enjoyed since the Public Health Act of 1875 to appoint, pay, treat and dismiss their staffs "at the pleasure of the Council".

At the beginning of the second world war NALGO were concerned about "astonishing" disparities in the pay and conditions of local government officers. They were convinced the only solution was collective bargaining on a national scale and that the existing National Council for administrative, technical and clerical staffs was powerless to overcome the opposition of many local authorities and their national associations. Their first approach to the Chamberlain Conservative government in February 1940 to achieve their objective received a dusty answer. Their second approach in August 1940 to Churchill's newly constructed National government gained a much more receptive hearing. Amid all the very serious wartime problems and nightly German air raids on London and other cities, the Minister of Health, Malcolm MacDonald, called a meeting of the local authority associations in November 1940 at which he urged them to form a joint committee with NALGO to build a truly National Whitley Council for white-collar staffs. Much wrangling and rancour followed, with the associations initially demanding abolition of all existing national and provincial negotiating bodies and that they alone should appoint employers' sides, fiercely opposed by those whose power and influence they sought to destroy. Concessions and compromises followed resulting eventually in a new national employers' side of 30 representatives, 15 appointed by the associations and 15 by the provincial employers. Thus LACSAB was conceived and created amidst tensions between the local authority associations and the provincial employers which have continued throughout its existence.

The employer representation for the manual workers' national negotiating body was reformed in a similar way at about the same time.

The establishment of LACSAB also virtually coincided with the start of nationally determined terms and conditions of employment in the three negotiating bodies originally within its scope. The first national "charter" for APT&C staffs (a formidable document of 42 sections) covering a wide range of pay and conditions, including measures to abolish patronage, nepotism and corruption, had been agreed after two years of intensive negotiations in January 1946. National basic rates of pay had been determined for manual workers and county council roadmen early in 1947, leaving national wages structures and national working conditions still to be negotiated in their two negotiating bodies. Such concepts as "pay years" and "pay rounds" were as yet unheard of.

So in those early post-war years as LACSAB's history begins and with the Attlee Labour government in control, and local authorities shedding responsibilities for electricity, gas and other functions, national collective bargaining was much in the ascendency in local government with widespread support from the local authority associations and their member authorities. This support could not however be regarded as entirely fulsome and voluntary as local authorities could be compelled by compulsory arbitration to apply the recommendations of national and provincial councils. There was thus much sense, whatever their real feelings about national collective bargaining as such, in their gaining membership to seek to exert some influence over national decisions they might subsequently be required to apply.

To help gauge the nature and flavour of negotiations of this era, an illustration is taken from the minutes of the NJC for APT&C services. In July 1946 a committee of the NJC met to determine whether or not baby cots should be taken into account in assessing "the number of beds available and which are erected and equipped" for the NJC's grading recommendations for masters and non-nursing matrons of public assistance institutions. The committee resolved -

"That 'baby cots' which are available, erected and equipped in the general and nursery wards of an institution shall be taken into account in determining the beds available under paragraph (b) of the National Council's recommendations, but 'baby cots' in maternity wards shall not be included for the purposes of such determination."

This is a chilling reminder of the immediate post-war context of "workhouses", with wards of segregated men and women, and the birth of children in such harrowing circumstances being accepted as a normal fact of life. It also demonstrates that the art of compromise and the formulation of negotiating "weasel words" is nothing new.

The first three Secretaries of LACSAB. Edward Bishop (centre) 1947-1957, Sir Reginald Griffiths (right) 1957-1972 and Brian Rusbridge (left) 1973-1987.

2 OFF TO A SOUND START

"His signal achievement was to turn into a universally respected process what many resented as new-fangled nonsense or interference in management's discretion."

(FROM THE TRIBUTE TO EDWARD BISHOP ON HIS DEATH BY SIR LEO SCHULTZ AND HARRY RAE IN "NEWS SUMMARY" OF OCTOBER 1975)

The context of LACSAB's first five years was of a relatively stable and tranquil period of pay bargaining when the Attlee government's formal wage policy succeeded largely due to the co-operation of the trade unions. LACSAB's sphere of influence was greatly extended to cover more negotiating groups. But it might be stretching credibility to describe it as a period of entirely successful negotiations in local government as national negotiators frequently resorted to arbitration and many local and provincial issues had to be determined nationally within the appeals machineries created.

POLITICAL AND ECONOMIC CONTEXT

The Attlee Labour government had been in power since 1945, issuing regular exhortations for moderate wage bargaining. Any thoughts of Government intervention had been dashed by the TUC making it clear towards the end of 1947 "that any attempt on the part of an outside body to regulate or directly control wage movements would have disastrous effects.... if there was to be any greater restraints upon wage movements it could come only from within the trade union movement itself". After much discussion the Government issued in February 1948 a White Paper - "The Statement on Personal Incomes, Costs and Prices" - which accepted the undesirability of direct Government interference in wage negotiations and called for a voluntary freeze of wage rates with very limited exceptions. The TUC, although somewhat resentful about lack of consultation, backed this policy. With committed support from the labour movement this policy was widely regarded as a qualified success throughout most of 1948 and 1949.

During 1949 the Government was concerned to preserve the relative cost advantage to be derived from devaluation. In November 1949 the TUC General Council recommended a one-year stabilisation of wage rates and the suspension of cost of living agreements (allowed under the 1948 policy) provided the retail price index did not move by more than 5%. With a general election imminent a TUC special conference in January 1950 endorsed this by a narrow vote.

There were many months of discussions in 1950 on the idea of a wages advisory council - a tripartite body of honest brokers, employers and union leaders to advise all collective negotiations on pay taking account of

Government views of the national interest – but because of many TUC reservations this was finally abandoned early in 1951 by the Chancellor of the Exchequer, now Hugh Gaitskell. In the Spring of 1951 short term factors predominated as the Attlee government issued more general pleas for restraint, at the same time strengthening price control and statutorily limiting company dividends.

The formal Attlee wages policy for 2½ years from 1948 to 1950 was reckoned to have been a considerable success in difficult circumstances and this is borne out by wage rate statistics: these had averaged 8 to 10% between June 1945 and March 1948; had fallen to average at around 3% from March 1948 to September 1949; dropped still further to about 1.4% after the 1949 devaluation; but then there was a sizeable jump thereafter to some 11% as the Korean war started in 1950. Much of the success of this policy could be attributed to the support of senior trade unionists and the moral influence of Sir Stafford Cripps and Ernest Bevin whose presence was greatly missed when they retired from the Government due to ill health.

The general election of October 1951 resulted by a small majority in a Conservative government initially led by Sir Winston Churchill committed to the dismantling of controls and freeing of the economy. But rearmament for the Korean war and seizure of the Abadan oil refinery in Persia led quickly to a serious balance of payments crisis. The Treasury view was that full employment was becoming impossible without wage restraint but after many attempts ideas of a White Paper on wage restraint were finally abandoned in 1952 by the Chancellor, R.A.Butler. Instead the Government raised the bank rate (to 4%!), increased profits tax, cut food subsidies, and urged trade union leaders towards moderation in wage bargaining – but they were reluctant to be seen to be acting in concert with a Conservative government. Ultimately the inflationary pressure abated largely due to other factors, including a sizeable counter-swing in commodity prices and a rapid recovery in the external account.

OVERALL LACSAB ACTIVITIES

The first five years from the establishment of LACSAB in November 1947 to its incorporation as a limited company on 31st December 1952 saw a marked extension of its interests; an increase in the number, responsibilities and authority of the negotiating bodies associated with it; and national determination of conditions of employment well established in all spheres. So the LACSAB secretary, Edward Bishop, was able in a report to the Board's meeting in October 1952 to comment that "starting out from modest beginnings in 1948 the Board has, during a particularly busy period, established co-ordination of policy in relation to those local government interests so far entrusted to it, serviced the various employers' sides with all the required information and advice, and in outside fields has established and consolidated a position of influence".

In this period the following wage negotiating bodies (additional to the original three) were added to the responsibilities of the LACSAB secretariat –

- National Joint Council for Local Authorities' Fire Brigades (1947 – extended to include Scotland)
- National Joint Council for Chief Officers of Local Authorities' Fire Brigades (1950 – extended to include Scotland)

- Joint Negotiating Committee for the Probation Service (1950) Joint Negotiating Committee for Local Authorities' (Building and Civil Engineering Craftsmen) (1951)
- Joint Negotiating Committee for Local Authorities' Services (Engineering Craftsmen) (1951)
- Joint Negotiating Committee for Approved Schools and Remand Homes in England and Wales (1952)

Additionally the NJC for APT&C was extended in 1950 by the establishment of the Standing Joint Advisory Committee for Staffs of Children's Homes (SJAC). The SJAC and the JNC for Approved Schools and Remand Homes covered supervisory staffs in residential establishments including those controlled by voluntary agencies as well as those local authority controlled – marking the first small steps by LACSAB beyond the direct local authority sphere of influence.

The growth of national settlements gave rise to the use of national disputes machinery. Edward Bishop reported in 1952 that each of the major national councils had several panels meeting in London regularly throughout the year to determine disputes relating to every aspect of their agreements in respect both of individuals and classes of workers. There seemed to have been insufficient acceptance in local government of the basic tenet of industrial relations that issues should be settled as near as possible to their source, with Bishop also commenting that there was an increasing tendency for disputes on provincial matters being referred for final settlement to the national bodies.

An interesting insight to the prevailing mood of the times is the fact that the Conditions of Employment and National Arbitration Order of 1940 and its successor, the Industrial Disputes Order of 1951, brought authority to the various national councils to act in place of the statutory arbitration tribunals with power to give decisions with equal validity and force.

Although these national negotiating bodies were empowered to adjudicate on differences between local authorities and their workers, this did not necessarily mean that they could always resolve their own disputes. Within these five years there were seven references to four different forms of independent arbitration affecting four separate negotiating bodies on a variety of issues, mainly pay-related. The LACSAB secretariat were not only immersed with the preparation of submissions to arbitrators on national disputes, as "in quite a number of cases" advice was given on arbitration affecting individual local authorities, in several of which the secretariat acted on behalf of, or attended to give guidance to, the local authority at the arbitration hearing. Advice was by no means limited to this, as it was reported that local authorities were taking full advantage of the opportunity to obtain information and advice from the LACSAB secretariat on a wide range of establishment problems and industrial relations issues.

The LACSAB minutes of this five-year period are much occupied with the extension of its sphere of influence and the consolidation of what had been achieved, such as seeking to nip in the bud an attempt by Middlesex County Council to set up negotiating machinery outside the NJC for APT&C staffs. Among the negotiating issues discussed in 1950 was a proposal by Surrey County Council to increase the hours of APT&C staffs from 38 to 40 per week: whilst at first sight this might look very reactionary it has to be seen in the context of many local authorities facing enormous increases in staffing costs as they gradually (and often reluctantly) implemented the 1946 "charter" for APT&C staffs. LACSAB decided against giving any advice on the Surrey proposal!

Other negotiating items included London weighting rearing its head for the first (but by no means the last) time with in 1951 the Burnham Committee Management Panel (outside the LACSAB sphere of influence then) seeking to abolish London weighting for teachers. LACSAB eventually agreed in 1952 that London weighting should continue, but decided against giving advice applicable to a particular service.

Close liaison was developed with other employers, in particular the National Joint Council for the Waterworks Industry, the Employers' Side of the National Council for the Passenger Transport Industry and the Municipal Passenger Transport Association.

MANUAL WORKERS

At their meeting in February 1947 the manual employers considered recommendations from the joint negotiating committee (i) to fix consolidated standard rates of wages; (ii) to establish two wage zones; and (iii) to provide a standard rate for general labourers of 94s. per week in zone A and 91s. in zone B with effect from 7th April 1947, and these were referred to provincial employers for their observations. A month later the employers were able to approve the joint negotiating committee's recommendations after arguments as to whether there should be a third lower zone C as advocated by the employers but opposed by the trade unions, with a compromise eventually emerging of the lower zone C rate of 88s. per week to apply for six months only.

The negotiations in 1948 were not only about pay rates but also on working hours as the trade unions early that year applied for a reduction to 44 hours per week. Again the employers sought provincial views, with some for conceding while others suggested this would be contrary to the Government's economic policy. It was in deference to the latter view that the employers proposed to the trade unions that the application should be deferred. At a meeting on 23rd March 1948 the trade unions would not accept this and referred the difference to the Ministry of Labour for arbitration. At the employers' meeting on 27th April the employers' secretary reported a communication from the Ministry of Labour but the minutes do not make clear whether or not this was an arbitration decision. Nevertheless that day agreement was reached on a 44-hour week to begin in October 1948 spread over five, five-and-a-half or six days. At the same time the two sides settled on a general increase of 6s. per week to apply from 5th July 1948 after the employers had optimistically suggested a forward date of 1st October 1948.

January 1949 saw the completion of a mammoth task of creating a national system of differential rates of wages together with a package of standard working conditions. The joint negotiating committee's report on these had been received in October 1948 and as usual put to provincial employers for comments. Agreement was finally reached at a meeting of the NJC on 26th January 1949 for the new national agreement arising from these wide-ranging changes to apply from 1st April 1949. All categories of manual jobs were placed in six wage groups for each of which there were rates for zones A and B ranging from 97s. per week for group 1 zone B to 113s. for group 6 zone A. The national working conditions covered the normal working week, overtime provisions, Sunday and rest day working, shift work and holidays.

Later in 1949 a trade union claim for adult females to be paid 80% of the male rate instead of 75% as hitherto was adjourned.

Well over a year elapsed before further negotiations on wage rates started in July 1950 with a claim by the trade unions for a substantial increase (later quantified as not less than 8s. per week). After talking around this claim for three meetings and receiving provincial views the employers finally tabled an offer of a 1d. per hour increase (3s.8d. per week) at the meeting of the NJC on 7th November. There seem to have been lengthy and serious negotiations as the minutes record the two parties separating on a number of occasions. After an improved offer of a 1 1/4d. per hour, a deal was struck on an increase of 1 1/2d. per hour with effect from 1st December 1950 and with women still at 75% of the male rates.

That agreement had operated for only four months when on 7th March 1951 the trade unions submitted three claims – (i) for basic rates to be increased having regard to movements in gas, water, electricity and transport; (ii) the London differential to be revised; and (iii) for zone B to be abolished. The first reaction of the employers that April was to say it was too soon after the December 1950 increase, but two meetings later in June they made an offer of a 1 1/4d. per hour increase. The trade unions expressed great dissatisfaction then, reiterated this in July when they declared a failure to agree and went to arbitration. Industrial Disputes Tribunal Award No.6 was received at the NJC meeting on 18th October but the minutes do not record its terms.

The next pay round fortunately was resolved by negotiation. After the trade unions had in December 1951 submitted a claim for a further increase of 7s.4d. per week there was evidently fruitful discussion in the joint executive committee in January 1952. At the NJC meeting on 14th February agreement was reached on an increase of 1 1/2d. per hour with effect from 3rd March 1952.

But it was back to arbitration the next time round. When in October 1952 the trade unions applied for a further substantial wage increase this quickly led to a failure to agree and a reference to arbitration with a hearing on 27th November. There was an incredibly quick decision as the Industrial Disputes Tribunal letter was dated 28th November, dealing with the core of the trade unions' arguments that local authority wages should follow those in the public utility services. The letter said that such a "formula does not commend itself to the tribunal as acceptance must of necessity stultify to a considerable extent the independence of the NJC as a negotiating body". The tribunal accordingly recommended that the parties should forthwith enter into further negotiations having regard to all other factors.

The tribunal decision was received at the NJC meeting on 10th December whereupon the employers offered an increase of 1d. per hour from 28th November 1952. The minutes drily indicate that the chairman declared that the employers' motion to this effect was not carried and that a failure to agree was recorded. So it was back again to the Industrial Disputes Tribunal and cold comfort to the trade unions when their award was received at the February 1953 NJC meeting as it did no more than endorse the employers' offer.

In 1953 it was the turn of the county council roadmen to go to arbitration.

They claimed parity of pay with that of manual workers in general which the employers refused to concede. The Industrial Disputes Tribunal established a differential between the two in their award, thus denying the parity sought by the county council roadmen.

APT&C STAFFS

In January 1947 the staff side asked for a substantial increase in the cost of living bonus then paid in addition to "charter" scales, which the employers resisted in line with the Government call for a wages standstill. They were however prepared to consolidate the bonus into salary scales with marginal rounding and small increases for juniors. When negotiations were resumed in October 1947 the employers' final offer represented little change except for juniors, and eventually in December the staff side sought arbitration. Counsel were engaged by both sides at the hearing of the National Arbitration Tribunal in January 1948. The award consolidated the bonus with the "charter" scales at the same level as previously offered by the employers, save for £25 increases at the top of the general division, £20 in the clerical division and £10 for women in the APT division.

Some time elapsed before the staff side lodged a further claim for a 20% increase in all salaries in January 1951, as in 1949 the TUC had called for an immediate halt to all wage claims following devaluation and as NALGO debated their tactics at great length. The employers agreed to look seriously at the claim on two conditions: first that the staff side abandon their demand that NJC scales were to be regarded as a minimum which could be improved locally; and secondly that they would consult provincial employers. Agreement was eventually reached on increases averaging 15% throughout the general division plus a shortening of the scale, with tapered increases in the APT grades and no increases at the then salary ceiling of £1,000 per annum.

In January 1952 the staff side (now led by Albert Nortrop) claimed increases of not less than 10% and for NJC salaries to be linked in future to the index of wage rates. The employers lost no time in rejecting index linking. Nor were they prepared to proposed any salary increase, insisting that local government should set an example in halting inflation although prices and pay elsewhere had risen since the 1951 settlement. This was unacceptable to the staff side who in April went for arbitration, this time by the Industrial Disputes Tribunal. Their award was for increases ranging from £10 to £25 in the general division and a flat £25 to those above, the percentage increases tapering from 5.6% to 2.5%. The staff side had sought an operative date of 1st January 1952 but the date awarded was 1st July 1952. On the other hand when the employers had argued that it would be unconstitutional to go beyond the salary ceiling of £1,000 a year, the chairman, Lord Terrington, had answered sweetly – "Indeed, I think that is a matter for the Tribunal to decide" ("White Collar Union", page 264) and proceeded to grant a £25 increase beyond that ceiling.

STAFFING AND PEOPLE

1952 saw the first of many proposals to change the premises occupied by the LACSAB secretariat. On this occasion it was suggested LACSAB should join with the County Councils Association (CCA) to acquire 13/14 Princes Gate, but this idea seems to have been quietly sidelined until it was revived in 1955.

The effect of all the negotiating activity at national level in this period 1947 to 1952 was to add substantially to the volume of matters referred to the LACSAB secretariat and correspondingly to increase its responsibilities. Yet Edward Bishop was able to report that, apart from typing, clerical and financial assistants, there had been only one addition to the permanent staff, that in 1947 of a senior assistant, D.S. (Derek) Bass, to cover the APT&C sphere - another like Harry Rae from the NALGO stable. Bishop's comment that this establishment bore favourable comparison with the industrial relations establishments in the public services and private industry was without doubt amply justified.

Scotland Yard in action. Police line up at a demonstration.

3 BISHOP'S FINAL FIVE YEARS

"The course of economic crises
Used to be wages chasing prices.
Nowadays we've reversed the stages
And start with prices chasing wages"
(Reproduced from a letter to "The Times", 23rd December 1955)

Relationships between the trade unions and the Government were more strained with a Conservative government in power than in the days of the Attlee administration, but nevertheless the industrial relations scene remained generally quiet and subdued. LACSAB continued to expand and consolidate its sphere of influence. Local government employers were able to clinch moderate pay deals in a period when the local government trade unions had few thoughts about embarking on industrial action. Edward Bishop retired from his post as LACSAB secretary in 1957, widely acclaimed as "the architect of whitleyism in local government".

POLITICAL AND ECONOMIC CONTEXT

The general scene in relation to pay and prices in this period is neatly encapsulated in the epigram quoted at the beginning of this chapter. Employment had risen to figures never attained before in peacetime and shortage of labour continued to cause staffing difficulties – a situation which the trade unions were not slow to exploit. Until about mid-1953 price increases slightly exceeded pay increases, but this position was not sustained and in fact in both 1953 and 1954 wages comfortably exceeded the rise in retail prices. The editorial comments in issues of "News Summary" in 1955 were full of doom and gloom foreseeing the consequences of the wage inflation then gathering momentum. Early in 1955 wages had raced ahead of prices but at the end of the year equilibrium had been restored with both indices having increased 5.5% during the year – alarming figures for those days. In May 1956 the Chancellor of the Exchequer, Harold Macmillan, claimed – "we are on a kind of plateau of stability for a year at least", exhorting that prices would rise only if salaries and wages rose. But he was rebuffed by the trade unions who made it clear that the move for higher wages was on: they were not prepared to co-operate with the Chancellor's appeal for restraint so long as the Government chose not to return to a planned economy. As "News Summary" commented in September 1956 – "the problem is not industrial: it is political". At the beginning of 1957 there seemed some hope of stability with pay increases of the order of 3% but these were dashed when the British Transport Commission added an extra 2% on to a 3% arbitration awarded contested by the railwaymen – plus a similar offer by the shipbuilding employers in Government-sponsored joint discussions. There were however important subsequent developments stemming from the recommendations of the ("Jack") courts of inquiry into the shipbuilding and engineering disputes that there should be established an authoritative and impartial body to consider the general movement of wages, costs and prices. As this period drew to a close debate on this proposal was well advanced with Harold Macmillan, by now Prime Minister, giving it his support.

Two particular events in the wider industrial relations scene had a particular impact on local Government negotiations, both stemming from Government decisions in respect of the Civil Service. Early in 1955 the Government approved proposals for equal pay for equal work for clerical and other non-industrial civil servants to be introduced by stages by January 1961. Women industrial workers employed by the Government were however excluded. Equal pay already operated in principle to a very great extent in many local Government fields of employment, as there was no sex differentiation in the administrative, professional and technical grades, nor for chief and other senior officers. There were nevertheless implications for clerical officers for whom the staff side of the NJC for APT&C staffs had already proposed equal pay should be introduced on a phased basis. Progress on equal pay for equal work for women manual workers seemed less likely given the Government's lack of action on their women industrial workers.

The other important outside development was the ("Priestley") Royal Commission on the Civil Service set up in November 1953 which finally reported at the end of 1955. On the principles for civil service pay Priestley plumped firmly for "fair comparison with the current remuneration of outside staffs employed on broadly comparable work, taking account of differences in other conditions of service". Elaborate methods of applying "fair comparisons" were proposed, with fact-finding work being separated from the negotiating process and done by different people, but still within the Civil Service. Taking account of this in pay levels Priestley awarded more to the higher ranks by "pulling out the concertina" but less in the lower ranges where in some cases there were reductions in take-home pay through reductions in hours and annual leave.

OVERALL LACSAB ACTIVITIES

The period from 1952, when LACSAB became a limited company, to 1957 was one of further expansion of its sphere of influence, much negotiating activity, coupled with the move in 1956 from Upper Grosvenor Street to 41 Belgrave Square, and culminating with the retirement of LACSAB secretary Edward Bishop. Local authorities were employing in 1952 in their various services over a million and a quarter workers (numbers of full-time and part-time workers) of whom just over 900,000 had their wages and working conditions determined by negotiating bodies associated with LACSAB.

Other negotiating bodies to be serviced by the LACSAB Secretariat were the new Police Council for Great Britain in 1953 and also in the same year the Joint Negotiating Committee for Justices Clerks. The Burnham Committee on teachers' pay remained outside the LACSAB umbrella, but it was agreed in 1954 that their local authorities' side should send a liaison representative to LACSAB meetings.

What might have been an important development in 1956 was a report on behalf of the local authority associations following a comprehensive review of the machinery for the settlement of wages and working conditions of nearly one and a half million local government employees. This report said "the key to the co-ordination of the activities of local authorities in the sphere of wages and salary negotiations is the centralised secretariat of the Local Authorities' Conditions of Service Advisory Board.....the effectiveness of which is a matter of cardinal importance". Recommendations included moves towards the integration of negotiating bodies, with medical and dental officers and public analysts being invited to join the Joint Negotiating Committee for Chief Officers (not then serviced by LACSAB) and/or the NJC for APT&C staffs as appropriate. To the 14 secretaryships then held by LACSAB, the report recommended the addition of the ("Soulbury") Committee for Inspectors and Organisers - at that time within the Burnham education group. Another proposal was that provincial employers' sides should be used as "sounding boards" on an extra-constitutional basis in relation to the pay of clerks, chief officers and craftsmen. There is no evidence of any early action to implement these recommendations until several of them were revived in April 1961 in a second report by the local authority associations on negotiating machinery in local government.

If the local authorities then had doubts about their negotiating efficacy they would have been reassured by comments in the "Firefighter" (organ of the Fire Brigades Union) of January/February 1956 - "The local authorities have learnt the lesson of solidarity. They have set up a Conditions of Service Advisory Board..... There is no disunity there. The employers speak with a single voice..... The employers' front is broad and unified...... It is in many ways a model which one could copy with advantage."

The LACSAB journal "News Summary" was launched in December 1953 as a means of communicating with constituent local authorities. The second issue in January 1954 commented that 1953 was a year of relative stability in the country's industrial relations scene, easily the best since 1947, but there were signs of serious pay problems looming ahead.

MANUAL WORKERS

At the end of 1953 the pay of manual workers was resolved by a reference to the Industrial Disputes Tribunal which awarded increases of 4s. per week for men and 3s. per week for women. A negotiated settlement for manual workers in 1954 met with much approval on all sides - combining a general wage increase with a review of differentials between the various group rates, plus the revaluation of "certain obnoxious jobs" - reached by agreement within the machinery "in a general desire to achieve a measure of stability for some little time to come". Further increases in manual workers' wages were agreed in May 1955. Another wages claim quickly followed as by early in 1956 indices of retail prices had gone up by seven points and wages rates by nine points. The principal problem facing the local authority employers was how far could industrial wages be allowed to go ahead of their own rates without imperilling essential services. The answer was to offer an increase of 3d. per hour from March 1956, as against the 4d. claimed by the unions. A further wage increase agreed as from May 1957 took the basic Group 1 Zone A rate to £8.2s.2d per week. Local government had once again been forced to follow the pattern of wage increases elsewhere, especially in the public services, with the electricity industry as so often the pacesetter.

Among many other matters discussed in the NJC for manual workers was the question of incentive bonus schemes. The decision in 1956 was that universal application of particular schemes according to a particular plan could not be recommended: it was for each local authority to decide whether or not incentive bonus schemes offered a substantial contribution to its labour problems.

APT&C STAFFS

Some time elapsed after the 1952 arbitration award before the staff side returned with a further claim in October 1953 by which time price movements had stabilised after the Korean war. The claim sought immediate increases ranging from £15 to £40 together with a reduction in the age of the general division maximum from 30 to 28, a £30 increment to all at scale maxima, and two additional increments to each of the higher grades. This was initially rejected by the employers who were not prepared to do more than consider changes in relevant circumstances since the 1952 award. In subsequent negotiations the employers offered increases of £10 to £20 in the general division and £25 for all in the higher grades from a forward date of 1st April 1954. At the meeting of the NJC in January 1954 the staff side accepted the offer under protest expressing keen disappointment with the inadequacy of the increases. This concern was reinforced by many subsequent protests by NALGO branches and led to the first special conference in NALGO's history requisitioned by branches in April 1954.

Whilst the Civil Service had its "fair comparisons" principle, in local government the NJC for APT&C staffs had then its "fair wages" principle – "Local government should not take the lead in determining salary standards, but should be in the first flight of good employers". This was taken into account in the first stage of the NJC's review requested by the staff side in April 1954 following the NALGO special conference earlier that month and eventually agreed in August 1954 for application from 1st January 1955. The former general division was superseded by a general division and a higher division, the clerical and higher clerical divisions were revised, and the former eleven administrative, professional and technical grades were replaced by seven grades. Important considerations in this review were the desirability (a) to introduce a two-tier system of recruitment of junior staffs related to educational standards, and (b) to provide in the higher scales a longer "length of life" in the incremental provisions. A further stage in the review of the APT&C scheme was reached in January 1955 with agreement on nationally prescribed pay levels for certain specific occupational groups. It was only in the case of sanitary inspectors that no agreement could be reached and a reference to arbitration necessary. At the arbitration hearing Edward Bishop described the staff side claim as "conceived in fantasy": a difference between claim and offer of £185 per annum was resolved by the Industrial Disputes Tribunal topping the offer by £20.

The employers were able exude some confidence that the APT&C review would be well received by their constituent authorities as they had prepared the ground by conducting extensive consultations culminating in a conference with provincial representatives. Such was not the lot of the staff side as the review outcome was bitterly opposed within NALGO whose branches quickly dubbed the new lower general division the "slave grade" – a move away from the 1946 concept of grammar school GCE entrants. A resolution carried by a decisive majority at a special NALGO conference in March 1955 represented a defeat for their national executive council and a "striking" (not to be taken too literally!) change in salary policy. NALGO's negotiators on the NJC staff side were instructed (i) to reopen negotiations to secure the abolition of the lower general division, and (ii) to use "the full resources of the Association" to restore salaries to their 1946 purchasing power. The employers regarded this claim as unrealistic, declined to negotiate upon it, and insisted on its withdrawal. So the NALGO negotiators went back to another special conference in November 1955 and secured a more realistic mandate, with the "back to 1946" claim being put to one side. Joint agreement quickly followed on "the most comprehensive revision of the APT&C scheme since 1946" to apply from 1st January 1956. The basic salary increase of 5% had regard to Civil Service and London County Council settlements earlier in 1955 and especially to recruiting problems confronting many local authorities. "Wage for age" rates disappeared to provide greater local discretion, and the general and higher general divisions were extended. There had evidently been some very shrewd timing by the APT&C employers who had been concocting their own proposals to alleviate authorities' recruiting problems, but had bided their time to allow NALGO's negotiators to extricate themselves from their predicament.

Given the 1955 backcloth it was hardly surprising that in 1956 NALGO's negotiators were disinclined to bite the bullet to reach a negotiated settlement for APT&C staffs. The staff side's case at arbitration for substantial increases rested principally on Civil Service post-"Priestley" pay movements. Edward Bishop for the employers contended that this case was inaccurate and misleading and that any general salary increase at that time was quite unjustified. In the event the Industrial Disputes Tribunal awarded 2.5% from lst October 1956. The next year it was back to a negotiated agreement operative from 1st September 1957 with yet further structural changes: for example, the existing seven administrative, professional and technical grades were reduced to five. Much stress was laid on examinations and qualifications to further the NJC's objective of a qualified (and thus more efficient) local government service.

Among the many other matters discussed in the APT&C NJC was adherence to national agreements, with the employers exhorting all local authorities that "an essential part of the Whitley procedure is the honouring by both employers and employed of agreements which are reached", especially on the national grading prescriptions.

FIRE BRIGADES

In the NJC for local authorities' fire brigades this period was dominated by disputes with the Fire Brigades Union (FBU) on manning issues. An article in "The Times" of 30th August 1954 succinctly summarises the issues as follows –

"The union are working for a closely integrated service composed largely of highly trained, full-time firemen, their hours of duty limited to 48 or fewer, their wages high, and their leisure completely their own. County authorities wish to continue and to extend the present intimate relationship between the brigades and the communities they serve, making full use of the local patriotism, knowledge and enthusiasm of part-time firemen in many small stations and, equally, of the enthusiasm and team spirit of the many full-time firemen who are anxious to add to their experience – and earnings – by volunteering to answer calls in off-duty periods."

The article went on to refer to difficulties because the FBU was in Communist hands and "seem to prefer an aggressive parade of militancy to the unspectacular negotiation of improved conditions for their members".

The NJC for fire brigades eventually in 1955 reached agreement on recommendations for flexible systems of duty for the fire service which were brought into effect by regulations under the Fire Services Act. This gave each fire authority a choice of four systems: the 56-hour week; the 60- hour week; the 80-hour week on the 24/24 hour system; and the day manning system. Local circumstances would be the guide, but any increases in hours had to be agreed with the firemen through their accredited representatives.

As to firemen's pay, there had been an enquiry into the FBU's "police parity" claim which followed the "spit and polish" strikes in November 1952. February 1955 saw the introduction of a new pay structure. A pay claim in December 1955 led to a quick settlement in February 1956. A further claim in April 1956 for a general increase in the existing scales plus an improvement in pay for the more senior firemen led to extensive negotiations over more than five months. At an early stage the claim for a general wage increase was withdrawn to allow discussions to centre round the problem of wastage of experienced men and to bring the wage structure into line with modern conditions. The eventual agreement made no change in the fireman's starting rate but made improvements elsewhere to encourage the retention of the more experienced fireman. There was another general wage settlement for firemen in 1957.

The emergence of the National Association of Fire Officers (NAFO) organising the junior officer ranks led to differences about representation on national negotiating bodies.

POLICE

1955 and 1956 saw a spate of arbitration awards covering all police ranks. At an arbitration hearing early in 1955 Sir Hartley Shawcross presented the case for more pay for chief constables resulting in an award of increases tapered from 10.7% to 6.7% at the top. Then a subsequent independent tribunal appointed by the Prime Minister awarded increases with effect from 16th December 1955 to the "federated ranks", i.e. constables, sergeants, inspectors and chief inspectors, ranging up to £130 a year, with constables doing best in percentage terms. This was regarded at the time as most favourable treatment for the police justified by the importance of manning-up the police forces in the national interest and with a shortage of policemen in many areas leading to what chief police officers had described as "a crisis in police administration". Superintendents and chief superintendents went to arbitration to seek pay increases to compensate them for additional duties arising from the reduction in the working week from 48 to 44 hours for the federated ranks. The outcome was a mere £25 a year with effect from December 1955 for provincial superintendents but nothing for chief superintendents nor for superintendent ranks in the Metropolitan and City of London forces.

March 1957 saw another arbitration on the pay of the federated ranks. Gerald Gardiner QC appeared for the official side to oppose a 7.5% claim and told the tribunal they had gone too far in their 1955 award because it had stimulated recruitment so much that police forces had more recruits than they could contend with. James Callaghan MP, at that time the appointed consultant to the Police Federation, presented the staff side case and claimed there was still a staff shortage. The arbitration award of 3% from 1st February 1957 was ironic as in negotiations the official side had been told by the staff side not to put forward "a miserable offer of 3%"!

Jim Callaghan MP in 1957, the appointed consultant to the Police Federation that time.

PROBATION SERVICE

There was an arbitration reference too in 1957 in respect of probation officers after the two sides of the JNC for the probation service had failed to reach agreement. The award of the Industrial Court in May 1957 was 18% at the minimum of the scale, tapered to 8.2% at the maximum.

STAFFING AND PEOPLE

Staffing and accommodation issues for LACSAB converged when Edward Bishop reported to the LACSAB Board in March 1954 that, as extra staff had been appointed to cope with the rapid expansion of activities, the existing premises at 37 Upper Grosvenor Street were "bursting at the seams" (by about this time the LACSAB staff had increased to a total of 20). The idea was revived early in 1955 of acquiring premises at Princes Gate to share with the County Councils Association but these were deemed not suitable for joint occupation. Other premises in Green Street were prospected subsequently but this fell through. Then 41 Belgrave Square came in sight in the summer of 1956, was quickly acquired and eventually occupied on 12th November 1956. So began the now well-established identity of national local authority pay negotiations with "Belgrave Square". "News Summary" commented that "Belgrave Square retains an air of quiet dignity" and added that No.41 had formerly been the town house of an Archbishop of York, the home of HRH Prince Arthur of Connaught, and had been recorded in the provisional list of buildings of architectural and historical interest (even before its LACSAB connections!).

Staffing issues were dominated by Edward Bishop's decision to retire. He had made it known to the LACSAB Board in March 1954 that he would be age 60 that May and did not wish to stay beyond May 1956. In 1955 efforts to appoint a successor came to nought with an ad-hoc committee reaching no agreement on this. However after some hesitations and inevitable delays it was decided in August 1956 to re-advertise the post and this led quickly to the appointment of Reginald Griffiths, then Director of Establishments, London County Council, in November 1956 and to Edward Bishop eventually retiring in September 1957.

Many tributes were paid to Edward Bishop on his retirement, particularly as the "architect of whitleyism in local government". John Warren of NALGO said his outstanding quality as an opponent was his certitude and grasp of facts: he had an eye for a situation and infinite resource in meeting it. Sir Horace Wilson (who had been Secretary of the original Whitley Committee which reported on industrial relations in 1917 and later became first Independent Chairman of the NJC for APT&C staffs) defined Edward Bishop's qualities as patience, perseverance, persuasiveness, devotion to the cause and above all a non-self seeking mind. In their tribute on Edward Bishop's death in "News Summary" of October 1975, Sir Leo Schultz and Harry Rae describe him - "Bland, imperturbable, impervious to pressure and insult from either side of the table, he was a shrewd master of strategy and tactics, inspiring loyalty in those who worked with him..." Sir George Mowbray, chairman of LACSAB, presiding at a function in Edward Bishop's honour, remarked that it was the first time he had presided at the retirement of a bishop - although he thought "Archbishop" would be a more suitable title.

A final postscript gives an interesting insight to the mood of this period. The minutes of the LACSAB Board of December 1954 record that - "The Secretary stated that due to the increasing volume of work he wished consideration to be given to an increase in the male staff". Nobody appears to have batted an eyelid at that in the all-male bastion of the day. It is difficult to imagine a similar statement being made without causing a great rumpus thirty years later.

4 PAY PAUSES AND GUIDING LIGHTS

"There are some signs that Whitehall favours an incomes policy which gives a regular increase of incomes in keeping with average underlying increase in productivity over several years. The regularity of annual wage increases is widely felt to be something now irrevocable."

(FROM A SYMPOSIUM OF ARTICLES PUBLISHED BY "THE TIMES" EARLY IN 1962)

As Reginald Griffiths took over from Edward Bishop as LACSAB secretary towards the end of 1957 the country was well into the 13 years of Conservative government which spanned 1951 to 1964, and had entered the post-Suez phase with Harold Macmillan as Prime Minister. The saying attributed to him – "You have never had it so good" – comes very much to mind. Eventually Selwyn Lloyd, the Chancellor of the Exchequer, introduced his pay pause in 1961 and subsequent pay policies in 1962. An apparent lack of will to hold to firm measures, especially when dealing with their own employees, led to a somewhat erratic "stop:go" series of Government measures. This had much impact on local government pay negotiations, with some exceptionally large increases flowing from special inquiries initiated by the Government. The local authority associations agreed to a considerable expansion of LACSAB's activities, notably in the education sector.

POLITICAL AND ECONOMIC CONTEXT

The proposal to establish an independent advisory body on wages, costs and prices and on their effect on the national economy led towards the end of 1957 to the Government setting up a Council on Prices, Productivity and Incomes chaired by Lord Cohen and intended to bring facts of the economic situation to the attention of the country and so mould public opinion. Although this Council was meant to be impartial, its creation was certainly not welcomed by the trade unions.

However, as 1958 began, nobody seemed anxious to precipitate a confrontation and there was something of a lull, as the TUC had in December 1957 accepted an invitation to confer with the Cohen Council despite serious reservations. The latter Council produced their first report in February 1958. They referred to the post-war period as years of economic success, the sharp contrast with the inter-war years being the current full employment situation, but the one big failure had been to prevent prices from rising, with the average annual price rise of 4 to 5% being unprecedented in the previous 100 years of British economic history. The Council pointed out that attempts by trade union members to continue the spectacular rises in wages of recent years would endanger their own future employment and standard of living. They hoped that, if any wage increases were granted in 1958, they would be substantially below the average of the last few years, so as to avoid further upward spiralling of prices. When they made their second report at the end of August 1958, the Cohen Council noted fewer wage increases had been granted so far in 1958, and those which had been granted had been smaller. If this trend continued throughout 1958 the outcome would be increases of about 3.5% – which was nevertheless still above the current rate of productivity increase. By the time the Cohen Council produced their third report in the summer of 1959 they were able to talk of a reasonable prospect of price stability, as the index of retail prices in June 1959 stood no higher than in June 1958 – something new in post-war experience. The opportunity had to be seized to raise output and real incomes without renewing the spiral of rising pay, profits and prices.

In 1960 however the dominant theme was not so much pay moderation as comparability. The "fair comparisons" principle was applied to the Civil Service, including senior Civil Servants through the recommendations of the Coleraine Committee. The main application of comparability outside the Civil Service was in the ("Guillebaud") Railway Pay Enquiry which had Edward Bishop as one their members (no doubt warmly welcomed by one of the trade union leaders, William Webber, who had worked very closely with Edward Bishop for many years as employers' chairman of the NJC for APT&C staffs). The "Willink" Royal Commission on the Police adduced their own special reasons for substantially improving police pay, as did the "Pilkington" Committee on the remuneration of doctors and dentists. The general reduction in manual and craft workers' hours from 44 to 42 per week had its effect too.

Not surprisingly prices increased by 5% per annum by summer 1961, leading Selwyn Lloyd first to appeal for "wage restraint" and then to announce on 25th July 1961 a "wage pause" in the public sector and nationalised industries. The first impact of this was on teachers as the Government decided not to approve the full increases recommended by the Burnham Committee (still outside the LACSAB umbrella at this point). Local authority association representatives expressed to the Chancellor "a general willingness to co-operate....in constraining expenditure", but the response of the public sector trade unions was predictably very hostile.

Subsequently in October 1961 the Chancellor called for a national wages policy and for both sides of industry to co-operate in assessing what wage increases could be afforded. The wage pause was obviously a holding operation and the Government's new policy on incomes became unfolded as 1962 began with the issue of a White Paper – "Incomes Policy: The Next Step"; a "guiding light" that pay increases should not be more than 2.5%; the creation of a National Economic Development Council (NEDC or "Neddy") – a tripartite gathering of Government, industry and the unions; and the proposal to establish a National Incomes Commission ("Nicky").

Caused in some part by the unprecedented harsh winter, production was stagnant at the beginning of 1963 and unemployment shot up to over 900,000, but the national economy improved sharply later in the year with growth in production close to the NEDC target of 4% a year. The Government's "guiding light" for pay increases to be 3 to 3.5% was generally observed in the public sector but towards the end of 1963 several major groups of industrial workers gained increases in the 5 to 6% range. A notable feature was the trend encouraged by NEDC towards longer-term settlements of two or three years' duration, including quite a few local government groups, seeking to achieve a period of stability.

1963 was proclaimed "National Productivity Year" with NEDC doing much valuable work to encourage both sides of industry to co-operate in increasing production as the Government strove to achieve expansion without inflation.

1964 was overshadowed by the anticipated general election. With the re-expansion of the economy turning into a boom, concerns were expressed about the effects of inflation, wage drift and serious labour shortages, but NEDC could not obtain any agreement on an incomes policy, due not only to the trade unions' reluctance but also to the employers failing to agree amongst themselves. No remedial action was taken in the 1964 budget and then the postmen's settlement at 6.5% (in advance of a pay research exercise) was widely regarded as having finally extinguished the Government's "guiding light".

Of the many other external influences on the work of local government national negotiating bodies, a few require specific mention. The first was the culmination of much pressure from the trade union movement to reduce working hours in the introduction of the 42-hour week – eventually flowing through to apply to local authority manual, craft and other workers in 1961. Towards the end of this period pressure was developing for a further reduction in working hours to 40 per week. A 40-hour week agreed by the Scottish plumbing and building industries to operate from November 1963 incurred the wrath of the National Incomes Commission when they condemned it in their first report in April 1963 as being in reality another wage increase of 7%. A subsequent shipyard settlement providing a phased reduction in hours from 42 to 41 in December 1964 and to 40 in July 1965 was criticised by the Government as they sought throughout 1964 to avoid the 40-hour week spreading to three million workers in the engineering industry.

Another important development was the Government decision announced by Iain Macleod, Minister of Labour and National Service, on 22nd October 1958 to end compulsory arbitration on industrial disputes – in force since 1940. Private sector employers largely welcomed this move, particularly since the 1940 ban on strikes and lockouts was removed in 1951, but the trade unions strongly opposed it, none more so than NALGO who claimed to be the largest "customer" of the old Industrial Disputes Tribunal following their victory to gain access to it in the famous House of Lords Bolton judgement of 1942. LACSAB sided with the public sector unions, telling the Minister they did not object to compulsory arbitration continuing for the local government service, otherwise "some means would require to be devised to ensure the universal acceptance of freely negotiated decisions". The bulk of cases dealt with by the compulsory arbitration procedures were "issues" through which voluntary collective agreements could be enforced on all employers, and NALGO had used this to good effect on behalf of their members employed by local authorities reluctant to adhere to nationally negotiated agreements. Eventually a residual provision was retained whereby under Clause 8 of the Terms and Conditions of Employment Act 1959 the Minister could refer to arbitration (the Industrial Court) claims from trade unions that employers were not applying generally recognised rates in the trade or industry.

Another important move in 1964 was the NALGO decision to affiliate to the TUC after many years outside it and much debate since the statement by their first general secretary, Levi Hill, in 1910 that "anything savouring of trade unionism is nausea to the local government officer and his association".

OVERALL LACSAB ACTIVITIES

This period saw further growth in the spread of LACSAB work over more negotiating groups, although a suggestion at a LACSAB meeting in December 1958 that the LACSAB secretary should be a substitute member of the Burnham Committee got nowhere on being "adjourned sine die". Municipal airport employees were brought under the LACSAB umbrella by extending the scope of the NJC for Manual Workers and the JNCs for craftsmen. Arising from the "Albermarle"" Committee report on the youth service the Joint Negotiating Committee for Youth Leaders was established and held its first meeting in February 1961 when Reginald Griffiths was appointed Joint Honorary Secretary to the employers' panel, alongside Sir William Alexander of the Association of Education Committees (AEC) who was also management panel secretary to the Burnham Committees.

A big step forward in the growth of the LACSAB "empire" stemmed from the second report of the local authority associations on negotiating machinery in local government in April 1961 which seems to have induced action which their first report of 1955 signally failed to do. The 1961 report proposed that, in order to achieve the maximum co-ordination and co-operation at secretarial level, the LACSAB secretary should be appointed either the employers' secretary or one of the employers' joint secretaries to eight additional bodies, which would extend his responsibilities to cover 23 negotiating bodies in all.

The proposed appointment as one of the joint authorities' side secretaries of the three joint negotiating committees covering chief officials (clerks of county councils: town and district council clerks: and chief officers) came amicably and as no surprise. At the beginning of 1959 the authorities' sides had faced arbitration hearings in respect of claims by the clerks, chief officers and "lettered scales" (senior and principal officers) for large increases in pay and had invited Reginald Griffiths to present their case for them.

The proposed appointment as joint honorary secretary to the five negotiating bodies in the "Burnham" group covering the education service was a very different kettle of fish. This had long been the sole preserve of the Secretary of the AEC (then Sir William Alexander) who was felt to enjoy the confidence of the teachers as an educationist himself. The impetus for change was doubtless the concern expressed at LACSAB meetings at the weakening of the total employers' front by concessions by the Burnham management panels. It was in the hands of the County Councils Association (CCA) and the Association of Municipal Corporations (AMC) – who represented local authorities – to do something about it. Much patient work was required by the LACSAB secretariat over many years to develop their position in teachers' pay negotiations to the point many years later in 1974 when one of several putative resignations by Sir William Alexander was accepted, opening the way for the LACSAB secretary to become sole management panel secretary of the Burnham group.

The two negotiating bodies where it was proposed that the LACSAB secretary should become sole employers' secretary were the Dental (Local Authorities) Health Service Whitley Council and Medical Committee C Health Service Whitley Council.

Another negotiating body in the "manual/craft" area was established in 1964 – the National Joint Council for Workshops for the Blind – and their first task was to reform the wages structure in the light of the Ministry of Labour departmental working party report of 1962.

A development which was to have increasing significance was the setting up in 1963 sponsored by the employers' side of the NJC for manual workers of the Local Government Work Study Group to encourage measures towards increased productivity by local authorities. It was reported to the LACSAB Board in June 1964 that already there were 326 local authorities in membership. From this small beginning was to emerge in due course the Local Authorities Management Services and Advisory Committee (LAMSAC).

Most of the issues discussed by LACSAB in this period are mentioned elsewhere covering the Government's economic and pay policies. Concern was expressed that the creation of ad- hoc bodies to consider pay issues (as in the case of police and probation) and the vetoing of pay settlements by Government ministers were undermining in the longer term the influence of and confidence in existing negotiating machinery. On several occasions in this period when the LACSAB Board discussed the co-ordination of pay negotiations they were perturbed by generous settlements elsewhere in the public sector. In the manual workers area the electricity supply industry were frequently quoted as the market leaders. In the white-collar area it was the generous treatment by the Government of their own employees in the Civil Service under the "fair comparisons" arrangements which led to considerable criticism as these put the pressure on local government to enhance their pay rates.

MANUAL WORKERS

Early in 1958 the employers' sides of the NJCs for manual workers and county council roadmen decided to respond positively to the unions' claim for an increase of 4d per hour by offering 2d per hour which was accepted. By the time they had made their move in August 1958 the indices of prices and wage rates risen by 5% and 5.5% respectively, and a pay movement for operatives in the public services had developed since that June. Earlier in 1958 a new pay scheme had been agreed after much patient work for school caretakers and cleaners, as well as a new grading structure for parks employees designed to provide career prospects based on training, qualifications and experience.

The manual workers' negotiations played an early part in the pay explosion of 1960 with a comprehensive package deal covering pay, hours, leave and zoning in February 1960. The pay increase of 7s.4d per week from 1st April 1960 brought the lowest grade up to a basic rate of £8.16s.11d a week but did no more than conform to general levels elsewhere. Hours were reduced from 44 to 42 per week following the trend in industry and other services: the implementation of this was however delayed until 1st January 1961 to help lessen the cost impact on local authorities and was accompanied by a joint statement on the full utilisation of working hours. An interesting facet is that there had been no claim by the unions for a reduction in the working week, but the employers felt this move was inevitable given trends elsewhere. Three days extra annual leave was conceded to employees with over 10 years' continuous service, bringing manual workers into line with the controversial decision in the NJC for APT&C staffs the previous year. A new standard formula was introduced for determining the zoning of local authorities to qualify for the extra 3s per week for Zone A and which was based on a combination of population and rateable value. This followed much criticism of the former arrangement whereby the allocation between zones had been determined by provincial councils and had led to many disputes. Next in this 1960 spate of activity was a scheme for the grading of ground staff at municipal airports coming into operation in April 1960 placing the airports into four classes for wage purposes. Then in July 1960 three years' patient negotiation culminated in the agreement on a grading structure for county council roadmen replacing the previous system of base rates and plusages.

Although the 1960 package was intended to remain firm for a substantial time unless circumstances changed materially, by November that year the unions had lodged a new claim. The employers had to acknowledge that subsequent wage movements elsewhere necessitated further adjustment and concluded an agreement in March 1961 on increased rates to apply from April 1961. The settlement also included transferring a large number of jobs out of the bottom Group 1, as well as trade union co-operation in the introduction of work study and organisation and method techniques.

The trade unions submitted a claim for an increase of 4d. per hour for manual workers early in 1962 following the Government's pay pause of 1961. The manual employers were clearly irritated by developments elsewhere as they faced another claim towards the end of 1962. They reckoned that their efforts to keep their pay negotiations on an even keel had been "rendered unduly difficult" by employers of much smaller groups of manual workers in the public services and the nationalised industries entering into fresh agreements, sometimes involving two substantial increases in a year, admittedly following frequent pay movements generally in the economy. They did eventually settle for a 2d. per hour increase in January 1963, but resisted pressure to backdate this – and in fact secured a forward operative date of the beginning of March 1963.

October 1963 saw a three-year pact for manual workers closely following that agreed for APT & C staffs and within the Government's "guiding light" of 3 to 3.5% increases. Under this, weekly wage rates for adult male workers would rise successively by 7s. per week in September 1963, September 1964 and September 1965, with the intention of providing stability during the period of its duration. There was also provision for a service supplement of 7s. per week from April 1964 to full-time employees with at least five years' continuous service. The Labour Correspondent of "The Times" commented that the local authorities preferred the service supplement to a further general increase as it excluded some 200,000 part-time workers, mostly women!

1962 also saw arbitration of a dispute over the wages and working conditions of school caretakers. At the arbitration hearing, Harry Rae for the employers accused the trade unions of speaking with two voices; when other manual workers' hours were reduced to 42 they had asked for a special pay increase for caretakers as they couldn't work a 42-hour week; but now they were not only asking for the pay increase but also saying they should enjoy the shorter working week as well! The arbitrators rejected the claim for a 42-hour week and awarded half the pay increase claimed – thus in effect endorsing the employers' offer.

With the increasing interest aroused in productivity encouraged by the National Economic Development Council (NEDC), the NJC for manual workers organised in January 1963 their (first) national conference on "Work Study as an Aid to Management" at Harrogate.

APT & C STAFFS

There was no adjustment in the national salaries of white-collar staff within the scope of the APT&C NJC during 1958. Negotiations arising from a staff side claim of November 1958 finally led to a settlement operative from 1st April 1959. The employers' position had not been helped by a Civil Service Arbitration Award during the course of negotiations based on information produced by the Civil Service Pay Research Unit on the "fair comparisons" principle giving 8.5% increases for Civil Service clerical officers at the top of their scale. The APT&C 1959 settlement provided varying increases of 3.5% or more. The controversial decision to concede three days additional annual leave for staff with at least ten years' service had been preceded by the examination of a long report on APT&C leave in 1958; this sparked off claims and subsequent settlements to extend this concession to other groups of local authority employees.

As the APT&C NJC concluded their agreement in September 1960 to operate from that month, their discussions were dominated by a backcloth of spiralling pay settlements in the rest of the public sector (including substantial increases in the Civil Service based on pay research and "fair comparisons") and increasingly serious shortages of professional officers in most parts of the country. The agreement included several special measures arising from a comprehensive review as well as general increases of the order of 5.9% rising to 7.6% for the highest grade to restore differentials. Subsequently in 1960 there were several changes in national grading prescriptions including a three-tier grading structure in social work in the light of the recommendations of the "Younghusband" Committee.

Selwyn Lloyd, Chancellor of the Exchequer in 1961 and instigator of a pay pause for public sector pay announed in July of that year.

NALGO had decided to defy Selwyn Lloyd's pay pause for public sector pay announced in July 1961 and followed this up that October with a claim for massive increases for APT&C staffs ranging from 20 to 25% based on arithmetical comparisons with the Civil Service. The employers argued that the claim was unacceptable and proposed an all-round increase of two per cent plus a few minor structural changes. Settlement was reached in July 1962 on a 3.5% general increase in line with movements elsewhere in the public sector and operative from 1st May 1962.

21st November 1962 was hailed as an historic occasion as agreement was finally reached removing the salary ceiling which had governed since 1944 the level of jurisdiction of the APT&C Council and bringing into its scope the "lettered grades" and other senior officers hitherto within scope of the Joint Negotiating Committee for Chief Officers. This was accompanied by the creation of a grading committee to consider matters specifically affecting the pay and service conditions of the various professional groups who were given special right of access to it.

Another constitutional change made at the same time by the APT&C Council provided specifically for the first time the right of either side to seek settlement of any dispute by arbitration.

The APT&C Council spent the first half of 1963 discussing the staff side's pay claim which sought massive changes in the lower end of the salary structure and increases throughout ranging from 11 to 20%. In sharp contrast the possibilities of a more modest settlement and a measure of stability by the exploration of a long-term agreement were the remit of the employer representatives in a joint working party. The three-year agreement reached in August 1963 in line with the NEDC recommendations and within the limits of the Government's incomes policy reflected closer proximity to the employers' objectives than to the unions' starting position.

Although the provincial negotiating machinery for both APT&C staffs and manual workers was changed by the reorganisation of local government in London in April 1965 under the London Government Act 1963, APT&C were more affected by the work of the London Government Staff Commission. It was at the latter's request that the APT&C employers wrote to all London authorities early in 1964 about late increases in pay, drawing attention to the Commission's opinion that "any upgrading solely or mainly as a preliminary step to transfer under the reorganisation might seriously impair the fair assimilation of staff".

Lord Hill of Luton at the time of his appointment as Independent Chairman of the APT&C Council in 1963.

Sir Thomas Phillips retired as Independent Chairman of the APT&C Council in 1963 after a 12-year period of office. Lord Hill of Luton who was appointed by the Minister of Local Government to succeed him was well-known as the "Radio Doctor" and former Cabinet Minister, and then occupied the chair for 15 years until 1978.

An interesting feature of the early part of this period was a number of exhortations to local authorities by the APT&C employers not to pay salaries above the levels settled in national negotiations for nationally prescribed grades. The tone of the admonitions in the 1950s contrasts sharply with the subsequent mood of the 1980s where greater flexibility became the order of the day.

The spread of three-year "Neddy" settlements continued with the agreements at the end of 1963 covering clerks of county councils, town and district council clerks and chief officers. These provided increases over a three-year period matching those agreed for APT&C staffs by a complicated formula revising the scales to give increases of 8% in April 1964 and a further 3.5% increase in January 1966. Medical and (Hospital) Dental Council Committee followed suit in April 1964 with a virtually identical agreement for local authority medical officers of health.

The LACSAB secretariat had been servicing the Whitley Council for New Towns Staffs since its formation in 1955. Whilst their settlements had normally followed the pattern set for analogous staffs under the APT&C Council, 1963 saw the start of a long wrangle in which the New Towns staffs' side (also predominated by NALGO) pressed for a firm salary linkage between New Towns chief officers and assistant secretaries in the Civil Service. This was strongly resisted by the New Towns employers who contended that a more appropriate relationship was with local authority chief officers.

FIRE BRIGADES

In the fire service 1958 began with Government intervention and the Secretaries of State refusing to approve recommendations for 1957 pay increases for firewomen in line with those agreed for firemen, followed by a further veto on a new pay structure hammered out for chief and assistant chief fire officers and firemasters to apply from 1st January 1958. Following a claim for increases of £1 per week agreement was reached on an increase of 7s.6d. per week for firemen, leading firemen and sub-officers with effect from 1st August 1958 with corresponding increases for other ranks.

The period between the 1958 and 1960 firemen's agreements saw the removal of the necessity to seek Government approval for them. The 1960 agreement operative from 1st April 1960 (and now expressed as annual salary) involved a major overhaul of the wage structure to restore their relative wage position; to encourage a better type of recruit; and to provide rewards for long service for those with no prospects of promotion – with an enhanced maximum rate being attained after nine years instead of after 15 years. Before negotiations in earnest the employers fully consulted fire authorities in a series of regional conferences in which there had been general recognition that significant improvements were necessary.

Following a 1960 campaign for its introduction by the FBU, the 48-hour working week quietly slipped into the list of approved duty systems in April 1961 as the Home Secretary withdrew his previous opposition to it.

Selwyn Lloyd's announcement of a "wage pause" for the public sector had come just as the FBU and NAFO were poised to lodge a claim for a £5 a week rise which they in fact tabled in August 1961. Manpower problems in the London and Middlesex fire brigades had led the employers to suggest interim plusages in those areas, but this move was seized upon by the unions as an attempt to destroy the national rate and to split the service. A typical big national campaign was mounted by the two unions to gain support from fire authorities to put the employers under much pressure. Agreement was nevertheless reached in December 1961 following another comprehensive review, substantially increasing pay and prospects; widening differentials between the provinces, the home counties and London; and emphasising the need for flexibility in hours of duty (with improved payments for more economical duty systems). In the provinces the increases at maximum were just over 19%. In order not to offend the Government's pay pause policy the new rates did not trigger until 1st January 1962, with the employers in frequent talks with Ministers pointing out to them that the agreement conformed to the principles which they had themselves applied in the Civil Service.

A further 3% increase to take effect from 1st August 1963 within the limits of the Government's incomes policy was agreed by the Fire Brigades NJC in June 1963 applicable to operational members of brigades and officer ranks. Having clinched a 1963 deal before the spate of three-year agreements, the Fire Brigades NJC brought themselves into line with other local government groups by concluding a two- year settlement in 1964 providing for annual pay increases of 3.5% within the Government's "guiding light" applicable from August 1964 and August 1965.

POLICE

There was no agreement in 1958 in Committee C of the Police Council arising from a 10% claim from the Police Federation who again resorted to arbitration. The Police Arbitration Tribunal were again unable to reach a unanimous award, the majority decision in September 1958 giving increases of 4 to 5% as from April 1958 in respect of constables, referring back to negotiation the pay of other federated ranks.

As with many other negotiating groups, 1959 was a fallow year for police pay negotiations. The 1959 development which was to have a profound impact subsequently was the announcement that December by the Prime Minister of the setting up of a Royal Commission on the Police headed by Sir Henry Willink QC with terms of reference including "the broad principles which should govern the remuneration of the constable...". Great expectations were aroused as most bodies giving evidence to the Royal Commission, including those represented on the official side of the Police Council, suggested special and substantial improvements in pay. These expectations were largely fulfilled in the Royal Commission's report published in November 1960. The maximum rate for the constable was increased from £695 to £910 after nine years' service (31% increase), with further long-service supplements leading to a rate of £970 after 22 years' service (nearly 40% increase). The official side's reaction to these Willink findings led to some criticism (especially from "The Guardian" whose editor had been a member of the Royal Commission) as they had quickly agreed to the pay increases recommended but had been at pains to distance themselves from the formulae by which the Royal Commission had reached their recommendations, which "The Economist" had described as "odd".

The Royal Commission had not made specific pay recommendations for ranks above constable but left these for subsequent negotiations which in the event evoked much controversy with views polarised as to how differentials should be maintained. The frequent jibe that remission of issues to the joint secretaries is often a step backwards in negotiations was disproved in this case: whilst the police authorities and the Police Federation had separate meetings, the joint secretaries provided a link between them and this eventually led to settlements by February 1961 backdated as in the case of constables to 1st September 1960 for all other ranks right up to chief constable, maintaining differentials by increases of 30% or more.

The effects of the Willink findings cushioned the police more than other public services to withstand the rigours of the 1961 pay pause. The 1962 discussions in Committee C of the Police Council heralded a bold new approach in line with the Willink proposals, moving away from the confrontation of claim followed by response towards a practice of a biennial joint examination of the case for pay adjustments in the light of wage movements in the economy as a whole. This new system led to a two-stage agreement being concluded in November 1962 with a 3.5% increase payable from 1st September 1962 (two years after the Willink improvements) and a further 2.5% increase payable from 1st February 1963 to run to 31st August 1964. It was hoped that this could have encouraging implications for pay negotiations in local government and in the public services generally.

With police pay sorted out until the end of August 1964, the Police Federation lodged a claim for a reduction in hours from 44 to 40 a week in July 1963. The official side were not prepared to contemplate an early reduction in hours because of manning implications, and with polarised views emerging, the staff side let it be known that they were considering arbitration. The "News Summary" report at that stage concluded with four innocuous words – "informal discussions are continuing" – and these evidently bore fruit as settlement was reached in October 1963 on a 42-hour working week to apply from 1st July 1964. Special transitional arrangements were hammered out for those police forces who could not reduce normal hours of duty by the date of implementation.

Following a further review under the arrangements introduced in 1964, revised rates of pay were agreed towards the end of 1964 for the police "federated" ranks to operate from 1st September 1964 to 31st August 1966 giving average increases ranging from 7.1 to 7.45%.

An important event in 1964 was the enactment of the new Police Act arising from the Royal Commission's recommendations of 1962. This provided for the Police Council to be the statutory negotiating body for the police service with a clear definition of negotiating powers; cadets to come within scope; and reference to arbitration where the two sides failed to reach agreement. Two Police Advisory Boards were created for consultation on "non-negotiable" functions.

PROBATION SERVICE

Probation pay came into prominence early in 1958 as the Home Secretary partially vetoed increases agreed in the Joint Negotiating Committee for the Probation Service in respect of senior, deputy and assistant principal, and principal probation officers. This came at the same time as intervention in fire service pay as the Government sought to exert some moderation in pay settlements in the public sector as the Cohen Council on Prices, Productivity and Incomes began its task. This particular probation pay issue had started way back in 1956 but had been delayed awaiting the arbitration outcome in 1957 for basic grade probation officers, with the resultant increases applying from 1st January 1957.

Early in 1959 the JNC for the Probation Service were in the final stages of negotiation on a claim for a substantial pay increase for probation officers when the Home Secretary appointed a departmental committee to enquire into all aspects of the probation service, including "the important questions of recruitment, training, pay and conditions of work". This meant that many months' thorough work by a JNC working party had to be put to one side to await the departmental committee's deliberations. During the course of 1960 while the departmental committee continued their review the probation service was not excluded from the general uplift in incomes when agreement was reached on revised scales with effect from 1st August 1960, providing increases of the order of 12.5%, and taking the maximum rate for a probation officer up to £1,025 a year.

The major recommendations of the departmental committee on the probation service in March 1962 included substantial increases in pay (for example lifting the maximum of the basic grade from £1,025 to £1,350 per year, i.e. an increase of 31.7%); the removal of the Ministers' right to veto negotiated recommendations; and uniform salaries for England, Wales and Scotland. Such large pay increases did not flow through to probation officers all at the same time, but by staged increases in January 1963, January 1964 and December 1964. The report of this phased agreement was accompanied by a statement pointing out that the agreement of a review to take effect from lst January 1966 would be that, having reached their new "plateau" in terms of salary, probation officers would make their contribution to stability by refraining from submitting frequent claims at short intervals - an expectation which appears to have been fulfilled.

STAFFING AND PEOPLE

The continued expansion in negotiating work led to considerable staff strengthening. Those appointed included Peter Fuller (later to become South Eastern provincial employers' secretary); David Thomas (subsequently LACSAB deputy secretary and then secretary); Alan Hoskins (later to become Yorkshire and Humberside provincial employers' secretary); Geoff Kelly and Alisdair Campbell. The award in 1962 of the OBE to Harry Rae, then LACSAB assistant secretary, was widely welcomed.

Haden Corser, former deputy general secretary of NALGO, died in September 1964. He had been widely regarded as a co- architect with Edward Bishop of national whitleyism in local government and had worked closely with Edward Bishop in the North West as well as at national level. It was much due to his perseverance that NALGO won the famous Bolton judgement of 1942 by the House of Lords establishing the right of local government officers to compulsory arbitration under the terms of the Industrial Disputes Order.

CONCLUSION

The end of this period was marked at Government level by a "sea change" as thirteen years of Conservative rule from 1951 to 1964 was brought to a close by the October 1964 general election outcome which put Labour into control with Harold Wilson as Prime Minister but with only a knife-edge Commons majority of six. Such major political upheavals have on occasions over the years resulted in dramatic revisions in incomes policies causing fundamental changes in the work of LACSAB. There was no sign of such dramatic change following the 1964 general election and this appears to be mainly due to the relatively tranquil scene at that time in local government pay negotiations with the overwhelming majority of employees in scope snugly cocooned within moderate long-term agreements of two or three years' duration stretching well into 1966 and thus largely immune from immediate change arising from external pressures.

LACSAB had actively encouraged the moves towards longer-term agreements and the stability which they created and so could be reasonably satisfied with the scene of industrial peace in local government which they could see at the end of 1964. When pay increases had been greater in recent years these had often arisen from Government intervention such as the Royal Commission on Police and the Departmental Committee on the Probation Service, or from the Government's treatment of their own employees in the Civil Service under the "fair comparisons" formula.

Barbara Castle, the newly appointed Secretary of State for Employment and Productivity in 1968.

5

LABOUR PAINS GIVING BIRTH TO STATUTORY PAY POLICIES

"This is an exceedingly interesting and exciting time to study industrial relations and to be involved in it. No man can tell where the processes of change will carry us."

Dr. W.E.J.("Bill") McCarthy introduced in 1969 the book – "Industrial Relations in Britain: A Guide for Management and Unions" with the above words. It was certainly a fascinating period as the Labour government elected in October 1964 tried in its early "honeymoon" days to create a voluntary policy for prices and incomes; then tried its hand at statutory policies from July 1966; but finally gave up in the wage explosion of 1970 preceding the general election which led to its removal from office. Local government pay negotiations co-ordinated by the LACSAB secretariat were fundamentally affected by these events.

POLITICAL AND ECONOMIC CONTEXT

George Brown, the Minister for Economic Affairs, had achieved his first target with the signing of a Joint Statement of Intent on productivity, prices and incomes by the Government, the CBI and the TUC on 16th December 1964. The next step was the establishment of the new National Board for Prices and Incomes (NBPI)) with the acceptance in March 1965 of the Chairmanship by Aubrey Jones (a former Conservative MP) and the winding up of the National Incomes Commission ("Nicky") the previous month. In April 1965 the Government moved into its third and highly critical stage with the publication of criteria for incomes levels pitched at a "norm" of 3-3.5% average rate of annual increase of money incomes per head consistent with stability in the general level of prices. There were four criteria for pay increases beyond the norm, one for notably increased productivity, and also one where the pay of a certain group of workers was recognised as having fallen seriously out of line (the escape clause which would allow Civil Service "fair comparisons" increases to continue unmolested). A special TUC conference of trade union executives endorsed the Government's policy on 30th April 1965, but difficulties were already looming ahead.

George Brown became Minister for Economic Affairs in the autumn of 1964.

The key question as 1965 unfolded was how the effects of the immediate measures on prices and incomes would facilitate the fulfilment of the long-term plan for the British economy which ambitiously aimed to increase the gross domestic product by 25% between 1964 and 1970. The NBPI under Aubrey Jones surged into a period of intense activity (and publicity), producing six main reports in their first nine months, and with many other references to them in the pipeline.

At the beginning of 1966, the Prime Minister, Harold Wilson, prophesied that it would be a "make or break" year and there were many Government exhortations on the twin needs for a faster rise in industrial efficiency and a slower rise in incomes. By early summer in 1966 the Government's incomes and prices policy was under heavy fire, with the NBPI's recommendations being ignored by both sides of industry. The moderate "Socialist Commentary" observed "we have reached the curious point where the necessity of an incomes policy is widely accepted, coupled with an equally wide determination on every side to get round it".

Aubrey Jones (left) on the Prices and Incomes Board in 1965.

The Prime Minister's announcement on 20th July 1966 of a general standstill on prices and incomes up to the end of that year (and a period of severe restraint in the first half of 1967) nevertheless came as a considerable surprise. The purpose was to give the country a breathing space in which productivity could catch up with the excessive increases in incomes which had taken place. A White Paper – "Prices and Incomes Standstill" – set out the Government's intentions in respect of existing and new agreements, the dividing line drawn at 20th July. Existing commitments, i.e. agreements already reached, were to be delayed by six months, and "new and stringent criteria" were to be drawn up for new agreements, while for the time being the incomes norm was zero. This sent shock waves through all the pay bargaining processes, not least in local government pay negotiations, with so much depending on whether or not an agreement was "in the bag" when the axe fell. In local government this led to the first of many circulars from the Ministry of Housing and Local Government and other "sponsoring" departments advising on the interpretation of the statutory pay policy in local government. LACSAB were consulted and able to exert some influence on how the incomes policy was applied in the particular circumstances of local authorities.

Although these stringent Government measures caused a sharp fall in industrial production and a disturbing rise in unemployment – thus severely denting the aspirations of the longer-term economic plans – they did nonetheless have the intended effect of halting the pay and price increases. The next Government White Paper published in December 1966 – "Period of Severe Restraint" – meant in effect that the standstill in incomes would continue until the end of June 1967 except in a very few cases.

The beginning of 1967 saw much debate about the future of the prices and incomes policy, with the CBI and the TUC uniting in their opposition to Government intervention and with both wedded to voluntary collective bargaining. The unions' earlier reluctant acquiescence in Government policy had now given way to an attitude of "hands off collective bargaining" leading to an unprecedented step at a special TUC conference on 2nd March 1967 when the TUC were given greater authority over wage claims. Unemployment had risen sharply to over 600,000 but there were signs of a marginal upturn in business confidence.

The Government's White Paper published in March 1967 – "Prices and Incomes Policy after 30th June 1967" – revealed only a slight retreat from their earlier inflexible stand on economic policy, despite the prospects of a head-on collision with the TUC. The key note was moderation: a voluntary incomes policy was to operate with the Government having reserve powers in case it failed. The norm for the next twelve months would still be zero, and increases would only be justified against four criteria on the lines of those which had applied for exceptional increases prior to 20th July 1966. These criteria were used to good advantage by LACSAB officers as they sought to repair the damage to many pay relationships shattered as the axe had fallen on 20th July 1966 between those who had secured firm agreements and those who were about to. Part II of the Prices and Incomes Act was activated giving the Government power to delay a price or pay rise for seven months on reference to the NBPI. This stage in policy was applied less severely than the previous one so that nearly everybody had pay increases in the second half of 1967, but it was tightened up again as further economic problems led to the Government decision on 18th November 1967 to devalue the pound sterling by 14.3%.

The keynote of the White Paper – "Productivity, Pay and Incomes in 1968 and 1969" – published soon after the Budget in March 1968 was that national economic strategy must be directed towards higher productivity and restraint on incomes. All increases in pay in the next two years had to be justified against the criteria and then held within a ceiling of 3.5% per annum. This policy and the further statutory powers backing it aroused opposition on all fronts, with the legislation scraping home in the House of Commons by small majorities because of many Labour abstentions.

The Government's prices and incomes policy was very much in the melting pot as 1968 drew to a close, with the Department of Employment and Productivity preparing a new White Paper for 1970 after exhaustive discussions with the TUC and the CBI. Despite evidence of improvement in the economy there were several causes for concern, with the retail price index reaching a new high level and discontent flaring up among the lower paid workers, notably local government manual workers in the "dustmen's dispute".

The end of 1969 and the beginning of 1970 saw a pay explosion. The Government's White Paper outlining its 1970 policy fixed a guideline for increases ranging from 2.5% to 4.5% a year. Barbara Castle, the Secretary of State for Employment, was at pains to point out this was not a "norm" in the old sense: the Government was merely saying what they thought was the most that was possible if prices were to be kept stable. Although she insisted on taking powers to delay pay increases for up to four months, she neither used them nor intervened even when, for instance, the builders negotiated a settlement raising their rates by 27% over the next 18 months.

The pay revolt in the public sector proceeded apace in the first half of 1970 with the teachers joining in with their industrial action in support of their interim claim. The prevailing mood was that new Government restrictions could be expected after the general election, whatever the outcome, and most workers were out to get what they could while the going was good. The Government's prices and incomes policy was regarded as defunct, with trade unions gaining increases far beyond the guidelines, and managements anxious to settle to avoid losses through strikes. Whatever intentions may have been behind the Government's inertia, the effect was a pre-general election pay bonanza.

THE "DONOVAN" REPORT

Other important features in the overall national context of this period were the inquiry, report and reactions arising from the ("Donovan") Royal Commission on Trade Unions and Employers' Associations. 1965 and 1966 saw the collection of a massive amount of evidence, including that of LACSAB and the local authority associations. LACSAB said the role of an employers' organisation was not merely defensive, as it should play a vital role to secure greater productivity and efficiency by linking pay with the maximum use of labour and other resources. "An effective representative employers' organisation is an essential part of the country's administrative framework in the public service as well as in industry" and "success in joint consultation depends on fully representative trade unions" were two major themes in the LACSAB evidence. LACSAB also held strongly to the view that agreements ought to be enforceable on both sides: employing authorities should pay neither more nor less than the agreed rate. The character of local government negotiating machinery came under searching scrutiny when the LACSAB chairman, secretary and other members were called to give oral evidence to the Royal Commission at the end of 1966, with the questions asked ranging from national or local bargaining to allegations of local authorities being low paying employers.

The Royal Commission's report, eventually published in 1968, was a weighty tome, recommending – inter alia – the registration of collective agreements; the establishment of an Industrial Relations Commission; the appointment of labour tribunals to cover disputes between employees and employers over statutory and contractual rights; and an independent review body to handle complaints by workers of unfair treatment by trade unions. They had examined at length the LACSAB view that agreements should be enforceable but had concluded this was virtually impracticable to achieve. Both the CBI and the TUC agreed that the Donovan report placed too much emphasis on local or plant bargaining, and too little on the value of national or industry-wide agreements.

The Government's White Paper – "In Place of Strife" – early in 1969 following the Donovan report proposed:-

(i) a commission on industrial relations to look into trade recognition problems and to promote trade union reforms;

(ii) a register of industrial agreements;

(iii) trade unions to be given the right to be furnished with certain information from employers;

(iv) the right to belong to a trade union to be part of all contracts of employment;

(v) power to the Secretary of State to require an employer to recognise and negotiate with a union;

(vi) discretionary power to the Secretary of State to require a 28-day "reconciliation pause"" in unconstitutional and some other strikes and to require a union ballot before a major official strike is called;
(vii) statutory machinery to safeguard employees against unfair dismissal;
(viii) a new industrial board with power to impose penalties for breach of an order by the Secretary of State, and also to hear complaints by individuals against unfair and arbitrary action by trade unions; and
(ix) trade unions to be required to register with a new registrar of trade unions.

Barbara Castle, the Secretary of State for Employment, incurred wrath on all sides for these proposals: from the TUC for going too far; from the CBI for not going far enough (as John Davies of the CBI put it – "taking a nutcracker to crack a cannonball"); and from LACSAB for not pursuing sufficiently the enforcing on national agreements. The main cause of controversy was undoubtedly the proposals to reduce the incidence of strikes by imposing a "cooling off" period and by making it compulsory in certain cases to ballot members first. These proposals were included in the subsequent Industrial Relations Bill and were the subject of prolonged negotiations between the Government and the TUC. A special TUC conference on 5th June 1969 resulted in an overwhelming majority (which included all the unions with members in local government) against penal sanctions on strikes. Only a few days later on 18th June the Government decided to drop the penal clauses from the Bill and to defer introduction of the Bill until the next session. In return the TUC General Council gave a "solemn and binding undertaking" to use their influence to settle unconstitutional strikes, mainly to be achieved by a strengthening of TUC Rule 11 giving the General Council wide powers to intervene in disputes likely to lead to stoppages. A writer in LACSAB's "News Summary" in July 1969 commented – "Local government officers are not particularly strike-prone, though there is a militant sector. The presence or absence of penal clauses may therefore be thought to be largely a matter of theory or principle." He would not have made such a complacent comment a year later.

A revised and emaciated Industrial Relations Bill was published in May 1970 but did not get through Parliament before the general election. Given the spate of disputes and strikes in the months leading up to the general election in local government and elsewhere, the TUC's "Solomon Binding" undertaking of June 1969 appears in retrospect to have been quite toothless. Indeed, the pay explosion of that time needs to be understood in terms of the inertia of both the Government and the TUC in that period.

One issue mentioned in the Donovan report which was taken up and pursued by legislation was that of equal pay for women on which they thought "the facts so disturbing and the social and economic implications so important". This eventually resulted in the Equal Pay Act 1970 which allowed women to claim equal pay with men if they were engaged on like work or work rated as equivalent, but not becoming fully operative until December 1975.

OVERALL LACSAB ACTIVITIES

Much of the time of the LACSAB Board during this period was occupied in co-ordinating local government pay negotiations as one phase of Government incomes policy succeeded another, as well as in giving evidence to the

("Donovan") Royal Commission on Trade Unions and Employers' Associations and reacting to the proposed legislation which flowed from the Donovan report.

Two important constitutional developments were the establishment of the Local Government Training Board (LGTB) in 1967 and of the Local Authorities Management Services and Advisory Committee (LAMSAC) in 1968. Both of these bodies had to a considerable extent grown out of the LACSAB organisation. The LGTB had first been suggested in a report of the Local Government Examinations Board (LGEB) which it absorbed. Its functions were to be similar to those of the nine statutory training boards set up under the Industrial Training Act 1965 but it would be voluntary not statutory. Lord Morris, formerly LGEB Chairman, was elected the first LGTB Chairman; Dudley Lofts, formerly LGEB Secretary, was appointed as the LGTB's first Director and David Thomas of LACSAB became its Chief Administrative Officer. The establishment of LAMSAC stemmed in large part from the increasing interest in productivity and work study methods fostered by the Local Government Work Study Group administered by LACSAB. It also arose from a recommendation of the National Board for Prices and Incomes (NBPI) in their Report No. 29 on the pay of local authority manual workers. LAMSAC's first Chief Advisory Officer was S.R.(Roy) Barnes.

An indication of the scale of activity in this period was the appointment by the LACSAB Board in December 1967 of a special sub-committee to co-ordinate responses to the NBPI who then had simultaneously three separate references affecting local government, i.e. manual workers, firemen and clerks/chief officers.

A decision which had considerable implications for the future work of LACSAB as well as for local government negotiating machinery generally was made in 1970 in accepting a recommendation of a working party of the APT&C and manual employers that the employers' secretarial arrangements at provincial level should, wherever possible, be unified and put on a full-time basis. The aim was to pursue unified policies at both national and provincial levels and for local government to operate as a single "industry". At the beginning of 1970 there were only five full-time professional provincial secretariats. LACSAB officers had serviced many provincial employers' sides on a part-time basis, and such arrangements were all eventually terminated as full-time provincial arrangements were made.

MANUAL WORKERS

The decision by the manual workers NJC in March 1965 to "open up" the three-year pay settlement and agree a 7s. per week increase as from 12th April 1965 was not felt to be a breach in that pact as the cost of living had increased beyond what could reasonably have been anticipated when the deal was struck in October 1963.

Demands for increased pay, supported by unofficial action by some members of the London Ambulance Service led after difficulties and discussions to the NJC approving an excess rate of 14s. per week from June 1965 to all the 100,000 manual workers (including ambulancemen) within its scope in London.

In October 1965 the NJC also agreed to reduce working hours from 42 to 40 per week from January 1966 against the background of encouraging efforts to increase productivity and efficiency "in accordance with the spirit of the Joint Statement of Intent on Productivity, Prices and Incomes". The 40-hour week had become widespread in most industries, but implementation was delayed until January 1966 to give local authorities the longest possible lead time.

The trade unions lodged a claim for an unusually large amount of 22s. per week to apply from September 1966 when the three- year pact expired, and the subsequent negotiations encountered several obstacles. In the closing stages pressure developed inspired by two of the three unions involved, GMWU and NUPE, for the claim to be referred to the NBPI. The publication at the end of June 1966 of the NBPI's report on industrial civil servants increased the possibility of a reference. Nevertheless a deal was struck at the NJC meeting on 7th July with Government clearance having been received and the likelihood of a reference to the NBPI having receded. The main features of the two-year agreement to last until September 1968 were a general increase of 11s.8d. per week from 5th September 1966; a further increase of 10s. per week from 4th September 1967; and the abolition of the Zone B rate in April 1967. But between agreement and implementation came the Prime Minister's announcement of a standstill on prices and wages. This meant that the manual agreement had to be deferred for six months from the original operative date of 5th September 1966 to 5th March 1967.

When soon afterwards the Government referred the pay of local authority manual workers to the NBPI the manual employers protested that there was no need for this as there was a two- year agreement extending into 1968. However they lost no time in preparing and presenting to the NBPI three memoranda later in 1966, two of which dealt at some length with the principles of pay determination for this group. Early in 1967 there was further written and oral evidence by both the employers and the trade unions.

The NBPI published in February 1967 their Report No.29 on the pay and conditions of manual workers in local authorities, the NHS, gas and water supply. They found the standard of labour utilisation in local government low; the complicated wage structure did not rest on any scientifically based system of job evaluation; and the spread of differentials was too low. They suggested the two sides should undertake a detailed examination of grades, occupations and relativities using job evaluation techniques. On the immediate pay issues the NBPI recommended that increases for county council roadmen and for manual workers in Scotland should be paid from 6th March 1967 as for manual workers in England and Wales although these had not been fully agreed by 20th July 1966. Local government contained large concentrations of workers among the lowest paid in the country: in the long term the solution of the low pay problem must be the more effective use of labour, such as incentive bonus schemes, measured day work and productivity agreements. To this end the establishment was proposed of national advisory services associated with the national negotiating machinery. As an interim measure pending the introduction of longer-term measures the NBPI proposed the introduction of a "rough and ready" scheme for interim payments to be negotiated by the NJC, suggesting a productivity increment of 10% of the basic wage rate payable on achievement of a 10% reduction in total labour costs. For the longer-term objective of linking pay to improved productivity the NBPI saw as important prerequisites (i) the need for higher standards of management; (ii) the need for better supervision; and (iii) a wide extension in the use of work study. They recommended the merging with the manual workers NJC of the Scottish NJIC, the NJC for county council roadmen, the wages boards for Glamorgan, Monmouthshire and Bristol, together with the transfer of ancillary staff employed by local authorities from the ancillary staffs council for the NHS to the manual workers NJC.

These were remarkably wide-ranging recommendations to stem from such a quick examination, but nevertheless the local authority employers were able immediately to state that at most points these coincided with their own policies. It was felt there might be general concern about the NBPI's strictures on low labour utilisation and there was some doubt about the suggested short-term productivity increment which seemed to fall short of the Government's stringent criteria. The employers quickly decided to appoint a firm of industrial consultants to examine the NBPI suggestion for an interim productivity scheme. The employers had been already well advanced in formulating ideas on the shape of a national advisory service before the NBPI inquiry. A review of the wages structure was also in hand, but it was not envisaged this would be based on sophisticated job evaluation techniques, although a job evaluation officer would be used.

The NPBI's recommendations on productivity and labour utilisation gave impetus to a movement which was already well under way. Over 200 local authorities were by then developing and using management service techniques. The Local Government Work Study Group, formed in 1963 with much support and encouragement by LACSAB and the manual employers had a membership of 300 management service officers and 450 authorities in corporate membership. The manual workers NJC had in January 1966 agreed a code of guiding principles for incentive schemes based on work study. LACSAB's "News Summary" had in the previous few years carried many articles on productivity, management services and work study to promote ideas and to stimulate action, and it was LACSAB and the manual employers who had initiated and organised the series of annual national conferences on management services at Harrogate. For example "News Summary" of May 1965 reproduced an article from "The Times" commenting on a recent survey showing that 77 local authorities were saving £2m a year through the application of work study.

PA Management Consultants who had been engaged by the manual employers concluded that an interim scheme to improve productivity side by side with increased earnings was practicable. They disproved the NBPI's suggestion that it would be possible to establish standard rates of output for the main classes of work which could then be applied nationally, but were fortunately able to propose a simple alternative which they were then asked to validate by implementing schemes in four local authorities willing to co-operate. These pilot schemes confirmed the practicability of the scheme recommended by PA and so the manual workers NJC were able in January 1969 to recommend an interim productivity scheme for adoption by local authorities. In May 1969 it was predicted in "News Summary" that by February 1972 125,000 out of 200,000 full-time workers and 110,000 out of 230,000 part-time workers would be on work-studied bonus schemes or other productivity schemes.

As to classification of manual workers' jobs, a study undertaken by the London

Boroughs Management Services Unit (LBMSU) commissioned by the manual employers confirmed their view that there was no need for a complete overhaul of the wages structure; that the NJC's system had over the years produced reasonable standards of grades and wage levels; but recommended that a limited use of job evaluation techniques would provide even more accurate results. These findings were accepted by the NJC and a series of officer working parties set up to review the main occupational group wage levels.

The merging of negotiating bodies as proposed by the NBPI was effected as from 1st July 1969 after all the necessary assents had been gained, with arrangements for specialist committees for county roadmen and employees in residential establishments, as well as a measure of autonomy for Scotland.

THE "DUSTMEN'S STRIKE"

"Perhaps the most astonishing thing about the 'dustmen's strike' was that the leaders on neither side had any idea they were sitting on a volcano until it erupted". Thus began a comment from an outside observer in "News Summary" of November 1969. There was an NJC executive committee meeting on 22nd September 1969 to discuss the outstanding aspects for a pay settlement. Much had been achieved on the revaluation of all occupational groups, and all that remained was to settle the amount of the basic increase and the top and bottom figures of the new structure, and to sort out some of the allocations to grades. When it became obvious because of the reclassification complications that negotiations would drag on for some weeks, Reginald Griffiths, the employers' secretary, suggested an interim increase. But the trade union leaders were confident there would be no trouble as long as they could fix an operative date, which they did for 29th September.

Yet that same night the Hackney branch of NUPE voted in favour of a strike for a £20 basic wage and the Hackney dustmen stopped work the next day. The strike spread with gathering impetus to other London boroughs and the provinces. Within a fortnight dustcarts had vanished from practically the whole of London and in many other areas of the country. Here and there other workers came out in support of the dustmen. Thousands of tons of garbage were piled in the streets, parks and lavatories closed, and funerals postponed. It was not at all clear why there had been this sudden rebellion, why it was dustmen, why in London, and how the employers and trade union leaders had been caught unawares.

Communication was certainly an important factor. The employers had originally been talking of an increase of 3.5% in line with incomes policy but on 19th September the Government conceded an 8.5% increase backdated to 1st July for their industrial workers (two of the three manual unions were involved in that deal) so it was obvious at the national meeting on 22nd September that an increase of only 3.5% was out of the question. When the Hackney NUPE branch made their decision that day they had not heard anything about the national meeting earlier that same day, but they had heard rumours of an offer of a minimum increase of 10s. a week which they regarded as wholly inadequate.

In the context of the prairie fire of spreading strikes negotiations could not be allowed to drag on and there was a paramount need for agreement when the NJC met on 9th October in Edinburgh. And there was final settlement there

A Council refuse collector.

providing increases ranging from 15s to about 35s. per week – even more in some cases. Dustmen got 30s. on their basic rate, those in London got another 11s. on their London addition, plus 9s. for those men who had no bonus scheme. Occupations were reclassified into seven new pay groups. The overall increase of 8.5% was at the time the largest ever for manual workers, and in London it was much more.

In retrospect, particularly in the knowledge of the mammoth job evaluation exercise in the 1980s, what is perhaps most incredible is how dustmen fared so well in the 1969 revaluation of posts.

Despite the magnitude of the Edinburgh settlement in October 1969 the trade unions presented at the NJC meeting on 23rd April 1970 their biggest claim ever, seeking an increase of £2.15s. (20%) to take the basic rate up to £16.10s. a week, as well as a 10% penalty on basic rates to all employees not covered by a productivity or bonus scheme and other subsidiary claims.

AIRPORTS

Airport staffs came into the news in June and July 1968 in a dispute at Manchester airport marked by a series of lightning stoppages. The root of the dispute was a demand by the airport staff at Manchester to break away from the municipal airports agreement and to follow the British Airports Authority (BAA) agreement covering Heathrow, Gatwick, etc. The dispute was settled after conciliation by the NJC's joint secretaries, Reginald Griffiths and Derek Gladwin. A study of the wage structure and job specifications for municipal airport ground staff was overtaken in the spring of 1969 by a reference by the Government to the NBPI of pay and conditions covering not only municipal airports but also airports run by the BAA and the Board of Trade. The NBPI published their Report No. 128 in October 1969 recommending in the interests of reducing friction and unrest the establishment of unified negotiating machinery covering all civil publicly owned airports. They made no explicit recommendations about pay levels, save to suggest that the principle of a London differential should be accepted. Problems at Heathrow had led meanwhile in 1970 to a court of inquiry led by Professor Robertson. The local authority employers had originally opposed unified negotiating machinery for fear of repercussions on the pay of their half million or so other manual workers, but speedily accepted the main NBPI recommendation as did the Government. The BAA strongly opposed unified machinery: they had their own domestic machinery (covering all employees) and their own problems – and did not wish to add to them. So the local authority employers made an offer of an increase of 35s. per week for employees in municipal airports as from 1st April 1970, linking future general pay increases to those agreed by the BAA, continuing to adhere to the local authority system of shift allowances, and reducing the number of classifications of municipal airports from five to two (only Manchester and Glasgow falling into the top category).

AMBULANCE SERVICE

The ambulance service was in this period still within local government. A working party on ambulance training had led to the adoption by the National Ambulance Service Advisory Council on 28th April 1969 of improved training standards, and this in turn was promptly followed by the NJC agreeing a revised wage structure for the ambulance service. The agreement envisaged a division of the service where practicable into transport and emergency services with pay enhancements for those ambulancemen trained to the new "Millar" standard (the working party had been led by Dr. E.L.M. Millar, Medical Officer of Health, Birmingham).

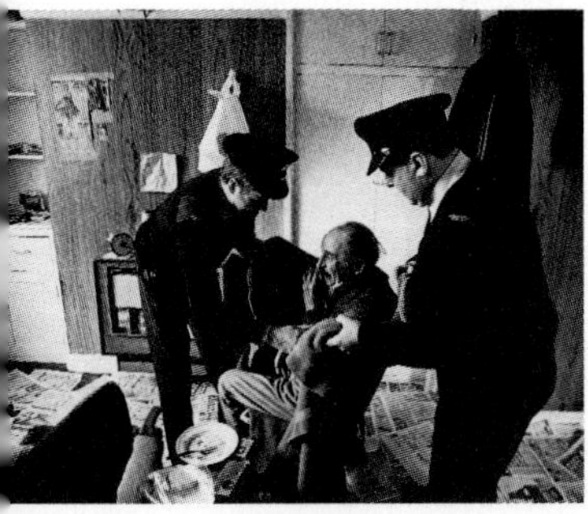

Ambulance men out on call.

Industrial action in certain ambulance authorities by supporters of the Federation of Ambulance Personnel led to the NJC asking in September 1969 Dr. W.E.J.McCarthy, then Research Fellow at St. Peter's College, Oxford, to enquire into the causes and circumstances of the dispute. Eric Wigham of "The Times" commented in "News Summary" of July 1970 – "Dr. McCarthy was given as ticklish a job as any industrial relations expert could have" as there were no precedents for dealing with a recognition claim by an organisation regarded by the recognised unions as a "break-away". His report published in May 1970 – "Representation and Collective Bargaining in the Ambulance Service" – showed that he based his judgements under three heads – representativeness, appropriateness and effects. He finally concluded that recognition of the federation would add to the existing inter-union rivalry and competition, recommending against recognition, although accepting many of the criticisms of the existing negotiating structure. He suggested a "Donovan"-style national ambulancemen's council involving rank and file ambulancemen representatives.

WORKSHOPS FOR THE BLIND

The recently formed NJC for Workshops for the Blind encountered tremendous problems in negotiating a new wage system for the blind to replace the system dividing take-home pay into "earnings" and "augmentation" which had been severely criticised by a Departmental Committee in 1962 because it provided no incentive to increase productivity. The employers made various proposals but these were all rejected by the National League for the Blind who made no counter-proposals other than to stay tied to the local authority manual rate as a guaranteed minimum. The National League pressed their claims for more pay vigorously and in May 1967 there were strikes in London workshops for the blind and a lobby of members of parliament. Following prolonged and sometimes bitter negotiations a new pay structure was eventually agreed early in 1968 which abolished the distinction between earnings and augmentation and linked blind workers to group 6 manual workers. Further difficulties arose in negotiations in 1969/1970 when the National League claimed a link with new manual category E following the restructuring of the wage grouping system for manual workers. This was eventually conceded although the employers had originally argued this was more than they were entitled to receive under the agreement providing for blind workers to receive any "general" increase in manual workers' pay.

APT&C STAFFS

As the 1963 APT&C three-year agreement extended through into 1966, direct pay negotiations for APT&C staffs did not form a feature of the 1965 scene. A significant development was a special conference in Cardiff in April 1965 when the national APT&C employers consulted their provincial colleagues on a variety of issues, especially to gauge opinion on pay structure for the 1966 negotiations. Early in 1966 the NJC set up a working party to examine the APT&C salary structure. Much work culminated in an agreement on 13th July 1966 by the NJC for a drastic reconstruction of the APT&C salary structure to operate from 1st August 1966 coupled with an all-round average increase of about 7% to last for two years. Clerical grades were fundamentally altered, a technical staff division was introduced as well as senior officers' grades and principal officers' ranges to emphasise career prospects. The full text of the historic agreement ran to 28 foolscap pages in the NJC Circular NO194 which also reveals the first steps towards the subsequently well-known pattern of a spinal column salary structure.

But this agreement too fell under the axe of the Prime Minister's announcement of a prices and incomes standstill on 20th July 1966 and its operation was delayed by six months to 1st February 1967. It had been the custom of the NJC's two committees covering residential staffs to follow the pattern of the main APT&C agreements. They were however caught on 20th July 1966 without firm agreements and it needed much effort and persuasion before they received increases corresponding to those in the main 1966 APT&C agreement, delayed in their case until 1st July 1967 under the Government's policy for the period of severe restraint.

Increases of the order of 3 to 3.5% conforming to the Government's incomes policy were agreed by the NJC in July 1968 to apply from 1st August 1968. The increases were slightly abated so that the money saved could be used to finance substantial increases of 10% or more for residential staffs also to apply from 1st August 1968 as allowed within the same negotiating group under incomes policy with support sought and gained from the sponsoring Government departments, notably the Home Office (Children's Department). Radical changes in the residential salary structure replaced over 30 existing categories with a system of five scales and one higher range, introducing a common charge for board and lodging instead of the multiplicity of charges hitherto.

After the one-year agreement of 1968, in 1969 the NJC reverted to a two-year APT&C settlement providing – in accordance with Government pay policy – increases of 3.5% from 1st August 1969 and a further 3.5% from 1st August 1970 to last for a further twelve months, subject to the right of either side to seek a further examination if there had been a major change in circumstances. There were larger increases for the clerical grade 1 and at other basic levels, together with the concession of a minimum salary at age 21 (then set at £635) which the employers were to rue for more than 20 years thereafter.

Whilst the employers could be reasonably satisfied with their 1969 pay bargain, the staff side leaders had clearly misjudged the feelings of their NALGO membership. A special NALGO delegate meeting that September "carried with general enthusiasm" a motion deploring the failure of their negotiators to achieve a reasonable increase and instructing that an improvement be sought immediately and negotiated without delay. Albert Nortrop, leader of the NJC staff side for many years, stepped down following much criticism and was replaced by Glyn Phillips. The increases eventually agreed of £80 at clerical grade 1 tapering sharply to £25 at senior officer level were described by the newly emerging NALGO Action Group as "so minute you have to put it under a microscope" but nevertheless were promptly accepted to leave the position clear to negotiate further increases from 1st August 1970. The hopes of the new staff side leadership that substantial increases would be forthcoming then as the 1970 pay explosion took off were not dashed and their claim for a 15% increase led to a quick settlement in June for an all-round improvement of 12.5% from 1st July 1970 - a month earlier than usual.

Although the inquiry by the National Board for Prices and Incomes (NBPI) on London weighting was primarily concerned with non-industrial civil servants, their eventual Report No.44 in 1967 had considerable implications for local government negotiators, especially APT&C. The APT&C employers were however able to face these with equanimity in the knowledge that the principles enunciated by the NBPI were largely those they had themselves suggested in their evidence to the NBPI.

One effect of the Government's incomes policy from 1966 onwards was that local proposals for regradings of APT&C officers had to be channelled through the employers' secretariat at Belgrave Square causing a great amount of work. A significant development arising from the difficulties of grading leapfrogging in London boroughs on the reorganisation of London local government in April 1965 was the creation at the instigation of the London Boroughs Association of a job evaluation system by the London Boroughs Management Services Unit (LBMSU) for the Greater London Whitley Council for APT&C staffs - the precursor of the model job evaluation scheme agreed nationally several years later.

A particular feature of the work of the employers in this period was the encouragement in the recruitment of APT&C staffs through careers conventions; national careers brochures (over 100,000 copies sold of one edition); and co- ordination of graduate recruitment.

The delicate balance of representation on the APT&C employers' side was marginally disturbed by the changes necessary on the reorganisation of London government in 1965. The strictly even 15 associations and 15 provincials which had prevailed since the 1940s was altered to 16 associations and 15 provincials. The Scottish APT&C Council was merged into the APT&C NJC in September 1969 on a basis similar to that on the Manual NJC, providing the Scots with four crucial seats on the APT&C employers' side.

TOP POSTS

Agreements for clerks and chief officers were due to expire at the end of July 1966 and, when the incomes standstill was announced on 20th July 1966, the authorities' sides were canvassing with provincial employers' sides under the extra-constitutional "sounding board" arrangements ideas of a 7% increase in line with that being proposed for APT&C staffs, coupled with structural alterations to seek to combat the extensive salary drift which had occurred. On 28th November 1966 the Government referred the pay of clerks and chief officers to the NBPI with wide-ranging terms of reference. The NBPI took much longer on this remit than on others and it was not until November 1967 that they finally produced their Report No.45 on the pay of chief and senior officers in local government service. In terms of salary levels they recommended increases from 1st July 1967 of 7% for those with salaries up to £3,000, tapering down to 3% for those above £6,000. The NBPI urged that pay should be related more closely to responsibilities and performance, criticising the existing pay system and the freedom it gave authorities which had resulted in a very high proportion paying at or near the permitted maximum, with nearly 25% paying over it. They suggested more numerous salary ranges related to narrower population ranges; deputies to be paid between two-thirds and 70% of their principals; a combined set of salary ranges covering county clerks, town and district clerks and chief officers; and a merging of the three existing negotiating bodies, to include the Greater London Council (GLC). Their long-term solution was job evaluation – to "provide a framework in which good management can be adequately rewarded ...no matter where the job is performed". Their suggestion for provincial representatives to be included on the employers' side of a new JNC was felt by the parties involved to be rather odd as none of them had made any reference to this in their submissions.

The JNCs quickly acted on the NBPI recommendation to increase salaries from 1st July 1967 but found it very difficult to make progress on most of the other proposals. When they reached agreement for 3% increases from 1st August 1968 they reported mixed progress on implementing the other NBPI recommendations. On deputies' salaries they went further by agreeing up to 75% rather than up to 70%, but instead of increasing the number of salary ranges they actually reduced them from three to two under 100,000 population. Little progress had been made on the other proposals. In fact, there was little further action on them, with agreements in 1969 and 1970 broadly reflecting those agreed for APT&C staffs.

When early in 1970 the Government proposed that the salaries of the most highly paid officers of local authorities should be determined by a panel of the Commission for Industry and Manpower – along with other groups such as members of parliament and senior civil servants – this was strongly opposed by LACSAB and the local authority associations because of its likely divisive effect on well-established negotiating machinery. The Bill to give effect to this proposal lapsed due to the dissolution on the general election later that year.

NEW TOWNS

In the Whitley Council for New Towns Staff 1965 saw agreement on the longstanding claim that the salaries of chief officers employed by development corporations should be linked to assistant secretaries in the civil service.

Of all the negotiating groups serviced by LACSAB affected by the incomes standstill on 20th July 1966, the Whitley Council for New Towns Staffs were entitled to feel most aggrieved. If they had met on 20th July rather than as they actually did on 21st July their pay agreement – providing for radical structural changes and the introduction of a simplified single series of scales – would have been delayed only until 1st February 1967, but instead they had to argue strongly before eventually securing its implementation. It was not until June 1967 that the

The Chief Architect of Washington New Town, Tyne and Wear.

Whitley Council was in a position to reach agreement on increases to be applied in two stages, first from 1st July 1967 and then secondly increases payable on 1st January 1968 but with retrospective effect from 1st July 1967.

The Whitley Council was unable to reach agreement on salaries to apply from 1st August 1969 and referred their difference for settlement by arbitration by the Industrial Court which awarded general increases of the order of 3.5% in line with APT&C staffs, and with increases up to 8.5% in their grade I.

FIRE BRIGADES

In November 1965 the unions submitted a claim for a substantial wage increase, overtime improvements, and acceptance of the 48-hour week as the standard system of duty. In subsequent discussions the employers' aim was to link pay improvements to better use of manpower, such as by extension of an improved residential (day manning) system, but this was rigidly opposed by the unions although the employers were prepared to concede an increase in excess of the Government's "norm". Negotiations were still in progress when the Prime Minister announced the incomes standstill on 20th July 1966 and were adjourned at a meeting the following day as by then it was known that the Government were immediately referring firemen's pay and hours to the National Board for Prices and Incomes (NBPI). The NBPI received evidence from both sides of the NJC early in 1967, the employers' evidence concentrating on suggestions covering both pay and duty systems. The NBPI Report No.32 on fire service pay published in May 1967 largely endorsed the employers' recommendations for a smaller and more highly paid service, save for an increase in the payment for extra availability and a change in its form. The NBPI commented that "working" hours in the fire service were not strictly comparable with those in industry since part of the fireman's time was spent waiting for emergency calls. The NBPI's main recommendations were a general pay increase of 7.5% from 1st July 1967 to last for two years; a pensionable payment (£170 a year at scale maximum) for extended availability; further discussions of the conditions under which the day-manning system would be more acceptable to the unions; the correction of the anomaly of firemen working a 56-hour week for the same pay as others doing 48 hours; and the formulation by the local authorities of a common practice on the provision of housing for firemen. Whilst the NBPI report was clearly acceptable overall to the employers, the Fire Brigades Union (FBU) expressed disappointment about the operative date of 1st July 1967, the two-year term, and that the report was silent on their claim for a 40-hour week. The NJC lost little time in reaching agreement on the employers' productivity proposals endorsed by the NBPI, with the emphasis on payment for greater availability thus putting into reverse the gradual post-war reduction from 60 to 48 hours. Under this firemen would receive at scale maximum a pensionable wage of £1,170 for a shift rota averaging 56 hours a week. The quid pro quo was that in return fire authorities would require fewer men.

At a meeting on 23rd January 1969 the NJC for fire brigades reached agreement on a general pay increase of 5.25% for firemen and fire officers from 1st January 1969 with no further review before 1st January 1970. However by the autumn of 1969 the unions were pressing for a review of the principles for determining the pay of their 30,000 members, referring to wage drift in industry which did not flow through to them, and a working party was established by the NJC to study the claim in depth. While this working party continued their search for a formula to relate firemen's pay to outside industry, the NJC in January 1970 agreed an increase of £45 for firemen from lst January 1970 together with improvements in the arrangements for payment of duty systems.

The report of the ("Holroyd") departmental committee on the fire service was eventually published in June 1970. One important recommendation was that the earnings of fully trained firemen with all-round operational experience should be comparable with the national average earnings of skilled craftsmen. A new grade of senior fireman with no supervisory duties was proposed for "encouragement for the large numbers of extremely competent firemen who do not seek promotion or who are unlikely to gain from it". The committee observed that the national joint negotiating machinery functioned reasonably well and should be continued. They also commended the system of employing part-time firemen and urged the NJC to increase its attractiveness by an early review of part- time fees.

A dispute which had embittered relations between the FBU and the National Association of Fire Officers (NAFO)) for nearly three years over the composition of the NJC's autonomous officers' committee was finally settled in July 1968. It had arisen through a move by the FBU to nominate a serving leading fireman as a representative on the officers' committee, and after many meetings a solution originating from the employers was found to bridge the gap between the two unions.

POLICE

Prolonged discussions foundered in 1965 in committee C of the now statutory Police Council for Great Britain on pay in areas where police forces were seriously undermanned. The official side sought that any departure from national rates should be subject to strict control and limited to large forces where a need was demonstrated. The staff side pressed for a two-tier addition which would give every constable another £260 a year, and over half as much again to those in undermanned forces. The issue was referred to arbitration by the official side and the cases of the two sides were heard by the Police Arbitration Tribunal on 24th and 25th November 1965. The arbitrators were obviously unconvinced by the staff side's case as their award was in most respects identical with the official side's proposals, thus vindicating their decision to exercise their right of unilateral access to arbitration. The award was followed by widely publicised criticism by the Police Federation who called the arbitrators "callous or unconcerned". This attracted considerable support in some sections of the press, although "The Economist" subsequently dubbed this "bobbyphilia".

The police did however receive favourable treatment under the Government's policy for the period of severe restraint as the Government considered that the police "are in a special position because of their importance in combating crime" (Michael Stewart, First Secretary of State, in the House of Commons on 22nd November 1966). Their next two-yearly pay review had been due to take effect from September 1966 and the Government eventually agreed after deputations to the Home Secretary by the Police Council to discussions on a pay increase to be made on 1st July 1967 with retrospective effect to 1st March 1967. These discussions led to agreement in April 1967 on a 9% increase.

In November 1968 increases of 5.25% from 1st September 1968 and 3% from 1st September 1969 were agreed for federated and superintendent ranks: the standard week was also reduced from 42 to 40 hours per week from 1st April 1970. The pay of federated ranks was increased by a further 8.5% from 1st January 1970 by agreement in committee C of the Police Council in February 1970. This was the first stage of the biennial review due in 1970, with the second stage expected to operate from 1st September 1970 following an examination of the existing pay structure.

The end of 1968 and the beginning of 1969 saw an unusual dispute between police authorities and police doctors. This arose through the introduction of breathalyser tests under the Road Safety Act 1967 and the issuing of revised recommendations by the British Medical Association (BMA) for the remuneration of medical practitioners assisting the police which they sought to have adopted (for the first time) on a national basis. The core of the dispute was whether it was for the police authority or the BMA to determine the extent of availability required, and the BMA proposed an increase in retaining fee from 50 guineas to £500 for their concept of availability. After the BMA recommended doctors to terminate their police contracts as from 6th January 1969, a dispute was reported to the Secretary of State for Employment on Christmas Eve 1968. The Home Secretary (by then James Callaghan – previously consultant to the Police Federation) received delegations from both sides on 7th January 1968, when he supported the management side view. Agreement was reached within a few weeks which provided a retaining fee of not less than £75 and not more than £250 per year.

PROBATION SERVICE

The probation service was another affected by the incomes standstill on 20th July 1966. Agreement had been reached and implemented on a 12% increase for main grade officers from 1st January 1966. The JNC had then agreed on increases ranging from 12 to 21% for senior and principal probation officers but the Government favoured 12% to 15% only. A joint deputation by the JNC to the Home Secretary on 21st July 1966 had an unexpected new dimension as the previous day's announcement meant they had also to argue against the unfair effect of the six months' standstill for the higher grades.

TEACHERS

1965 saw the Remuneration of Teachers Act 1965 and new arrangements governing negotiation and arbitration of teachers' pay as well as active involvement in teachers' pay negotiations by the LACSAB secretariat, with Reginald Griffiths now installed as joint honorary secretary of the management panels. Burnham pay talks broke down following which there was a reference to arbitration. The main argument was on the basic scale for qualified assistant teachers with the teachers' panel claiming £900 to £1,700 against which the management panel had finally offered £710 to £1,400. The award was for £730 to £1,400. "News Summary" commented – "The award is a clear vindication of the realistic way in which the management panel had approached the matter of teachers' pay and was almost a complete confirmation of the proposals which they had put forward." The revised scales were effective for two years from 1st April 1965 and it was estimated that the overall cost was about 13%. One interesting facet was a reference in the management panel's arbitration submissions to teachers' hours being less than that of their analogues which led to bitter recriminations from the teachers' unions about teachers being regarded as part-time workers.

In 1967 the teachers' panel claimed pay increases of 30%, the management panel proposed an overall increase amounting to 6%, and once again there was a reference to arbitration. The principal effect of the arbitrators' award was to endorse the management panel's offer at the lower salary levels, but to improve the increases for the more senior posts. The teachers had pressed for adjustments in the system for above- scale posts to reduce the primary/secondary differential but the arbitrators decided against any such change. The teachers fared much better on their claim for safeguarding of salaries on reorganisation with an award for full safeguarding of salaries in perpetuity. The total cost of the award was 6-7% and the revised scales applied from 1st July 1967 (delayed because of Government pay policy) to 31st March 1969.

There was deadlock too in the 1967 negotiations in the Burnham further education committee with a reference to arbitration.

Sir Ronald Gould, leader of the teachers' panel for many years, was very anxious to secure a negotiated settlement in his final series of negotiations in 1969 and ultimately had his wish fulfilled in the agreement of the Burnham primary and secondary committee early in 1969 on new scales to operate from 1st April 1969 to 31st March 1971. The negotiations were not however without their difficulties in seeking to reconcile the teachers' aspirations with the ceiling imposed by the Government's incomes policy. At a critical stage in the negotiations Sir William Alexander welcomed an "end-loading" device suggested by the Secretary of State which he would probably have roundly condemned had he known that it had in fact originated at Belgrave Square.

The Burnham further education committee again failed to settle pay in 1969 and once again went to arbitration. The award of the arbitral body gave overall increases of nearly 6.5% to last for two years from 1st April 1969 – broadly in line with the agreement for schoolteachers.

The 1969 settlement was not well received by the teachers' unions and their members. As pay movements elsewhere accelerated, in October 1969 the teachers' panel of the Burnham primary and secondary committee lodged a claim for an interim increase of £135 a year to operate from 1st April 1970. A tense series of negotiating meetings ensued, with the management panel gradually edging up their offer from £50 to £100, but by this time the teachers had embarked on industrial action in support of their claim in various parts of the country, gaining a great deal of public and press support. The management panel linked their offer to a proposal for a major review of the teachers' salary structure, and suggested arbitration. Agreement was eventually reached on 3rd March 1970 on an interim increase of £120 a year from 1st April 1970 coupled with a review of the teachers' salary structure to be partially implemented from 1st January 1971, and thus enabled the teachers' unions to call off the industrial action. The proceedings on 3rd March were bizarre: at one stage the representatives of the Secretary of State were insisting on his behalf that the offer could not be increased, yet at the same time the Secretary of State was privately meeting teachers' leaders offering to improve the offer. The local authority representatives did not protest as much as might have been expected in such circumstances, no doubt with impending local elections and teachers' votes looming largely in mind. Ultimately it was perhaps the teachers who could feel that they were sold short as the increases they gained were modest compared with settlements achieved by others in the 1970 pay explosion.

STAFFING AND PEOPLE

The great explosion in negotiating work caused by the introduction of a statutory incomes policy had a considerable impact on the workload at LACSAB especially as nearly all proposals for changes in pay and service conditions emanating from local authorities had to be monitored at Belgrave Square as part of the Government's "early warning" arrangements. Some additional posts were created but the situation caused some disquiet among the more senior staff about their salary levels. This led eventually to LACSAB commissioning the London Boroughs Management Service Unit (LBMSU) to undertake a confidential job evaluation of the senior LACSAB posts below assistant secretary level. The results of the LBMSU evaluation were accepted by the LACSAB Board in March 1969 and these resulted in substantial upgradings.

Accommodation at 41 Belgrave Square was becoming inadequate in 1965 for the expanding staff but attempts to lease No.40 Belgrave Square next door were abandoned as an office development permit could not be obtained. This problem subsequently eased on the establishment of the Local Government Training Board in 1967 with the consequential transfer to it of staff of the old Local Government Examinations Board from 41 Belgrave Square.

One unfortunate event was the death on 9th November 1969 of Sir George Mowbray who had been chairman of LACSAB since its establishment in 1947. Sir George had been chairman of the Royal County of Berkshire from 1944 to 1946 and from 1960 to 1965, as well as chairman of the County Councils Association (CCA) from 1950 to 1956. As "News Summary" of December 1969 put it - "He carried the duties of that office (chairman of LACSAB) with dignity and understanding and was widely respected among those concerned with local government service conditions at national level". The influence and work of LACSAB had been greatly enhanced under his quiet but effective leadership. Sir George was succeeded as LACSAB chairman by Alderman H.G.Lewis.

CONCLUSION

The main impact on the work of LACSAB over the period 1965 to 1970 was undoubtedly the introduction of a statutory incomes policy and the inevitable traumas of the first few years as that policy was developed and then allowed to disintegrate. There were however other very important features, especially the increasing militancy of many of the trade unions in the local government sphere, extending to teachers - and even to police doctors. Until that time the generally accepted thinking was to keep pay negotiations away from media interest and against having to negotiate in public "in the middle of Trafalgar Square". The police and teachers in this period developed communications strategies and were prepared to engage in high-profile publicity campaigns to further their causes. Life at Belgrave Square would never be quite the same again as it had been in the relatively more ordered and sedate years hitherto.

A traffic warden gives advice on parking in Maidstone, Kent.

6 HEATH AND COUNTER-INFLATION

"If employers and unions connive and collude at phoney and bogus agreements in order to evade the policy requirements, then they are debasing the whole of their own collective bargaining processes in the future. It is no more possible to have slightly dishonest bargaining specifically designed to beat the policy than it is to take refuge in the fact that one is only a teenzy weenzy bit pregnant."

This period covers that of the Conservative Government led by Edward Heath until his general election defeat early in 1974. It also coincides with the end of an era in local government history as on 1st April 1974 over 1,400 existing local authorities were replaced by 456 new authorities in England and Wales created by the Local Government Act 1972. An important event for LACSAB was the retirement of Sir Reginald Griffiths at the end of 1972 and the appointment of Brian Rusbridge to succeed him.

POLITICAL AND ECONOMIC CONTEXT

The above quotation taken from an article by Derek Robinson, deputy chairman of the Pay Board, in "Personnel Management" reproduced in the September 1973 issue of "News Summary" aptly illustrates the nature of the problems in coping with pay bargaining under a statutory incomes policy. The statutory incomes policy of 1972 to 1974 was not an entirely new ball game as negotiators – often both sides working together – had become adept in squeezing the last pip out of policy criteria in the statutory policies of 1966 to 1970. LACSAB could not be entirely exempted from such strictures as indeed it was at about this time that the Pay Board and the Ministry of Housing and Local Government changed overnight all their officials facing the LACSAB secretariat in order to take a more rigid line and to avoid too much flexibility in the operation of Stage 3 of the Government's counter- inflation policy.

The Conservative administration of Edward Heath which took over after the general election of June 1970 had to contend in July with the first official national dock strike since 1926 which led to the Pearson court of inquiry and substantial improvements in dockers' pay and conditions. They were reluctant to interfere directly in industrial relations, believing competition to be the most effective means of safeguarding consumers in the private sector, but took a tough line with price and wage increases in the public services. The pattern of inflationary settlements which had begun early in 1970 continued unabated throughout that year, with the "Scamp" settlement for local authority manual workers attracting much publicity (and much criticism in Downing Street). The Government's "laissez faire" attitude to inflation, together with the decision to disband the National Board for Prices and Incomes (NBPI) received a barrage of criticism. "News Summary" of December 1970 reported prices up by 7.5% per annum by September 1970 and weekly earnings up by 14% by August 1970. By August 1971 the Government had met with some success in the public sector in a determined effort to keep pay increases below 10% but the price had been widespread strikes and industrial action. This was in the context of Fords settling for 33% over two years and other generous settlements elsewhere in the car industry and in the private manufacturing sector. The atmosphere was suddenly improved by Chancellor Barber's purchase tax and hire purchase concessions in July 1971 which it was hoped would raise the growth rate to 4 or 4.5%. "News Summary" of October 1971 reported – "wage claims more massive than any in British history". The TUC were floating proposals for cost-of-living "threshold clauses", i.e. additional payments to trigger if the index of retail prices rose above a certain point during the currency of an agreement.

The Government's policy of de-escalating wage increases had achieved considerable success in getting increases down to 7 or 8% but was seriously dented by a costly settlement following the miners' strike early in 1972 which it was said was to be regarded as a special case. As 1972 continued the Government faced the dilemma of containing inflation and at the same time allowing the economy to grow but their efforts to stimulate the economy were not succeeding. A series of tripartite Downing Street talks between the Government, the CBI and the TUC on pay and prices began in July 1972 but broke down that November on Edward Heath's plan for a £2 a week limit on wage increases coupled to a 5% limit on price rises, linked to the aim of a 5% growth rate.

Prime Minister Heath's announcement on 6th November 1972 of a standstill on pay and prices (Counter-Inflation Stage 1) did not therefore come as so much of a surprise as the Wilson standstill of 1966. In fact it had been well signalled a few weeks earlier at Belgrave Square when negotiators on both sides in police pay talks were informed by the Home Office that they had a "fleeting opportunity" to do a deal.

Counter-Inflation Stage 2 followed early in 1973, extending the freeze by a further 60 days and setting out the statutory prices and incomes controls to operate from 1st April 1973 until that October. These restricted pay increases to £1 per week plus 4%, but no individual was to receive an increase of more than a £250 a year. There were also controls over prices and limitations on profits, as well as the establishment of two new bodies, a Price Commission and a Pay Board given powers over prices, pay, dividends and rates for three years.

The Stage 1 standstill had resulted in the TUC adopting an attitude of "reluctant acquiescence" but had succeeded in halting increases in earnings. However at February 1973 the prices index showed an embarrassing annual increase of 7.9%. By June 1973 "News Summary" featured an article entitled – "Are the industrial troubles over?" – with reports of booming trade, falling unemployment and comparative industrial peace, thus raising optimism that the worst of the Government's industrial problems were over. Most unions who had threatened to defy Stage 2 had drawn back, because the promise of increases of £1 plus 4% proved too attractive, and so the TUC attitude moved to "resentful acquiescence".

All through the summer of 1973 talks about the form of Stage 3 of the counter-inflation policy were held against the background of the sliding value of sterling. The Government were now interested in threshold agreements to protect the real value of earnings, but by this time the TUC opposed this idea which they themselves had sponsored two years earlier. Stage 3 of the counter-inflationary policy eventually came into force for pay on 7th November 1973. The main innovation was the provision of a threshold payment of 40p per week if the price index rose by 7%, plus another 40p for every 1% above that level. Its other main provisions were (i) a maximum of 7% of the average paybill up to £350 a year; (ii) a further 1% to remove anomalies; (iii) extra payments for genuine efficiency schemes; (iv) premium payments for "unsocial hours"; and (v) New Year's Day to be a bank holiday (this might well in retrospect prove to have been the most expensive provision as it heralded the era of the long Christmas/New Year break). It was estimated this would overall add about 10 to 11% to the annual wage bill, which the CBI criticised as inflationary whilst the TUC were utterly hostile over the rejection of food subsidies after food prices had increased by 15% a year. "The Guardian" on 9th October observed – "Mr. Heath has staked everything . . . on being able to sustain growth through the next 12 to 18 months".

Edward Heath's gamble failed. The electrical power stations dispute leading to the three-day week seriously damaged any prospect of growth in the economy. Early in 1974 he went for a general election to seek support for the Government's stance but suffered defeat, bringing a Labour government headed by Harold Wilson, but initially only as a minority administration without an overall majority.

INDUSTRIAL RELATIONS ACT 1971

In this period 1970 to 1974 the consequences of the Donovan Royal Commission's report continued to unfold and the Industrial Relations Act 1971 eventually reached the statute book. The previous Labour government's Industrial Relations Bill had fallen because of the 1970 general election and following that the question was what Heath's Conservative government would put in place of it. The first step in the autumn of 1970 was a consultative document on industrial relations. LACSAB's comments again included the suggestion that collective agreements should be presumed to be enforceable contracts unless they provided to the contrary. LACSAB doubted whether local government would need to make much if any use of the proposed statutory agencies because of their adequate existing machinery, and also expressed reservations about proposed requirements for the disclosure of information. The next step was the Government's introduction late in 1970 of the Industrial Relations Bill. It took some time for the final shape of this to emerge as substantial changes were made during the committee stage in the House of Commons, so much so that in April 1971 "News Summary" reported that Robert Carr, Secretary of State for Employment, had tabled 13 new clauses, a new schedule and 97 new amendments. The CBI were broadly in support despite having the main changes they sought rejected, but a special TUC meeting on 18th March 1971 decided to try and prevent it from working.

The Industrial Relations Act 1971 which eventually received Royal Assent on

5th August 1971 after a most tortuous parliamentary passage was a major piece of legislation intended to provide a civilised framework for the conduct of industrial relations. The seven main elements of this complex Act were:-

(1) a code of industrial relations practice;

(2) new rights and protection for the individual;

(3) a new concept of unfair dismissal practice;

(4) new methods of settling disputes over the recognition of trade unions and their bargaining rights; and new methods for improving procedural agreements which lay down the arrangements for dealing with industrial relations;

(5) a new system of registration for trade unions and employers' associations;

(6) a new system of informal and expert judicial institutions – the Industrial Court – and an extended system of industrial tribunals; and

(7) new protection for the community in emergencies.

The trade union movement collectively continued to oppose the legislation, including the new system of registration, but with some hesitations as Robert Carr regarded the confinement of legal immunities to registered unions as one of the pillars of the Act.

An important development as far as LACSAB was concerned was the publication in December 1971 of the LACSAB guide to the Industrial Relations Act. This guide, largely the work of Frank Walton, then LACSAB assistant secretary, which examined the Act clause by clause and provided check lists illustrating action to be taken, was very well received by local authorities and initiated a significant area of LACSAB activity in advice and guidance on employment legislation.

LOCAL GOVERNMENT REORGANISATION

A major piece of legislation to impact considerably on the work of LACSAB was the Local Government Act 1972 leading to the extensive reorganisation of local authorities outside London effective from 1st April 1974. Under this the existing 1,400 local authorities in England and Wales disappeared and were replaced by 456 new local authorities. Six metropolitan areas were created with systems broadly akin to London, together with a simplified two-tier system of county councils and district councils elsewhere. A statutory Local Government Staffing Commission was established to deal with such matters as staff transfer and recruitment arrangements for the transition. The essence of the Staff Commission's work was redeployment of existing staff to avoid redundancies – which could not be entirely reconciled with Secretary of State Peter Walker's earlier brave words about bigger authorities, bigger jobs and salaries attracting the best people to fill them. (The LACSAB secretariat were later to have to spend much time giving in-depth advice to members of several authorities wishing to part company with their most senior officers appointed under the redeployment measures). To avoid problems experienced in the London reorganisation of 1965 there was concern to "nip in the bud" any moves by the old authorities to award improvements in pay or status to their staffs which would give them an unfair advantage on transfer. Advice and guidance to this end was issued by LACSAB, the local authority associations and national employers' sides in February 1972 and this was given statutory backing by a provision in the Local Government Act 1972. Once again, as in statutory incomes policy phases, LACSAB became the monitoring agent on behalf of central government and all local authorities were required to submit proposals to them for local increases in pay. The LACSAB secretariat were heavily involved in scrutinising many local proposals and advising whether or not they satisfied specified criteria. It is a sign of the times and of the relationships which then existed between local authorities, LACSAB and central government that these arrangements were with only isolated exceptions accepted and operated without much ado.

Staffing structures for the post-reorganisation situation were much influenced by the "Bains" working party report on management structures for the new local authorities. One particular development arising from this was the broadening out from the traditional "establishment" role to the "personnel management" role already widely recognised outside local government. It was soon afterwards that the Society of Chief Personnel Officers in Local Government (SOCPO) was formed.

Another important dimension of local government reorganisation affecting the work of LACSAB was the negotiation of salary provisions for chief executives and chief officers of the new authorities which is covered later in this chapter.

Local government reorganisation and the consequent regrouping of the local authority associations led quite naturally to speculation about the future of the central organisations of local government, including LACSAB. However. Laurence Welsh's ideas in the September 1973 issue of "News Summary" that the wider scope of personnel management should be recognised by giving LACSAB "the better-sounding and more descriptive title of Local Government Manpower Advisory Board" was, to say the least, not generally well-received beyond Belgrave Square.

The end of 1973 and beginning of 1974 were marked by a controversy arising from allegations that the salary costs of the new authorities would be considerably higher than those of the predecessor authorities. Graham Page, then Minister for Local Government, called for an investigation and agreed LACSAB should undertake it. The subsequent LACSAB report – "Survey of Local Authorities' Salaries" – published later in 1974 showed that, compared with those of the former authorities, the salary costs of the new authorities were 9.4% more; the number of staff had increased by 4.7%; and average salaries had increased by 4.5%. Many reasons were given to explain (not entirely convincingly) these increases accruing when there was much scope for rationalising local authority services. In retrospect the increase in local authority staffing costs in the early 1970s – not only the "big bang" of reorganisation nor forgetting the huge expansion of social services presided over by Secretary of State Keith Joseph – contrasts sharply with the tough attitude of the next Conservative administration from 1979 onwards in controlling local authorities' spending and staffing.

OVERALL LACSAB ACTIVITIES

As in earlier periods much of the discussion at meetings of the LACSAB Board in this period 1970 to 1974 centred on the major issues of the time. The Board considered at some length the Government's voluntary and statutory incomes policies; the passage of the Industrial Relations Bill leading to the 1971 Act; and the various impacts of local government reorganisation.

The unprecedented and lengthy period of unrest of the manual workers' dispute of 1970 led to the LACSAB Board in December 1970 to seek to examine the question of general relationships of LACSAB to individual negotiating bodies. This resulted in the Board agreeing in February 1971 to experimental arrangements whereby a small group of LACSAB members would meet whenever required at short notice so that the chairmen of national employers' sides could confer with them at important stages in their specific negotiations. But little seems to have come of this.

One issue which commanded much attention by the LACSAB Board was London weighting. A LACSAB deputation to Maurice Macmillan, Secretary of State for Employment. on 12th September 1973 told him of "extraordinary pressures upon local government to make substantial increases in London weighting" and that this required the urgent and intensive attention of the Government. The Government's response was to refer the issue to the Pay Board whose massive investigation meant that their report did not materialise until June 1974, by which time NALGO had for the first time initiated industrial action, spurring the London boroughs to seek to find an interim solution.

MANUAL WORKERS

Any hopes that the 1969 Edinburgh 8.5% settlement would produce industrial peace were shortlived when the manual trade unions tabled their massive 1970 claim in April 1970. Negotiation began against the background of militant noises from trade union leaders hitherto known for their moderation but now disturbed by the loss of control of their membership in the spate of unofficial strikes leading up to the Edinburgh deal. A main plank in the unions' case was that their gains at Edinburgh had gone because it was followed by the subsequent wage explosion elsewhere, which for example had resulted in the Government offering their own industrial workers 13.5% following a report by the National Board for Prices and Incomes (NBPI). Neither a working party nor the NJC themselves could find common ground for a settlement by September 1970 and the trade unions rejected the employers' proposal of arbitration. By this stage the employers had (after extensive consultations with the provincial network) tabled a revised offer of 36s. per week and other improvements, including the important and novel suggestion of a guaranteed minimum earnings level. Both sides went to the Department of Employment to seek conciliation, but Secretary of State Robert Carr decided not to intervene – which Alan Fisher, General Secretary of NUPE, described as wrecking the Department's conciliation functions. Industrial action ensued with the unions concentrating their publicity on the pay of the few workers in the lower grades whilst mobilising for strike action key workers all on higher grades. The overwhelming majority of authorities favoured further negotiations rather than accept the unions' terms, although 35 out of 1,600 authorities in the United Kingdom were willing to concede.

After a new employers' offer had been rejected on 21st October, a committee of inquiry headed by Sir Jack Scamp was set up by the NJC – with the employers agreeing in advance to be bound by the results. The final settlement recommended by the Scamp committee in November was for a 50s. a week increase (close to the unions' claim of 55s.) to operate from 9th November 1970 and was recognised by the committee to be "very expensive". It nevertheless had to be seen in the context of such close adherence in the past by the local authority employers to Government incomes policies that local authority manual earnings were among the lowest in the country; the Government's prior agreement to a 13.5% increase for their own industrial workers; the Government's subsequent quick decision to settle on the same terms for health service ancillary workers; but perhaps above all the lesson in 1969 that strikes pay dividends had not been lost on the unions' hitherto quiescent membership.

Sir Jack Scamp

The Scamp settlement aroused much public and political criticism as inflationary and damaging to the Government's efforts to halt inflation, incurring the wrath of Prime Minister, Edward Heath. However when the LACSAB Board came to reflect on the Scamp settlement at their meeting on 16th February 1971 they were encouraged by reports in "The Times" that the Scamp terms were more reasonable than at first thought - and moreover compared favourably and cost less than the award of the concurrent Wilberforce inquiry into the pay of electricity power station workers. (It had taken some time to catch up with the Government's ruse in claiming the Wilberforce cost to be 10.9% by measuring this by the addition to overall paybill after taking into account of savings resulting from proposed productivity measures, and for it to be realised that actually earnings would go up by more than 15%!)

As the first stage towards equal pay for equal work, women's manual wage rates were raised to 82.5% of men's rates from 6th September 1971.

The 1971 manual claim submitted by the unions in August of that year included two novel features as well as asking for an increase of £2 per week. They sought a cost-of-living threshold clause as advocated by the TUC and also deliberate employment creation through the expansion of local authority services. After the bitter industrial action and intensive negotiations of the preceding two years, there must have been considerable relief on both sides of the table when they clinched a deal on 30th November, the employers having "moderately improved" their earlier offer. The effect of the agreement was to increase male manual workers' rates by amounts ranging from £1.20 to £1.50 (post-decimalisation) per week according to grade with effect from 8th November 1971. The employers were not prepared to take the lead in conceding a threshold clause, but instead resurrected their 1970 proposal for a minimum earnings guarantee, and agreement was reached on this at a level of £19 a week for full-time male workers. The employers also rejected a claim for a 10% penalty payment by authorities who had not introduced productivity agreements: their counter-proposal led to agreement on a self-financing lead-in payment of £1 per week not to be triggered before 1st March 1972.

The lead-in payment did little to assuage the mounting frustration and cynicism of the manual unions at the lack of progress towards the introduction of productivity and bonus schemes since these had first been considered the air, with the employers assuring the unions they would continue their efforts to stimulate action by local authorities, but insisting nevertheless there must be a clearly discernible end-product in the form of a viable pay and productivity scheme before the lead-in payment could apply.

The force of argument rather than the argument of force may well have been the raison d'être for the 27-page document of arguments in favour of a four-point 1972 claim the manual unions submitted that summer. They sought a £4 increase; protection against price rises; shorter hours; and longer holidays. A long list in "News Summary" of December 1972 of local authority pay increases exempted from the Government's incomes standstill of 6th November 1972 includes the manual 1972 settlement and registers the fact that the signal of a "fleeting opportunity" to settle police pay had not been lost on other local government negotiators. The manual settlement was reached on 6th November only hours before the axe fell and provided for increases of £2.40 per week from that date raising the lowest grade basic rate outside London to £19.85 per week and the top grade to £23.15. The employers conceded two extra days holiday a year but on hours did no more than agree in the time-honoured formulation to "keep the matter under review".

The pay settlement for manual workers from November 1973 provided for increases adding up to a 9.8% increase in the paybill, including some restructuring of ambulancemen's pay. This agreement also provided for changes in holiday entitlements and unsocial hours to apply from April 1974.

APT&C STAFFS

The 1971 pay round for APT&C began with the national employers consulting provincial and Scottish employers at a two-day conference in April at Eastbourne on that year's pay negotiations as well as job evaluation, productivity bargaining for white-collar staffs, and adherence to national agreements. Pay negotiations began that same month as the staff side lodged a claim for a 14% increase plus other improvements. After prolonged negotiations settlement was eventually reached late in July on revised scales to operate from 1st July 1971 providing tapered increases varying from between 10.5 and 11.5% at lower points to 7.5% higher up, at an overall cost of just under 8.5%.

The 1972 APT&C negotiations took a remarkably similar course to those of the previous year and again tapered increases were in vogue, broadly in tune with the Government's emerging policy at that time. The staff side had in April claimed a 12% increase together with other improvements, including a reduction in hours to 35 per week. The agreement arrived at on 5th July provided for increases from 1st July 1972 ranging from 11% at the age 21 point to 7.7% at the top. The employers made an important concession in reducing hours from 38 to 37 hours (36 in London) from a forward date of 1st January 1973 linked to exhortations of "continued co-operation towards maximum efficiency". This hours concession was however caught by the Government's incomes freeze of 6th November 1972 and implementation was delayed for some considerable time.

Perhaps the most noticeable aspect of the 1973 APT&C pay negotiations was the marked contrast between the original aspirations of the staff side and the final end-product. The staff side claim was for pay increases ranging from 20 to 25% with other improvements. The agreement reached in July was for increases from 1st July 1973 in line with Stage 2 of the Government's counter-inflation policy of £1 per week plus 4%. At the NALGO conference that June little was said in support of the Government's policy but the decision nonetheless was to work within it, very much in line with the general "resentful acquiescence" of the trade union movement at that time.

1971 saw the emergence of the generic social worker in the newly combined social service departments following the 1970 recommendations of the Seebohm committee. The APT&C NJC agreed in January 1971 new national salaries for social workers and other groups in social service departments to apply from 1st April 1971. A major change in the salary structure for residential staffs was agreed to operate from 1st January 1972. The hours of residential staffs had been a matter of concern for many years and the agreement of October 1973 set out a timetable for a phased reduction to an eventual 40-hour week from 1st April 1976.

Throughout this period 1970 to 1974 the APT&C NJC were discussing the possibility of introducing a scheme of job evaluation following what had been done a few years earlier by London boroughs. In 1970 the employers commissioned from LAMSAC work on a scheme and this was completed by 1971, but then there were very lengthy deliberations within the NJC before final agreement was reached early in 1974 on a model scheme which authorities could decide whether or not to apply. The points rating matrix was much on the lines already used by the London boroughs but there were important differences in the procedures recommended. Very few authorities however adopted the model scheme in subsequent years, due in no small part to local trade union opposition, but also because increases based on job evaluation were stopped under counter-inflation policies whereas increases based on added responsibilities were allowed. LACSAB had in 1973 secured the services of Derek Ward, formerly of the GLC and LAMSAC, who was undoubtedly the recognised national expert on job evaluation in local government. Derek unfortunately died suddenly after moving to LACSAB and it must be a matter of conjecture whether job evaluation would have been more widely adopted had he been able to continue to exert his influence.

The period ended with the difficulties on London weighting on which LACSAB members were pressing for Government action and leading to widespread industrial action by NALGO members for the first time in NALGO history. The discussions on London weighting for APT&C staffs were unusually complicated: not only had the Government participated in discussions, imposed the limitations of their incomes policy, and eventually referred the issue to the Pay Board; but also there were lengthy discussions at provincial level in London leading to an interim offer on an issue normally reserved for national negotiation. It was not until well into the summer of 1974 that this matter was finally resolved.

TOP POSTS

No agreement was reached when in 1972 the town and district council clerks claimed increases of 47.7% to establish a direct relationship with the pay of the higher civil service and the issue was referred to the Industrial Arbitration Board. Their award of June 1972 rejected the claim and referred the issue back for further discussions between the two sides which should have regard to the salaries of other local government officers – the main point stressed throughout in negotiations and at arbitration by the authorities' side. Agreement was reached soon afterwards on that basis for increases from 1st July 1972 for town and district council clerks and for chief officers too.

A major task in this period was to determine the salary provisions for the chief executives and chief officers of the new local authorities created under the Local Government Act 1972 to operate from 1st April 1974. The protracted negotiations were beset by serious delays arising from the introduction of the successive stages of the Government's counter-inflation policy. The new "shadow" authorities were anxious to proceed with their staffing appointments – naturally starting with their top posts – and were seriously hindered in this by the delay in determining the salaries for them. Agreements were finally reached on a new salary structure for chief executives of new authorities in March 1973 and for chief officers in June 1973. Because of incomes policy criteria the pay levels had to reflect those currently being paid in existing authorities of a similar size. For both chief executives and chief officers the salary schemes provided for the first time for salaries to be related to the precise size of the authority based on static, additional and projected population. For chief officers the fulcrum principle was introduced whereby all individual scales were related to the fulcrum point based on the authority's size. To comply with the requirements of counter-inflation policy and the Pay Board all salary proposals were monitored at LACSAB. Further serious delays ensued because the Pay Board were reluctant to endorse salary proposals (at one critical stage LACSAB officers late one Friday evening refused to allow a Pay Board official to go off on annual leave until he had cleared some proposals). The Pay Board's delaying tactics continued until the summer of 1974 when the Pay Board were insisting on carrying out their own investigations of the salary levels of senior officers employed by three sample new authorities. No decisions on these had been reached by the Pay Board before its demise.

FIRE BRIGADES

The negotiations in the second half of 1970 to replace the fire brigades pay agreement which expired at the end of that year got off to a bad start with the FBU conference declaring they had no confidence in the capability of the national negotiating machinery to settle the claim they intended to submit. Reginald Griffiths, LACSAB secretary, was quick to point out how this sharply contrasted with the Holroyd committee's conclusion that the joint machinery worked reasonably well and should continue, and indeed with the FBU's own evidence to Holroyd. The FBU asked the Home Secretary to intervene and appoint an independent inquiry into fire service pay. Reginald Maudling, the Home Secretary, agreed with them that a valuation of the job of the fireman was required but this was a matter for the NJC. Talks in the NJC on increased pay and shorter hours for firemen, and on the possibility of devising a formula for fixing their pay in the future, started in November 1970 against the background of industrial action in the home counties over a dispute on London differential payments. No agreement was reached in the NJC and seven weeks of industrial action ensued when FBU members refused to undertake other than emergency duties. The dispute was eventually resolved by an agreement to increase firemen's pay by 5.5% from 1st January 1971 coupled with the establishment of an independent committee of inquiry into fire service pay and hours to be chaired by Sir Charles Cunningham. A reduction of hours for pay calculation purposes from 46 to 44 per week from 1st April 1971 – a feature of the 1970 agreement – resulted in a further 6% increase in earnings.

Evidence to the Cunningham committee by the employers' side dealt at great length with the perennial problem of firemen's hours, especially highlighting the advantages of a day-manning system recommended by the NBPI, the Holroyd committee and the employers themselves, but operative in only a few places because of strong FBU opposition. As to pay levels, the employers argued that the principle factor was whether the pay attracted and retained enough people of the right quality, rejecting the proposition that firemen's earnings should be linked to those of skilled craftsmen as too imprecise. New rates of pay were agreed by the NJC on 9th December 1971 in the light of the recommendations of the Cunningham inquiry which said there was insufficient evidence to support the view that weekly earnings in the fire service were grossly out of line with those in other employments drawing on similar sources of labour. But other considerations – the number of hours worked and the degree of danger and unpleasantness associated with the work – must be taken into account. All pay rates should be expressed in pence per hour and revised rates for firemen ranged from 43p to 58p an hour with effect from 1st October 1971 related to a basic working week of 40 hours. This gave a fully qualified fireman working 56 hours annual earnings of £1,850 – an increase of 15.7%.

There was a much speedier conclusion to the fire pay talks in 1972 with agreement well in advance of the operative date of 1st October 1972. For firemen the pay rises ranged from 4p to 5.5p an hour. It was agreed to defer a claim for a shorter working week until publication of the report of a Home Office working party on the better utilisation of manpower.

1973 was the year for substantial improvements in firemen's pay and conditions. The NJC's objective in protracted discussions was "to establish the fireman as a technician skilled and occupied in using the most modern equipment, methods and techniques to undertake the full range of fire fighting...". Full advantage was taken to extract the maximum benefits permissible under Stage 3 of the counter- inflation policy published early in November 1973. The main effect was to introduce a 48-hour working week in all brigades from 8th November 1974 with the same earnings as for 56 hours based on the improved rates operative from 7th November 1973. The agreement also introduced a weekly payment of £2.43 per week for working unsocial hours and the 1% flexibility margin specified in Stage 3 was also used. The NJC agreement contained many pious clauses referring to better utilisation of firemen, maximum use of hours, etc. The agreement was approved by the Pay Board but with such serious misgivings that shortly afterwards it was "all change" as every Pay Board officer and many Ministry officials facing the LACSAB secretariat were replaced overnight.

POLICE

There were lengthy discussions on police pay to operate for the two years from

1st September 1970. At a meeting of committee C of the Police Council in September 1970 the official side offered a general addition of broadly 10.5% which, taken together with the 8.5% interim increase from 1st January 1970, represented an increase of about 19% for the two-year period. Subsequent discussions hinged on the increasing problem of premature wastage, as 50% of all those joining the service were resigning before pension entitlement. The final agreement provided for a general increase of 10% throughout the scales for the federated ranks together with a number of special measures to combat premature wastage estimated to cost just over another 6%, including a steeper rise to the constable's maximum – now reached in six years (instead of nine) and an additional long service increment.

As in the previous two-year period, interim pay rises were agreed – in this case 6.5% backdated to 1st September 1971.

As already mentioned, the risk of being caught by an incomes standstill was very much in the minds of negotiators on both sides when they met in October 1972 to negotiate a two-year settlement to run from 1st September 1972 which was the date of implementation of a new simplified police rank structure. The signal of a "fleeting opportunity" to settle was not lost on them and a 15% deal was clinched with alacrity.

Stage 2 of the Government's counter-inflation policy meant that there was an entitlement to £1 plus 4% under the formula so an interim pay settlement on that basis was agreed at meetings on 18th July 1973 to operate from 1st September 1973 for all ranks from constable to chief superintendent.

The width of the services already then provided by the LACSAB secretariat is illustrated by the other main issue apart from pay dealt with by the Police Council in the period 1970 to 1974. For 1972 saw the culmination of much work in committee E and agreement on a wide range of improvements in police pensions coinciding with major reviews of other local government and public service pension arrangements.

PROBATION SERVICE

The main event in this period in the JNC for the probation service was the publication in August 1972 of the report of the Butterworth inquiry into the work and pay of probation officers and social workers. This had followed prolonged and difficult negotiations in the JNC in 1971 when they had finally to conclude an agreement on "the only terms acceptable to the Government" but in the knowledge that the Butterworth committee of inquiry was being established. Their job evaluation exercise had revealed "a difference, not great but clearly discernible, between the job size of the experienced main grade probation officers and corresponding levels of social workers" and "a marked difference in the career prospects of new entrants" (to the advantage of the social workers). The most controversial Butterworth recommendation was the creation of a new non-supervisory section of the main grade, splitting into A and B scales. Annual selection for the B scale was to be decided by each probation committee based on assessments of professional experience, performance and potential. The JNC quickly settled on a revised salary structure with effect from 1st July 1972 giving effect to the Butterworth recommendations. The difficulties in achieving a fair system of selection to the B scale were to bedevil negotiations for many years.

TEACHERS

In the bitter negotiations on the 1970 interim increase for primary and secondary school teachers the management panel had made it clear they linked their improved offers to a proposed major overhaul of the teachers' pay structure. The existing structure was a basic scale on which all teachers, including heads, were paid to which could be added a plethora of allowances. The management panel's proposals tabled in October 1970 replaced all the existing complicated system by five specified and published scales for all teachers, apart from heads and deputies who would have separate scales. Such a structure would for the first time offer and identify full and improved career prospects to all teachers and would apply from 1st April 1971. Protracted negotiations, including four meetings within two weeks in February/March 1971, ended in total disagreement: the teachers – with the NUT having the majority say – rejected the revised structure: they pressed for 40% increases: they refused to go to arbitration: and, when the independent chairman ruled there should be a reference to arbitration because of the deadlock, they refused to make nominations to the arbitral body. Despite the teacher unions' reluctance the issue went to arbitration and the award of the arbitral body in July 1971 was to a large extent a vindication of the policy pursued throughout by the management panel, accepting their new structure and marginally increasing the money available from 9.7 to 10.8% to last for two years, plus about 1% per annum flow through costs for a number of years.

Although the 1971 award was supposed to last for two years, the teachers sought a flat rise of £250 from 1st April 1972, to which the management panel responded positively by an offer of a 6% increase which they upped to a final 7% in March 1972. Again there was disagreement and a reference to arbitration. The arbitral body headed by Lord Pearson awarded a 9% increase with slightly higher increases for the lower paid.

A primary school teacher and her pupils.

It is doubtful whether the 1972 arbitration award had even been implemented before the teachers lodged their 1973 claim for improvements totalling 20% at the Burnham primary and secondary committee on 20th July 1972. The fact that there was settlement in the Burnham committee on revised salary scales from 1st April 1973 did not necessarily mean that all was by then sweetness and light, but had much to do with the fact that Stage 2 of the Government's statutory counter- inflation policy was in force with the trade union movement reluctantly acquiescing in it. The NUT in particular were by now most dissatisfied with the operation of the Burnham negotiating machinery, particularly the Government's interference exercised through their representation on the management panel and the use of their veto on the overall amount of any offer (under the 1965 concordat between the Government and the local authority associations). They suggested later in 1973 replacing the existing Burnham machinery with a non-statutory national joint council dealing with conditions as well as pay and excluding the Government.

Difficulties in the Burnham committees were unfortunately not confined to pay negotiations for school teachers as, when talks broke down in August 1971 in the Burnham Further Education Committee after the teachers' panel refused to budge from their 37% claim, this was the third time in three consecutive negotiating rounds that there was a reference to arbitration. The 10% award backdated to 1st April 1971 of the arbitral body headed by Professor J.C.Wood was the same amount as had been offered by the management panel in their final offer. Further education fortunately broke the mould in March 1972 by reaching agreement on a 7.7% increase to apply from 1st April 1972. It was noted at the time that a great deal of the success was due to the willingness of both sides to enter into informal but realistic talks under the guidance of the independent chairman - an unusual feature in the teachers' pay bargaining of that era.

An important event in terms of impact on the work of the LACSAB secretariat was the resignation of Sir William Alexander as joint honorary secretary of the Burnham and allied committees with effect from 1st January 1974. The LACSAB secretary, Brian Rusbridge, became sole management panel secretary with the bulk of the employers' negotiating work coming over to Belgrave Square from the Association of Education Committees. For long there had been a strong view prevailing among teachers that only educationists could understand teachers' jobs and pay, and consequently much suspicion of LACSAB. The views of the NUT general secretary, Edward Britton, had been profoundly influenced at a LACSAB function in December 1972 when he had met quite a number of representatives of other LACSAB "customers", such as town clerks, chief constables, chief officers and many long-established professional groups - and when he must have wondered what was so special about teachers after all!

STAFFING AND PEOPLE

As far as LACSAB people were concerned, the big landmark in this period 1970 to 1974 was the retirement of Reginald Griffiths as LACSAB secretary at the end of 1972 and the appointment of Brian Rusbridge to succeed him as from 1st January 1973.

Many tributes were paid to Reginald Griffiths for his 15 years' "hard" service. Although renowned as a "tough operator", his unfailing courtesy was widely recognised. Once when questioned in terms of victory or defeat he retorted - "Settlements are what matter. The real question for any negotiator is 'At the end of the day can you, through negotiations, reach a settlement?'" He was much respected by his working colleagues at Belgrave Square for his utter professionalism, approachableness and his willingness publicly to back decisions they had taken (whatever he might say otherwise in private). He keenly studied the "chemistry" of every meeting: after absorbing the facts of any issue he would then concentrate his attention on those he would face and how they would react at various stages in the negotiating process. He often played a few holes of golf at first light before facing yet another weighty day at Belgrave Square. It is probably a quite apocryphal story that he addressed the golf ball he was about to hit in terms of the trade union leader he would be facing later that day! The fact that he had many times to argue local government's case very strongly in Whitehall, sometimes incurring ministerial wrath, did not fortunately prevent his receiving a well-earned knighthood in the 1973 New Year's Honours List on his retirement.

Brian Rusbridge, who succeeded Reginald Griffiths, came from British Rail where he had senior managerial appointments for personnel and operating functions, and previously he had had extensive managerial experience with ICI.

There was a considerable strengthening of the LACSAB secretariat in this period. Frank Walton came as assistant secretary in 1971 and was redesignated senior assistant secretary in 1973 shortly before he took charge of the Burnham committee area of work as it came over fully to Belgrave Square. Also in 1973 Derek Bass, assistant secretary on APT&C since early 1950, had to retire because of ill-health and Ron Hayward was promoted to succeed him, while Ken Clark was appointed as additional assistant secretary.

On the provincial scene there was the retirement in 1972 of Stanley Eaton who had been employers' secretary of the North Western and North Wales provincial councils since 1951. Stanley Eaton had served with Edward Bishop since 1933 in the North West and elsewhere in setting up the network of provincial councils. He was succeeded by his assistant, Helen Pott.

There were changes too in the chairmanship of LACSAB. In 1971 Alderman H.G. Lewis had to resign because of ill-health and Alderman Sir Frank Marshall, Leeds City Council and AMC, succeeded him. Sir Frank resigned in March 1973 and Alderman Leslie Freeman, GLC, was then appointed chairman. But Leslie Freeman had only been in office a few months when the Conservatives lost the GLC to Labour and so he lost his power base and the LACSAB chair. So in 1973 Sir Leo Schultz, Hull City Council and Yorkshire provincial employers took the LACSAB chair. It was also in July 1973 that Councillor Sid Dennett, Wimborne District Council and South Western provincial employers, became vice-chairman of LACSAB, a position which he was to continue to hold until he himself was appointed as LACSAB chairman in 1989.

Consideration was given in 1971 to a proposal to move the LACSAB office to Alembic House on the Albert Embankment, where the LGTB had been situated, but it was eventually decided in 1972 to remain at 41 Belgrave Square. By the time this period ended early in 1974, 41 Belgrave Square was once again bulging at the seams because of the strengthening of the LACSAB secretariat and something needed to be done to alleviate this situation.

CONCLUSION

So this was another turbulent era in the history of LACSAB. It had started with strike action by groups as remote as manual workers and teachers, continued with other unrest such as the firemen's dispute, and ended with even the hitherto moderate NALGO roused to industrial action over London weighting.

The period also marks the introduction of a second attempt at a statutory incomes policy with LACSAB and trade union officials now more adept in the techniques of stretching the policy constraints and not so much engaging in confrontation with each other, but rather working together to circumvent the incomes policy. It also saw the LACSAB secretariat heavily involved in monitoring on behalf of central government pay proposals by local authorities relating to (a) the counter-inflation programme; (b) late increases in pay prior to local government reorganisation; and (c) salary proposals for chief officers of the new authorities.

At the end of the period early in 1974 LACSAB faced a period of much uncertainty with the new secretary, Brian Rusbridge, at the helm as the new post-reorganisation local authorities took off at April 1974 and as Harold Wilson's Labour government succeeded Edward Heath's Conservative administration after their general election defeat in February 1974. One effect of local government reorganisation was the emergence of a new breed of ambitious younger local politicians who lost little time in making their presence strongly felt on the national negotiating scene. A former LACSAB officer in the early 1970s referred rather unkindly to a group of elderly employer members as "geriatrics anonymous" as they staggered up the steps of 41 Belgrave Square one lunch-time. But that was the end of one era: one of a very different kind was to follow.

7 A PERIOD OF EXPANSION

"My hands are poised over the keys – what tune do you want me to play?"

(Brian Rusbridge at conference of local authority associations, September 1979)

Politically this period encompasses the Labour administrations of Harold Wilson and James Callaghan and is taken through to the first year of Margaret Thatcher's Conservative government so as to include the completion of the comparability studies of 1979/1980. Economically the "social contract" with the TUC resulted in hyper-inflation with price and pay increases topping 30% by 1975 followed by another dose of statutory pay policy which eventually fell apart completely as the Government interfered in the manual pay negotiations and suggested comparability studies. In the main local government pay negotiations there were periods of relative calm in the first few years of the statutory pay policy, but also turbulent times such as the prolonged firemen's strike of 1977. This was a period of great expansion of LACSAB's staffing and activities. But in the longer term perhaps the most significant development was the more direct linkage introduced between local government's pay negotiations and their funding by means of rate support grant settlements and cash limits.

POLITICAL AND ECONOMIC CONTEXT

It took several months for the pay policy of the new Labour government to emerge in the first half of 1974. Some important facts were nevertheless elicited when a deputation from LACSAB, the local authority associations and major employers' sides went to see Anthony Crosland, the new Secretary for the Environment that June. They were then told that the Government expected the statutory pay controls to be lifted before the end of July and that the basic aims thereafter were:-

- to end the period of restraint in an orderly fashion;
- to restore to employers and trade unions responsibility, with the social contract, to conduct negotiations; and
- to give maximum autonomy to local authorities subject to such statutory responsibilities as that of the Secretary of State for Education in relation to teachers.

The Government had welcomed the TUC document – "Collective bargaining and the social contract"; they hoped settlements in the immediate future would fall either within the terms of Stage 3 of the counter-inflation policy or the parameters of the TUC papers; and they were anxious that there should be at least 12 months between settlements. Negotiators could take account of the need to promote efficiency and reduce unit costs; raise the level of low pay; move further towards equal pay; and improve non-wage benefits like holidays or hours of work.

The TUC document identified a central negotiating objective as the maintenance of real incomes achieved either by claiming compensation for the rise in the cost of living since the last settlement – taking threshold increases into account – or by negotiating arrangements to keep up with the cost of living during the new agreement. Eric Wigham writing in the July 1974 edition of "News Summary" commented – "it is clear that wage movements will still be somewhat inflationary even if everybody does as advised. The main question however is whether the unions will observe the TUC recommendations". Given the vague terms of the Social Contract and the inflationary context, his remarks could hardly be termed prophetic: the question was not so much whether there was to be a wage explosion, but more realistically about how great its extent would be.

By August 1974 it was all doom and gloom as economic commentators talked of the most grave economic crisis since the war. The retail price annual increase of over 17% was expected to continue whilst average earnings increases would rise from the existing 15.8% to about 20% by the end of the year. With a general election already called, the TUC marshalled virtually unanimous support for the Social Contract whilst unilaterally without consultation adjusting the minimum wage target from £25 to £30 per week.

With the October 1974 general election over and Labour confirmed in office with a working majority, there was growing anxiety as 1974 drew to a close about the fate of the Social Contract as many settlements were reached in the private sector blatantly in breach of it. The TUC avoided open criticism of this, the CBI backed away from issuing their own guidelines, and Government ministers appealed over and over again for wage restraint. But the salient facts were that average earnings had shot up by 29.0% by the end of 1974 while prices rose by 19.1% with no signs of stabilisation. By the early summer of 1975 "The Economist" spoke of hyper-inflation and collapse of the Social Contract, contending that the reintroduction of a statutory incomes policy was merely a matter of time. It was felt that the Social Contract finally collapsed with the miners' and electricity supply settlements. As 30% wage increases became the norm, the price index soaring towards the same level, and the unemployment figures topping the million mark, ministerial pleas for restraint became more frantic, and there was no abatement in talks searching for ways to combat inflation.

The Government's eventual response came in the White Paper in July 1975 – "Attack on Inflation" – setting down the requirements to be observed on a"voluntary" basis for pay and prices in the year 1st August 1975 to 31st July 1976. The term "voluntary" was felt to be something of a misnomer as the Remuneration Charges and Grants Act 1975 gave statutory backing to the policy and there was no voluntary element in the public sector: in local government authorities breaking the rules were liable to have their rate support grant cut. £6 per week increases were allowed up to a salary limit of £8,500. The introduction of new incentive bonus and productivity schemes were prohibited as were group upgradings. But increases under incremental arrangements were permitted, drawing immediate criticism from the CBI. Worries about inflation and mounting unemployment enabled the Government's measures to be strongly supported at the TUC conference in September where there was much criticism of the cuts in public expenditure, especially from the public service unions.

As the new policy was almost universally observed, the Government's measures began to bite on earnings and prices by the end of 1975 with the annual rate of pay increases falling to 14% in the second half of 1975, but unemployment soared up to 1,430,369 – the highest level since before the war.

The Government gained the support of the TUC for the second stage of the incomes policy for the year beginning 1st August 1976 which allowed for increases up to 5% of the individual's earnings, with a minimum of £2.50 per week and a maximum of £4 per week to apply to all incomes above £80 per week.

LACSAB's concern that local government had insufficient voice in shaping pay policies led to the whole Board having a two- hour session with Albert Booth, Secretary for Employment, on 23rd February 1977. It was LACSAB's firm view that a third phase was needed for the year commencing 1st August 1977 and they elicited the fact that this was indeed the Government's intention. Many points were covered in what LACSAB members hoped was the first step in a continuing dialogue. The LACSAB view was that rate support grant negotiations should not tie the hands of negotiators and that increase orders were the means for tidying up the financial position after negotiations had taken place. Phase 2 held well and it was possible to report in July 1977 that 85% of employees covered by major agreements had settled within the guidelines and that there had been no breaches of the policy, although average earnings had increased by 7.5%.

The main general principles set out in the Government's White Paper – "The Attack on Inflation after 31st July 1977" (this time without TUC backing) recommended that all employers were to base their approach to pay negotiations on getting inflation into single figures, and to provide for a general level of pay settlements moderate enough to secure that the national earnings increase was no more than 10%. It was generally felt it would be very difficult to get workers to accept increases of less then 10% which would be thought of as a minimum, while the annual rate of inflation remained at 17%. Problems loomed for local authorities whose cash limits for the year to April 1978 were five to six per cent.

A Government letter of 25th November 1977 to local authorities asking that central departments should be given 14 days' notice of any projected local government pay deal led to a delegation from LACSAB and the local authority associations meeting on 5th December Peter Shore, the Secretary for the Environment, and other ministers. The local government representatives pointed out that there was already a practice of keeping Government departments aware of what was happening, and this would continue. They took the opportunity again to stress the importance of Government spokesmen not embarrassing the local government employers by statements in Parliament, to the press or to the trade unions.

Despite earnings looking like increasing by between 12 and 14%, rather than the 10% pay policy ceiling, the outlook seemed brighter at the beginning of 1978 with the annual retail price increase having fallen to 12.1%. By June 1978 John Ardill could comment in "News Summary" that there was no real smell of confrontation in the air, although the unions were speaking incessantly of unfettered collective bargaining whilst the Prime Minister talked of the inevitability of continuing Government intervention. But the force with which the Government had inflicted pay guidelines on central and local government employees had left a legacy of smouldering resentment with the unions.

The publication in July 1978 of the Government's White Paper – "Winning the Battle against Inflation" – setting out their pay policy from 1st August 1978 marked a clear parting of the ways between the Government and the TUC whose General Council voted with only one dissenting voice to reject the Stage 4 5% guideline. The Labour party conference in October similarly condemned the 5% guidelines by a large majority vote. The many reasons for the unions' vocal fury at the new pay policy could be attributed to their wish to be left alone and trusted to negotiate responsibly, as well as to the rigidity in failing to deal with anomalies and pressures at both ends of the pay spectrum.

The Government nevertheless did succeed in bringing inflation down to single figures during 1978, with the annual rate of increase below 8% that October. The parameters for local government pay negotiations were to some extent set by the Government's proposals in November 1978 for the rate support grant and cash limits for the financial year 1979/1980 which were calculated to reflect the Government's assumption that pay settlements would as in previous years accord with their pay policy. The trade union reaction was voiced by Geoffrey Drain of NALGO who said"they are not providing councils with enough funds to pay their workforces adequately". The tough line on public service pay was in marked contrast to more generous deals in the private sector. But the pendulum soon swung rapidly in the other direction.

A relatively small chink in the Government's pay policy rapidly became a gaping chasm on the issue of comparability. Government interference in the local government manual pay negotiations towards the end of 1978 and early in 1979 during the "winter of discontent" led to the Government establishing an independent standing commission to undertake a comparability study for local authority manual workers, NHS ancillary staffs, ambulancemen and university manual workers.

At a press conference in February 1979, Peter Shore, the Environment Secretary, maintained that the arrangements for comparability for local authority manual workers were regarded as "very exceptional" and it would need very exceptional circumstances for other groups even to be considered for similar treatment. Yet before many weeks had elapsed comparability was in vogue and virtually every negotiating group in local government negotiated a comparability study (except police and fire whose index-linked pay arrangements obviated the necessity). The 9% concession to the local authority manual workers as a result of Government intervention was also to become the norm for other groups thus effectively rendering null and void the original 5% guideline for that pay round.

As the general election of May 1979 resulted in the defeat of the Labour administration of James Callaghan, one immediate question was how the new Conservative government led by Margaret Thatcher would regard the inflationary comparability studies under way. The answer soon came, but was two-edged, as the incoming Chancellor of the Exchequer, Geoffrey Howe explained – "On pay in the public services, while we will honour the commitments...entered into by our predecessors, in general we will limit the adjustment of cash limits so that substantial off-setting economies will have to be found".

EMPLOYMENT LEGISLATION

An important part of the Social Contract of 1974 was the Government's pledge to repeal the Industrial Relations Act 1971 and to replace it by legislation more acceptable to the trade unions. Little time was lost in introducing the Trade Union and Labour Relations Bill which was expected to have only limited effect because much of the 1971 Act had become a dead letter by trade union opposition. The new bill generally restored the legal position to what it was before the 1971 Act, but in some respects tipped the balance of power a little more towards the trade unions, in particular in extending immunity from civil action for inducing breach of contract in the course of a trade dispute. The closed shop was to be formally legalised and it would be regarded as fair dismissal to dismiss an employee for not belonging to a specified union where there was a union membership agreement except where there was objection on religious grounds. The bill was subsequently enacted as the Trade Union and Labour Relations Act 1974 (TULRA) but had been modified by amendments during its passage through Parliament.

A further important development was the publication of the Government's Employment Protection Bill in May 1975 which proposed the largest single piece of industrial relations legislation affecting the rights of individual employees ever to be passed in this country. LACSAB felt that the measures to be introduced were of such significance to make available to local authorities forthwith a booklet describing the proposals of most relevance so that the implications could be considered well in advance. Amongst much other legislation the Trade Union and Labour Relations (Amendment) Bill was also introduced to give legal effect to the Government's closed shop proposals which had been lost during the passage of the 1974 Act.

The Employment Protection Act finally received Royal Assent in November 1975 and provided for its various measures to be introduced in stages. In February 1976 LACSAB produced their "Employee Relations Handbook", by far the most compendious tome yet published by them, covering not only the Employment Protection Act, but also the TULRA provisions, the Sex Discrimination Act, the Redundancy Payments Act, the Contract of Employment Act and the Rehabilitation of Offenders Act and how each Act affected or amended another. For each group of provisions the handbook explained the legal provisions, assessed their implications for local authorities, and gave a check list for the use of managers. The handbook, with its 168 pages containing some 100,000 words, was sold to local authorities for only £1.20 and quickly became an indispensable tool for thousands of officers grappling with all the new employment legislation (17,500 copies were sold in the first two months).

Health and safety at work was also very much on the agenda. Much useful work on this was done by LACSAB who set up a working party in 1975 in conjunction with the local authority associations and who also met to exchange views with the TUC local government committee. "Giving appointed workpeople the role of safety dogs...backed by the force of law will give a tremendous impetus to make Britain a healthier place to work in" declared Bill Simpson, chairman of the Health and Safety Commission early in 1976, but in November of that year the Government had to postpone the implementation of the health and safety at work regulations until October 1978 because of the need to restrict expenditure, but LACSAB encouraged local authorities that much could begin on a voluntary basis in advance of the statutory enforcing regulations.

After such a major piece of legislation as the Employment Protection Act 1975 it was hardly surprising that there was in subsequent years some respite in terms of initiating legislation but much effort was nevertheless involved in employers coming to grips with the various parts of the 1975 Act as they were brought in by stages.

As this period drew to a close and the Callaghan administration was succeeded by Margaret Thatcher's Conservative government, James Prior as Secretary for Employment appeared to adopt a "softly, softly" approach and there were as yet few indications of the extent to which industrial relations legislation was to continue to be a dominant political issue.

LOCAL GOVERNMENT CONTEXT

Perhaps the most significant development affecting the work of LACSAB in this period was the much more direct linkage between local government funding and pay negotiations.

Although the LACSAB report of 1974 – "Survey of Local Authorities' Salaries" – had attempted to justify the increases in staffing costs arising from the major local government reorganisation of that year, this was by no means the last word on the subject. An article by Muriel Bowen in the "Sunday Times" of 4th August 1974 complaining that reorganisation had pushed up top salaries in local government became the centre of much controversy and much righteous indignation from local authority organs. The front page of "News Summary" of April 1975 was devoted to a defence of local government pay levels as it became the "whipping boy" of the media who blamed such extravagance in part for the country's economic problems.

It was in 1975 that Anthony Crosland, the Secretary for the Environment, made his famous statement that "now the party is over", introducing a much more stringent attitude by the Government towards the funding of local government staffing and pay increases. In the rate support grant settlement for 1975/1976 the Department of Environment contemplated the limitation of expansion in staff numbers to the small increases necessary to meet inescapable commitments. The introduction by the Department of Environment in March 1975 of the quarterly joint manpower watch system would enable a scrutiny at national and local levels of staffing on a thorough and consistent basis on a scale never before attempted. It was agreed that LACSAB, who were already in the process of assembling a team whose functions were to include the development of pay and manpower statistics, be asked to undertake the work of compiling the joint manpower watch on behalf of the Department of Environment and the local authority associations.

The Government's cuts in public expenditure as part of their 1975 "Attack on Inflation" policy came soon after the start of the collection of joint manpower watch figures. So although there were increases in manpower numbers until June 1976, this was followed by a long period of reductions until numbers started to move up again from September 1978 onwards, by which time the grand total recorded in full-time and full-time equivalents was 2,104,117. Eight public service unions decided towards the end of 1976 to combine to protest and engage in forms of non-cooperation against cuts in public expenditure. NALGO went further than the others by deciding in January 1977 to impose a national overtime ban from 1st April 1977 which was largely ignored by NALGO members and local authorities alike.

Another manifestation of the stronger connection between local government funding and pay negotiations was the growing interest by leading local "policy and resource" members, several of whom made their presence sharply felt in national pay negotiations and who added a new dimension to the already familiar "ability to pay" argument. The hitherto cosy arrangement of post-hoc endorsement of local government pay deals by means of supplementary rate support grant increase orders was to come to an end as cash limits were imposed by the Government.

OVERALL LACSAB ACTIVITIES

The minutes of the LACSAB Board in this period 1974 to 1979 show that much of their business was responding to the steady stream of Government initiatives on pay policy, but a series of delegations to ministers developed into a useful two-way flow of ideas in which local government members were able to have more of a voice than hitherto. Prior to "The Attack on Inflation" policy of 1975, the LACSAB Board had been disturbed at the profound effect on local authority salaries of the "Boyle" report for the higher civil service and the "Houghton" report for teachers.

The LACSAB Board were particularly concerned that, after all their efforts which had led to the major review of London weighting by the Pay Board in 1973/1974, by the end of 1974 the eventual outcome was entirely unsatisfactory with widely differing levels, steps and boundaries as between their own local government negotiating groups. LACSAB attributed this untidy situation in large part to the contradictory terms of the Pay Board's conclusions which, whilst recommending levels for inner and outer London based on the principle of cost compensation, permitted negotiators to achieve different results by a "kittying" process. This criticism was not entirely fair as the first local government agreement for London weighting post-Pay Board was for APT&C staffs and was skewed to the benefit of outer London (because the London boroughs' earlier interim increase had done so) to an extent such that other negotiating groups could hardly ignore it. The 1974 negotiations introduced the fringe area allowances immediately outside London to ameliorate the "cliff edge" heightened by successive London weighting awards and to absorb many local allowances paid because of problems of recruitment and retention of staffs.

In September 1975 as the LACSAB Board were informed of a crop of seven arbitrations there was a note of disquiet that these would do little to provide satisfactory and lasting conclusions as there was a lack of continuity in the arbitration panels appointed. The latter aspect became a point of particular concern as LACSAB faced at about the same time three arbitrations on the same issue of London weighting.

The strong influence of the APT&C employers' representatives on the LACSAB Board was felt in 1976 when they managed to reverse a LACSAB decision to improve redundancy provisions for the 41 to 49 age group, and again in 1977 when their "nothing more than minimum statutory provisions" line was accepted on maternity provisions. Although only three out of the 30 LACSAB members directly represented the APT&C employers, no fewer than nine LACSAB members served on the APT&C employers at that time, six reaching the LACSAB Board by other means.

A frequent issue confronting the LACSAB Board in this period was Government interference in local government pay negotiations. This was a particular problem early in 1978 on firemen's pay and hours, but the issue really came to a head in the 1978 manual pay negotiations in late 1978/early 1979 when the Government eventually wrenched the initiative from the local government employers, met the general secretaries of public sector unions, and offered them a 9% increase plus a comparability study.

In terms of the range of activities of the LACSAB secretariat this period 1974 to 1979 marks a substantial advancement in areas beyond the direct national pay negotiations in the various groups. Reference has already been made to the growth of the advisory service in the employment legislation area and the handbooks published on major pieces of legislation. As well as responding to many requests for guidance from local, provincial and national levels, LACSAB was pushing out a steady stream of regular advice on employment law through its frequent advisory bulletins widely welcomed and respected throughout local government for their authoritative nature. Although these were "employer-only" pronouncements every opportunity was taken informally to ensure their terms were largely acceptable to the trade unions.

The other significant extension of activities of the LACSAB secretariat stemmed from the decision in June 1974 by the LACSAB Board in the light of a report by the secretary, Brian Rusbridge, to create a unit for the development of pay and manpower statistics. LACSAB established in conjunction with the LGTB and LAMSAC a working party of local, provincial and national officers to plan the co-ordinated development of the provision of reliable, available and up-to-date pay and manpower statistics to be of value to individual authorities and also for a variety of uses at national level. The decision to ask LACSAB early in 1975 to undertake the joint manpower watch exercise was welcomed inasmuch as this work would be done by local government and its own agencies rather than by central government, but nevertheless diverted the LACSAB officers concerned from their work on the general development of statistics. As well as taking the lead in the development of more reliable pay and manpower statistics, LACSAB also did much to co-ordinate manpower information systems. As Ken Woods, LACSAB deputy secretary, put it in a "News Summary" article of February 1976 – "local government must know what it's about as an employer. The happy improvisation of a jazz ensemble is no longer possible. A big band needs a score". [This evidently was not the specific score sought subsequently by LACSAB secretary, Brian Rusbridge, when he made his famous comment in September 1979- "My hand are poised over the keys – what tune do you want me to play?"] An important example of the work initiated on manpower information systems was the LACSAB document published later in 1976 – "Guidelines for the development of personnel record systems in local authorities" – which was relevant both to manual and to computer-based record systems. In the field of pay statistics much was done to improve the reliability of the various pay and manpower surveys undertaken by LACSAB so that in a relatively short time these became accepted for their reliability and integrity, not least by the trade unions, in national pay negotiations.

1975 saw the setting up of a further negotiating body under the LACSAB umbrella – the joint negotiating committee for coroners, an ancient office dating back over 800 years, covering 179 appointments, of which 22 were full-time.

The LACSAB journal took on a new lease of life at the beginning of 1978 as it changed its title from "News Summary" to "Local Government Manpower".

MANUAL WORKERS

The agreement of the manual workers NJC on revised rates of pay from 4th November 1974 was one of the first to follow the endorsement by the TUC that September of the Social Contract. The unilateral revision of the TUC's target for a minimum wage from £25 to £30 was allowed to flow through immediately to form the basic Group A rate. All threshold payments were absorbed, the adult rate would be paid at age 18 instead of at age 19, the minimum earnings guarantee was discontinued, and shift working enhancements improved in line with those for APT&C staffs. This was "in the view of the parties, within the terms of the TUC/Government Social Contract".

A dispute arose however early in 1975 between the two sides of the NJC over a claim by the trade unions' side for the restoration of the value of pay differentials between the grades in the manual pay scheme determined in 1969. This was strongly resisted by the employers who claimed this could not be dealt with outside the annual pay negotiations and that the November 1974 agreement had to operate as agreed until November 1975. They asserted that the claim for restored differentials was an after thought to extricate the unions from their problems of solving the Glasgow and Liverpool refuse collection drivers' strikes and had not been mentioned in the claim which led to the November 1974 deal. The unions denied they had changed their tack and claimed that they had reached the November 1974 agreement because of an assurance given that negotiations could continue on the grading issue. The dispute was referred to ACAS who set up a board of arbitration. The award in the summer of 1975 was a classic "on the one hand...on the other hand...therefore..." compromise recognising improvements for the low-paid must involve compression of differentials but the top rate was only £3.25 a week higher than the £30 minimum conceded on low pay grounds. So some slight improvements were awarded "to be regarded as a first step in improving the pay structure" conceding an extra £2 for the highest rate at an annual cost of less than 2%.

Sewage workers

The manual worker pay negotiations of 1975 were the first in local government following the Government's introduction of their "Attack on Inflation" policy in July 1975. Both the terms of the trade union claim and the quick settlement at the end of September 1975 conformed with the new pay policy, providing for a £6 per week supplement with effect from 4th November 1975 which would not count for bonus, overtime and other similar enhancements. There were to be no further pay increases or improvements in service conditions at local, provincial or national levels during the twelve-month term of the agreement, and it was also decided that no further productivity schemes or lead-in payments could be introduced.

With the TUC in 1976 again supporting the Government's pay policy – "The Attack on Inflation: The Second Year", the NJC for manual workers quickly concluded their 1976 pay agreement early in October 1976. The deal was in line with pay policy limits and provided for a weekly earnings supplement of £2.50 or 5% of total earnings, whichever was the greater, subject to a maximum of £4 with effect from 4th November 1976.

The manual trade unions' 1977 claim was of a very different order and has to be seen against the context of the TUC not supporting the Government's policy – "The Attack on Inflation after 31st July 1977". They claimed a substantial increase in basic rates, consolidation of the 1975 and 1976 supplements, a reduction in the working week, maintenance of employees' purchasing power, improved annual leave and other changes. When the NJC met on 24th October 1977 the employers tabled an offer strictly in accordance with the Government's guidelines and which provided consolidation of supplements and new money increases which were expected to yield a 10% increase in earnings over the twelve-month period. The unions took the offer away to consult their members and came back to a further NJC meeting on 19th December 1977 to accept it. The revised rates applied from 4th November 1977.

THE WINTER OF DISCONTENT

The manual pay negotiations for 1978 were expected to be much more difficult with both the TUC and Labour party conferences having decisively rejected the Government's policy – "Winning the Battle against Inflation" – limiting pay increases to 5%. The trade union side submitted a claim containing several major elements, including a fully-consolidated basic rate of £60 per week; a reduced working week of 35 hours without loss of pay; improved annual holidays; and cost of living protection. This claim was presented and argued at the NJC meeting on 30th October. The employers returned to the next NJC meeting on 12th December with an offer consistent with the Government's pay policy to apply from 4th November 1978. This included staggered increases in basic rates ranging from 60p per week to £3.25 per week to restore the 1969 job evaluated differentials and introduced the concept of a minimum earnings guarantee with a minimum earnings level for each grade for 40-hour workers pitched well above the Government's £44.50 figure for lower incomes. By this time several groups of manual workers in the public sector including local government were taking various forms of industrial action during what became known as the "winter of discontent". Subsequent intervention by Government ministers eventually led to a very different and improved employers' package offer at the NJC meeting on 21st February 1979 after much confusion about the Government's precise intentions. The trade unions recommended acceptance of this improved offer which consisted of four major elements:-

(i) £3.50 on the basic rates from 4th November 1978;

(ii) the outstanding £5 supplement consolidated from 22nd February 1979;

(iii) a supplement of £1 from 22nd February 1979 for those working 35 hours or more to be offset against any sum due from the first stage of the comparability study; and

(iv) agreement on a comparability study to be undertaken by an independent standing commission which was to produce a first report by 1st August 1979, with 50% of any recommendations to be implemented on 1st July 1979 and the remaining 50% on 1st April 1980, with the next annual settlement due meanwhile in November 1979.

The amended offer was not only significantly different in its form but also regards quantum. Instead of keeping within the 5% Government guideline it offered 9% plus the hope of more to come from the comparability study. Environment Secretary, Peter Shore, welcomed the agreement as fair – even generous – and said he regarded the arrangements for comparability for local authority manuals as "very exceptional", but a subsequent Government statement encouraged negotiators in the public services to consider comparability exercises to be conducted by the independent standing commission they had established.

The report of the Standing Commission on Pay Comparability chaired by Professor Hugh Clegg was published on 1st August 1979 as promised after employers and unions had submitted evidence. There were obvious shortcomings arising from the very limited five months allowed for their inquiries. They did not favour binding recommendations but preferred the parties themselves to negotiate changes arising from their report; they had to limit their study to a few representative benchmark jobs using both factor analysis and job-for-job comparison methods; they firmly rejected indexation as a basis for comparisons as sought by the unions; they took account of all elements of the total remuneration package including pensions and job security; they rejected the unions' arguments of projecting awards forward by six months; but overall felt that the results were credible as, although not clustering around a single figure, they all pointed in the same direction.

Both sides of the NJC accepted the Clegg recommendations; 50% of the resultant increase came into effect from the pay week including 1st August 1979, with the remaining 50% being brought into effect from the pay week including 1st April 1980. (LGM of September 1979 reports on the Clegg inquiry at length and comments – "The numerical results of the inquiry are by now well-known" – and quotes no details of them)

One constitutional issue worthy of note in this period was the decision in January 1977 to widen the scope of the NJC for manual workers to include Northern Ireland and to establish a Northern Ireland Joint Industrial Council.

CRAFT WORKERS

A significant issue was the claim of the electricians for a pay increase to bring the basic pay of local authority electricians into line with electricians in the electrical contracting industry which was eventually referred to arbitration in 1975. The award was – inter alia – that the parties should revise the wage system to provide a higher basic rate incorporating some of the bonus element, and that the basic rate should bear a closer relationship with the rate paid to electricians in outside industry. The employers and the union were at odds in the interpretation of the award and its validity, with the employers pointing out that the board of arbitration made no specific finding on the basic rate as requested. These differences were however soon rendered academic in view of the Government's £6 limitation on wage increases.

The agreement for a comparability study for local authority manual workers led to comparability studies in 1979/1980 for the craft groups, with building and civil engineering and electricians opting for the Standing Commission and the others going for an "in house" job-for-job comparison. By late 1979 it was recognised that these studies would take some time to complete and this led to negotiations for immediate increases pending their outcome. Bearing in mind what had flowed from the manual comparability exercise, the craft employers offered comparability increases in advance of the results which would be taken into account and subsumed when the results were published. This cleared the way for quick deals for the 1979/1980 pay round which included a 13% increase from November 1979 and agreement that the eventual comparability award would be payable from 1st April 1980. LGM of July 1980 was able to report agreement arising from the "in house" study for engineering craftsmen effective from 1st April 1980, but it was not until the January 1981 issue that agreements were reported for building and civil engineering craftsmen and for electricians following the publication of Report No. 10 of the Standing Commission for Pay Comparability. A particular feature of the agreement for building and civil engineering craftsmen was the introduction of a two-tier structure of nationally agreed bonus calculator rates.

In 1977 the joint negotiating committees for building and civil engineering craftsmen and for engineering craftsmen introduced provincial machinery for settling differences between local authorities and their employees.

APT&C STAFFS

The 1974 APT&C negotiations were a long drawn out affair. Although there was much discussion in the early half of the year governed by Stage 3 of the former Heath government's counter-inflation policies, the eventual agreement in September 1974 was in terms of the new Labour government's Social Contract. A demand for closer links with civil service pay was a major feature of the 20% claim submitted by the APT&C staff side in March 1974, with NALGO publishing a booklet explaining the claim. They particularly drew attention to the erosion of differentials vis-à-vis manual workers and the extent to which clerical salaries in local government had fallen behind comparable levels elsewhere. The very detailed claim was examined by an NJC working party which identified "priority areas" for the 1974 settlement. After lengthy discussions the working party on 5th September recommended to both sides of the NJC a settlement within the Social Contract and which would increase the overall salaries bill by 14%. It included a measure of restructuring and the correction of anomalies, pay increases ranging from 11 to 13.5% and more favourable treatment for the lower paid. The deal was ratified by the NJC on 18th September. There was subsequently much justified criticism by local authorities of the concessions for the lower paid, especially the combination of the bottom two clerical grades, conceived to circumvent pay policy restrictions which had since been lifted.

NALGO's preparations on the 1975 APT&C salaries claim began earlier than usual in the hope a report could be made to their annual meeting on 9th June of a settlement or on progress reached. In the wake of the criticism by local authorities of the 1974 settlement, the employers' preparations had commenced even earlier with extensive officer-level discussions towards the end of 1974 followed early in 1975 by member-level consultations. There was a universal view that at lower salary levels local government salaries were highly competitive if not actually "up market" and that any settlement should not exceed the cost of living to accord with the Social Contract. The staff side eventually claimed £10 per week plus 15% with an operative date of 1st May 1975, two months before the due date of 1st July 1975. The employers' position had in the meantime been made more difficult by the generous pay research settlement for the non-industrial civil service operative from 1st January and 1st April 1975. LACSAB officers were mystified by this as the Social Contract made no mention of comparability as a basis for pay increases. At a meeting on 30th May the employers proposed an increase of 21.7% which "News Summary" reports laconically as not acceptable to the staff side. Because of the consolidation of flat-rated threshold payments this employer offer was heavily skewed in favour of the higher paid to counter-balance the effects of the 1974 settlement and in sharp contrast to the staff side claim weighted again in favour of the lower paid. The staff side were placed in the dilemma that to redistribute the money available they would have to reduce the increases for the higher paid already on offer by the employers. Although the May offer was rejected by the staff side, they decided to publish it in detail and to recommend negotiators to improve it rather than to press their original claim. Towards the end of June the employers put forward an improved package the total cost of which was estimated at 25% of the existing paybill, and this was agreed at the July NJC meeting. The package included increases of 22% on all points with effect from 1st July 1975, revised grading provisions for several occupational groups and other aspects. One feature of this settlement which achieved many employer objectives was to bring the salaries of all APT&C officers (except those on chief officer scales) on to the common spinal column of 51 points.

The APT&C settlement effective from 1st July 1976 was virtually the last major agreement under the Government's "Attack on Inflation" policy and strictly conformed with it with supplements of £6 per week for those earning up to £8,500.

1977 saw a claim and an agreement in terms of Stage 2 of the pay policy providing an earnings supplement of £2.50 per week or 5% of total earnings subject to a maximum of £4 per week with effect from 1st July 1977. There was some delay as the employers were obliged to make an assessment of the cost of the incremental system before they were satisfied it was of insufficient significance to justify any reduction in the pay offer.

A more detailed claim was submitted by the APT&C staff side in 1978 when, in addition to seeking a substantial and equal percentage increase in earnings for each individual, they sought the introduction of a 35-hour week. There was subsequently strong pressure within NALGO to ignore the Government's 10% guidelines but this was decisively defeated at a special conference on 2nd June. Settlement was eventually reached by the NJC on 5th July at Bournemouth to operate from 1st July 1978 on increases of 9.94% throughout, consolidation of the

Stage 2 earnings supplement and other features. Problems had arisen at a late stage concerning the application of the Government's guidelines which led to a deputation from the employers meeting the Environment Secretary, Peter Shore, at short notice at a critical stage in the negotiations. The employers insisted on adopting a realistic attitude on the costing of certain elements of their proposals instead of the mechanistic one which Government officials sought to impose.

The period between the 1978 and 1979 APT&C pay negotiations was certainly no interlude as both sides were heavily preoccupied with the protracted social worker dispute and negotiations. The Government's Stage 4 pay policy guidelines had been substantially modified by the time the APT&C negotiators got down to business for the 1979 pay review and comparability was now the name of the game. Earlier unfruitful discussions in the NJC's executive committee made an immediate settlement look highly unlikely when the NJC met at Norwich on 6th July yet after a long hot summer's day the gap was bridged and agreement reached (subject to ratification by the trade unions). The agreement provided for consolidation of Stage 1 supplements plus a 9.4% increase in pay from 1st July 1979 together with a comparability study to be conducted "in house" by the NJC and implemented in one stage with effect from 1st January 1980. As the comparability study would of necessity be complex and comprehensive, a joint steering group was established by the NJC to oversee the exercise. Whilst much of the information would be on a broad base, not related to specific jobs or occupations and largely relying on already published material, there would be a job profile exercise to examine salaries actually paid for specific jobs and job-types. The steering group were confronted with many difficulties in reaching any conclusions as the wide array of data failed to point incontravertibly in one direction. But the positions of the two sides became polarised when the employers, conscious of difficulties looming because of stringent rate support grant levels and cash limits, introduced the "ability to pay" argument early in 1980. An employers' offer ranging from 6% at the bottom to 12% at the top was rejected out of hand by the staff side and NALGO instructed its members to take industrial action. Local authorities believed the employers were reneging on their undertaking on the comparability study; an avalanche of local authority protests descended on Belgrave Square; and several local deals struck. These were initially ignored by employer members but on 21st March LACSAB encouraged the employers to reconsider their position and joint talks resumed quickly thereafter. A series of quick meetings resulted in a settlement on 28th March for increases ranging from 9.5% at the bottom to 18% at the top as from 1st January 1980 (as against the 6% to 12% originally offered). Very little industrial action had actually been necessary by NALGO members as it was the local authorities who insisted on the employers fulfilling their obligations in respect of the comparability study. It was estimated later that the delay by the employers in responding to local authority pressure could have cost local government up to £50m. extra through the concessions gained by the staff side when their negotiating position had become stronger.

Given the problems in resolving London weighting in 1974 and the widely diverging settlements stemming from the Pay Board's report it was hardly surprising that the 1975 APT&C London weighting negotiations were difficult, lengthy and inconclusive, finishing up with a reference to arbitration, along with the teachers and GLC APTEC staffs. LACSAB did all they could to ensure as much consistency as possible in the arbitration awards and to that end got the same chairman, Professor John Wood, and employer member. The common employers' sides' cases took the line that allowances should be derived from the updated Pay Board recommendations; regard should be had to financial restraints; and there should be no increase in fringe area allowances. Another important aim for the employers was to reduce the excess spending beyond the Pay Board "kitty" arising from the 1974 settlements. The arbitration award effectively supported the employers' case in principle by reaffirming the Pay Board "cost compensation" approach. Some 70% of the 1974 excess over the Pay Board "kitty" was retained, comparing favourably with 80% for GLC APTEC staffs and 100% for teachers.

An emotive issue on the NJC agenda for a lengthy period was the subject of motor car allowances. The employers believed a radical review was justified as the situation on car ownership had changed dramatically since the scheme had first been introduced in 1947. Employer proposals were formulated, put to the staff side early in 1976, and led to intensive negotiations. Towards the end of 1976 an impasse appeared to have been reached and arbitration seemed likely, but then further urgent talks eventually resulted in January 1977 in a settlement on a new formula for essential car users, but there was no agreement on casual car users which the staff side took after some delay to arbitration. The eventual arbitration award in August 1977 amply demonstrated the folly of referring highly technical issues to ad-hoc arbitrators. The award produced a scheme much more administratively cumbersome than either side had contemplated. This plus an arithmetical error by the arbitrators led the NJC to agree on a simpler system than had been awarded.. Huge problems were also created through the award being backdated to 1st January 1977 as efforts to produce a "ready reckoner" for calculation of arrears foundered because of the variety of local practices in operating a "national" scheme.

A difficult issue resolved in 1977 was in respect of maternity leave when the existing contractual provisions were integrated with the statutory rights under the Employment Protection Act 1975 by a two-tier scheme depending on whether or not the officer had one or two years' continuous service.

The main 1975 pay settlement had also mopped up many outstanding grading issues with the exception of laboratory/ workshop technicians which was eventually referred to arbitration. The outcome was a very detailed, cumbersome and confusing structure which caused many problems in the next decade. Whilst the arbitrators could be (and were) criticised for this, much of the cumbersome nature of the award could be traced back to the employers' proposals.

1978/1979 SOCIAL WORKER DISPUTE

Undoubtedly the biggest grading issue in this period 1974 to 1979 was the social workers which suddenly exploded when, on 8th August 1978, the employers rejected out of hand a staff side claim to abolish the national grading prescription. The response of NALGO was to initiate strike action from 14th August in 12 different authorities, leading to a prolonged and ugly dispute. The employers quickly confirmed that authorities were virtually unanimous in wanting the continuation of national grades and to act together through the national employers rather than be exposed in isolation to local action orchestrated nationally by NALGO. In September the employers commissioned an immediate but comprehensive enquiry on social workers' pay, quickly brought the results together to provide a basis for national negotiations, and by early October had initiated exploratory joint talks by the leaders of both sides of the NJC. Intensive confidential discussions ensued as the strike action continued and by November both sides of the national working party made a joint recommendation which the employers ratified. Extensive employer consultations then took place on the proposals which set out five pay bands for social workers and welfare assistants each related to typical levels of responsibility. There was a good measure of support for these proposals but reservations were voiced stemming in large part from the secretive nature of the national discussions; the feeling that authorities were faced with a "fait accompli"; and especially the knowledge that a new agreement on these lines would involve much work and bargaining locally. It was not until 6th February 1979 that the NJC finally approved the working party recommendations and the strike action was called off by NALGO, bringing to an end – not without many recriminations – the most bitter dispute yet in the APT&C sphere. Many lessons were to be learned from this dispute which started with a union demand for abolition of one national grade and resulted in five new pay levels replacing two existing levels. One lesson for the employers was the great cost of a blunt rejection of a staff side claim rather than the time-honoured Whitley approach of thrashing problems out. A lesson for NALGO was the great drain on their funds through paying full pay to the striking social workers and which led very quickly to a change of rules.

Whilst the social workers overall gained substantially in pay from the 1978/1979 dispute, their increases were relatively modest compared with those which residential officers received from their 1979 agreement although the latter never hit the headlines as did the social workers. The employers seized the initiative from the outset when they decided in September 1978 to extend the urgent but comprehensive enquiry to cover residential staffs as well as social workers. This led to the formulation of proposals for a more simplified system of a framework of national guidelines within which pay levels could be selected locally according to the contribution required of each residential officer. Joint agreement was eventually reached by the NJC in April 1979 after extensive joint working party discussions. The magnitude of increases for residential officers arising from this could not be assessed immediately as much depended on local application. It was subsequently found that in the two years April 1979 to April 1981 their average salaries had increased by just over 75%, compared with the 48.5% of APT&C staffs generally (all having benefited from the 1979/1980 comparability study).

Another follow-on from social workers was in respect of nursery staffs as the employers accepted that staffs in day nurseries should also benefit, but not to the same extent as residential officers whose inclusive salaries recompensed for unsocial hours and weekend working which did not arise in day nurseries. The staff side pressed for substantial increases beyond those proposed by the employers and also for inclusion of nursery staffs in schools and classes, and the issue eventually went to arbitration. The arbitration award in 1980 mainly upheld the employers' proposals, accepting the principle of a pay differential for residential officers over day nursery staffs to reflect unsocial hours and weekend working and leaving the pay of nursery staffs in schools and classes largely unchanged.

One manifestation of Britain's entry into Europe was the EEC directive on poultry meat inspection which caused the APT&C employers many problems from 1976 onwards. These led to a series of tripartite talks involving also the Ministry of Agriculture and the British Poultry Federation, and to the provincial and national employers' network having to co-ordinate training courses to ensure an adequate supply of poultry meat inspectors to comply with the EEC directive.

This was a period when the APT&C employers concentrated much work and resources in studying the jobs, training, pay and grading of many specific occupational groups. The report in 1978 on staffing in environmental health was a good example of collaboration between the national organisations of local government. This comprehensive document discussed the organisation, staffing and training of environmental health staff, helped local authorities decide their own requirements, and identified ways in which their decisions could be aided by national decisions. Much similar useful collaborative work was also done in the same period in the social services area, and the knowledge and experience gained had unexpectedly to be redeployed to produce the proposals to resolve the 1978/1979 social worker dispute.

The end of 1975 was marked by the publication of the eighth edition of the national scheme (the "Purple Book") which it was hoped would by its system of regular updating by amendment sheets have an infinite duration. This edition of the scheme consolidated the familiar spinal column system of salaries, providing a comprehensive yet simplified national salary structure.

Lord Hill of Luton resigned in 1978 as independent chairman of the NJC after a 15-year stint. An effective chairman who rarely wasted words, he once expeditiously concluded an agenda of over 20 items before one LACSAB secretary could find his papers. Lord Hill, who unfortunately died in 1989, will long be remembered for his after dinner speeches at NJC functions with his fruity voice and earthy wit.

TOP POSTS

When in 1973 the joint negotiating committees for chief executives and chief officers had reached their important agreements on salary levels for the new local authorities on the 1974 reorganisation of local government there was a proviso for the scales to be reviewed not later than April 1975. This review was delayed year after year for a variety of reasons including pay policies. One significant development was early in 1975 when the Government suggested the review should be undertaken by an ad-hoc independent committee under the chairmanship of Lord Boyle, which would also have within its ambit the NHS, the water industry and chief constables. This proposal was stoutly resisted by LACSAB and the local authority associations who argued that a structure of negotiating bodies had been built up for the determination of salaries and their functioning should not be abrogated. When they met ministers in February 1975 they were able to persuade them to think again.

Top salaries in local government fared very badly in 1976 and 1977 under Stages 1 and 2 of the Government's "Attack on Inflation" policy. In 1978 the strict interpretation of the Stage 3 guidelines would have meant offering chief executives, chief officers and deputies less than APT&C staffs. The employers felt this would be unfair, so directly the APT&C NJC concluded their 1978 pay deal at Bournemouth in July 1978, a similar package was forthwith offered to and accepted by the chief executives who also happened to be in conference at Bournemouth, and to the chief officers a few hours later back in London. For this contravention of pay policy guidelines local government was later fined £3m in the next rate support grant settlement.

In June 1979 the pay negotiations for chief officers and chief executives went in different directions. The chief officers quickly agreed on an "in house" comparability study, with an increase of 9% from 1st July 1979, leaving the implementation of any increase beyond 9% for further discussion. But the chief executives insisted on an interim payment of 15% from 1st July 1979 and in addition 9% or an appropriate cost of living increase. As the employers would not agree to this, there was a reference to arbitration. The award of January 1980 was a 9.4% increase from 1st July 1979 plus a further 8% to be set aside to reform the salary structure to take effect from 1st January 1980. At a JNC meeting in February 1980 the employers offered the chief executives a revised salary structure conforming with the arbitration award and reflecting greater differentiation as between authority types. Meanwhile for chief officers the employers offered 12% from 1st January 1980 following the chief executives' arbitration award. But at a JNC meeting on 25th March 1980 in the light of the comparability study (and the APT&C settlement) the employers upped their offer to 17% from 1st January 1980, giving a total increase of 28% over 1978 levels, and a deal was struck on that basis.

FIRE BRIGADES

After the mammoth 1973 package for firemen's pay, the Social Contract agreement reached to apply from 7th November 1974 was a straightforward increase in pay levels. A small working party was set up by the NJC to carry out a job evaluation/productivity investigation into the work of the qualified fireman, and following that the NJC would examine the feasibility of a working week of 40 hours as claimed by the FBU.

In May 1975 the FBU banned all but emergency duties in support of a claim for interim pay increases and a shorter working week pending the completion of the job evaluation/productivity investigation, notwithstanding the revised rates from 7th November 1974 were supposed to last for 12 months. Following this there was a series of NJC meetings to seek to resolve the situation when the union submitted a number of claims. The employers made it clear they would need to have regard to the pay policy about to be introduced by the Government. A recalled delegate conference of the FBU at the end of July decided to escalate the programme of industrial action and this caused serious fire cover problems in some areas. The Home Secretary intervened with a proposal to set up an inquiry into the question of a 40-hour week and other problems associated with the dispute, following which the employers expressed willingness to co- operate in an inquiry. Noting that the 40-hour week issue had been taken up by the

A fireman at the scene of a blaze.

proposed Home Office inquiry, the NJC reached a settlement in August on the basis of immediate joint talks on the issue of the whole-time retained duty system; a continuing review of the work of the fireman; and a £6 supplement from November 1975 within the terms of the Government's pay policy.

October 1976 saw an annual settlement for firemen's pay in accordance with the Government's pay policy Stage 2 £2.50/5%/£4 limits operative from 7th November 1976.

The NJC working party set up to examine changes in the fireman's job since 1971 eventually produced in the spring of 1977 a composite job description for the fully qualified fireman in a document entitled – "The Qualified Fireman's Job". The NJC agreed to establish a small working group formed of NJC members and chaired by an independent chairman, Lord McCarthy, to compare the agreed fireman's job description with those of other occupations. The group eventually concluded in their report in September 1977 that the range of knowledge and skills required and the variety of situations encountered by the fireman meant that any comparison should ultimately be with the generality of jobs and not with specific analogues. Following publication of the McCarthy report, the FBU submitted a claim based on a comparison with the broadest range of occupations plus an element for what they saw as the special factors of the fire service. The employers estimated that the claim if conceded would increase firemen's pay by about 36%, far beyond the limits of 10% of earnings under Stage 3 of the Government's pay policy. The employers' counter-offer was (i) to increase earnings by 10% from 7th November 1977; (ii) agreement in principle to introduce a 42-hour week without loss of pay from November 1978; and (iii) implementation in two stages at November 1978 and November 1979 of a pay formula to link firemen's average earnings with the upper quartile of adult manual workers.

1977/1978 FIREMEN'S DISPUTE

A delegate conference of the FBU in November 1977 decided (against the advice of their executive) to call a national strike as from 14th November 1977 in support of a claim based on male average earnings plus 10%. As the strike action proceeded and the army were called in with their "green goddesses" the two sides continued talks and attempts to find a settlement. Deputations by the FBU to the Home Secretary and the Prime Minister evoked the response that any immediate increase had to be within pay policy limits. The FBU sought TUC approval for a nationwide campaign against the 10% pay guidelines but this was refused, with the TUC general secretary saying that the union should accept the package offered. Whilst the Government were not prepared to breach pay policy by improving the 10% offered for 1977, they went so far as to agree to the full implementation of an agreed pay formula for the future by equal stages in 1978 and 1979, backed up by rate support grant funding. There was eventually a return to work by FBU members on 16th January 1978, followed the next day by an agreement in the NJC. When the terms of the final settlement were compared with the employers' offer well in advance of the strike action, it was clearly evident that little if anything had been gained by the strike action on top of the concessions arising from the Government's clumsy interventions in the negotiations. This strike had significance far beyond the fire service as the

Government's reaction was looked upon by all and sundry as the touchstone of its determination to reduce inflation. Commitment of over 20,000 servicemen for nine weeks in a strike-breaking role put much pressure on the TUC's tacit acquiescence in a continuation of pay policy. The FBU failed by only one vote in the TUC general council to get the support of the trade union movement as a whole – a measure of how easily the dispute could have gone a different way.

The early part of 1978 was taken up by extensive and protracted negotiations on the introduction of the 42-hour week, with fire authorities especially concerned about the manpower implications of the shorter working week. Despite substantial employer concessions, difficulties continued in the discussions about the introduction of the 42-hour week and the employers were frustrated in their attempts to resolve this by arbitration by a provision in the 1975 Employment Protection Act. Eventually Professor John Wood, chairman of the Central Arbitration Committee was invited as an independent third party to whom both sides could submit for clarification and record the position reached. Following a report from Professor Wood critical of both sides, exploratory talks took place between the leaders of the two sides, and this led eventually to agreement towards the end of 1978. The outcome was generally satisfactory to the employers when assessed in relation to their three main objectives of (a) minimum increase in manpower; (b) more time available for working routines; and (c) more disciplined approach to industrial relations at local level.

There was hope that the pay of firemen would cease to become an issue for confrontation with the introduction of arrangements for index-linking with average male earnings by two stages from November 1978 and November 1979 under the terms of the final agreement of the 1977/1978 dispute of January 1978. These arrangements provided a continuous means of maintaining relativities with the rest of the economy and thus obviated the need for a comparability study as arose for most other local government groups in 1979/1980.

POLICE

The 1974 police pay agreement concluded well in advance of the operative date of 1st September 1974 was stated to be within the limits of the previous Government's Stage 3 guidelines and gave increases to police constables ranging from 16.7% to 23%. The agreement also provided for a review of the police pay structure which was then undertaken by a joint working party of the Police Council and which produced a 60-page report in May 1975 setting out an objective analysis of the facts surrounding the policeman's job. The report echoed earlier inquiries into police pay in the view that the policeman was unique among subordinates in the degree of responsibility he had to exercise. Whilst the fundamentals of the job had not changed, there was greater pressure of work than hitherto on the individual, and more emphasis on specialist skills. Conditions of service had deteriorated in one respect in that the number of assaults on the police had risen dramatically in recent years. The working party came down firmly against consolidation of rent allowance into pensionable pay and concluded there was no single principle for determining the general level of police pay. They agreed that the maintenance of the value of police pay should be achieved by linkage to the earnings index as well as the wages index.

Following the working party's deliberations 1975 negotiations commenced the same month on a claim for improved police pay when the initial offer by the official side was turned down. New scales of pay for all ranks up to superintendent were soon agreed at subsequent meetings and these reflected the restructuring recommended in the joint working party's review as well as compensation for increases in the cost of living. Substantial increases in pay levels arose, increasing the overall police paybill by 26.5% (29.8% over the previous 12 months). Police were in fact the last major group to conclude a settlement before the introduction of the Government's "Attack on Inflation" policy which limited increases to a £6 per week supplement. The general feeling at the time was that police had been dealt with very generously in benefiting from a settlement outside the £6 per week limit although their operative date of 1st September 1975 fell within the period covered by the new pay policy.

When a major dispute on pay arose in the next year, 1976, between the Police Federation and the official side, the initial reaction was that the stance of the Federation was, to say the least, bizarre in view of the beneficial treatment in 1975. The Federation claim was that they should receive the £6 per week on top of the large increases awarded in 1975. The official side would not agree so the Police Federation met the Home Secretary who confirmed that the 1976 settlement should be under the terms of the Government's new Stage 2 guidelines (£2.50/5%/£4). Although in pressing their £6 per week claim the Federation were in direct conflict with the Government and the TUC (not to mention the official side), their response was to withdraw from the Police Council, no longer recognising it for the purpose of pay negotiations, and to conduct a publicity campaign in support of their claim. The Home Secretary continued to refuse the claim for £6 but accepted there should be a review of the negotiating machinery for the police service. 1977 began with an idea from the Scottish Police Federation (who had not withdrawn from the Police Council) of the appointment of an independent person to bring the two parties together in pay talks, and the official side agreed to support this. The next step in 1977 was taken by the Home Secretary in imposing a Stage 2 settlement from 1st September 1976 which had been on offer by the official side eleven months previously. The strong reaction to this from the Police Federation included a decision to seek the right to strike. The Government agreed to set up an independent inquiry into the Police Federation which could look at the issues of the right to strike and of affiliation to the TUC on top of the independent review of the negotiating machinery. Meanwhile the official side urged that the focus should now be on the 1977 round, to use the flexibility offered within the Stage 3 guidelines, and to proceed with the compilation of comprehensive data to undergird the 1977 talks.

As 1977 proceeded the independent review body to look at police negotiating machinery was established under the chairmanship of Lord Edmund-Davies, while the Police Council undertook the 1977 pay review in the absence of the police federations for England, Wales and Northern Ireland. In order to accommodate the views of the latter bodies, a without prejudice offer was made to them to participate in pay talks outwith the Police Council on an ad-hoc basis with an independent chairman acceptable to all the parties. The Police Federation continued to refuse to negotiate with representatives of the police authorities either inside or outside the Police Council. In the summer of 1977 they launched, with attendant publicity, a massive claim for increases ranging from 78% to 104%. An impasse was reached with a situation where pay talks could not begin, and with the Conservative opposition calling for an independent inquiry into police pay - which would cause yet further delay.

The Police Federation eventually got their way to a large extent when after intensive three-way negotiations in the autumn of 1977 between the Home Secretary, the official side and the federations, agreement was reached that the independent inquiry chaired by Lord Edmund-Davies should review police pay as well as negotiating machinery. Coupled to this was an agreement for a 10% increase in police pay from 1st September 1977. The official side view had been that there needed to be a substantial revision of police pay which could readily and quickly be done within the Police Council, but they finally assented to the establishment of the pay inquiry in the interests of resolving the very serious situation. The terms of the Edmund-Davies committee of inquiry were accordingly widened to include (a) a review of police work in the light of changes in responsibilities and workload; (b) the pressures and dangers to which the police were exposed arising from social changes; (c) the restrictions placed on the police individually and as a force; and (d) to determine police pay levels in the light of those factors. Separate evidence was submitted to the committee of inquiry by the various parties, including the Government home departments (who indicated they did not endorse all the official side's evidence although they had been involved in preparing it). The core of the Police Federation's argument was that they should negotiate directly with central government to the exclusion of the authorities whose view, they claimed, had predominated on the official side (in flat contradiction to their other argument that the local authorities could not settle anything on their own without the prior clearance of Government). The official side went as far as they could to meet the federations' views, agreeing with them in urging the removal of the Home Secretary's power of veto, the appointment of an independent chairman of the Police Council and the establishment of an independent secretariat.

The report of the Edmund-Davies committee of inquiry published in July 1978 recommended substantial increases in pay from 1st September 1978 throughout all the police ranks up to chief constable, with percentage increases ranging from 29.7 to over 40 and appeared largely to justify the Federation's policy of massive pay claims and their tactics of undermining the negotiating process. Nevertheless the official side welcomed them because they went a long way to improving police manpower and morale, although this might have been more than the situation warranted in some areas. The committee said there was no justification for changing the existing system of separate rent allowances but did not explain their reason for this. They also advocated a national rate of pay which in future should be index-linked by reference to average earnings. On negotiating machinery, the Edmund-Davies committee recommended the establishment of a Police Negotiating Board with, as largely expected, an independent chairman and two independent vice-chairmen, supported by an independent secretariat, with the local authorities still represented on the official side - which meant that one important aspect of the Federation's objectives had not been achieved. After negotiations based on the Edmund-Davies recommendations for pay increases from 1st September 1978, the new

Police Negotiating Board was set up and met for the first time on 15th August 1979. At this first meeting revised rates of pay were agreed with effect from 1st September 1979 in line with the Edmund-Davies recommendations on index-linking.

PROBATION AND MAGISTRATES COURTS STAFFS

It was not long before the probation staff side were claiming for a reversion to one salary scale for the main grade of probation officer in view of many difficulties in operating the separate A and B scales arising from the Butterworth recommendations, and this was eventually agreed because of the widespread unpopularity of this measure.

A sign of the times and the increasing industrial turmoil is a report in September 1979 in "Local Government Manpower" of threatened industrial action by the hitherto quiescent staffs in magistrates courts. This was however averted by a substantial settlement for a 9% increase from 1st July 1979, a further 5% increase from 1st October 1979, plus a reference to Professor Clegg's comparability commission.

Probation officers were one group not to have a separate comparability study in 1979/1980 and agreed instead to reflect increases for social workers arising out of the APT&C comparability study. This led to an agreement of a common 16% increase throughout the probation pay scales from 1st January 1980.

TEACHERS

This period 1974 to 1980 is marked in respect of teachers' pay negotiations by a flurry of activity as it starts with the Houghton inquiry and report, another burst of action as it closes with the Clegg comparability study, with a relatively quiet interlude of several years in between dictated by the Government's pay policy.

The growing dissatisfaction of the teacher unions about the negotiations on teachers' pay led eventually to the Government setting up in 1974 a committee of inquiry into teachers' pay under the chairmanship of Lord Houghton of Sowerby. The inquiry had wide coverage extending to all teaching staffs in schools, further education, colleges of education and farm institutes in England and Wales and Scotland too. It was not concerned with conditions of service, but the Secretary for Education, Reginald Prentice, asked that it should consider pay structure as well as pay levels. The latter part of 1974 was largely devoted to a mass of evidence being submitted to the Houghton committee by the many parties with interests in the pay of all the staffs covered by the inquiry, with extensive submissions prepared at Belgrave Square on behalf of the various management panels.

THE HOUGHTON REPORT

The report of the Houghton committee of inquiry into the pay of non-university teachers was eventually published in December 1974 and recommended increases ranging from 15% to 40%. Considerable structural changes were recommended, for example improved weighting for younger children substantially improved the career prospects of primary school teachers. A common incremental spine of salaries was recommended for assistant teachers in primary and secondary schools (but surprisingly not for other groups of teachers) and the number of scales for assistant teachers was reduced from six to five. In further education increases recommended in the proportion of promotion posts improved career prospects, and the unions at last secured the abolition of the assistant lecturer scale. The committee also suggested alignment of scales and merging of negotiating machinery in line with the Government's plans to integrate teacher training with other forms of higher education. The immediate reaction of the teacher unions was to criticise the unexpectedly small increase at the lower end of the structure and they pressed in the subsequent Burnham discussions for improvements beyond the Houghton recommendations. The management panel successfully resisted this, having in the interests of good industrial relations refrained from expressing their misgivings at the large increases at the top of the structures, particularly in further education, which were bound to cause repercussive problems on other negotiating groups and for which there was scant evidence of sufficient justification in the committee's report. Agreements were quickly reached by most of the Burnham and allied committees to reflect the terms of the Houghton recommendations.

The Soulbury Committee was not however able to agree on the effect of Houghton on inspectors and organisers and asked a board of reference to determine whether the principles on teachers' salaries should be applied to Soulbury-paid staff. The arbitration board ruled in the negative on this but expressed opinions on the affinity with teachers of subject and general advisers and educational psychologists. Much effort and time was needed for the two sides to translate the arbitrators' views into a satisfactory pay settlement.

It might have been hoped that a major award such as Houghton would settle the dust for a while but that was not the way of teachers' pay negotiations. Such slender hopes which may have been held were soon dashed. The teachers claimed increases of 26% to apply from 1st April 1975 and the management panel had to point out this conflicted with the Houghton recommendations and also exceeded the terms of the Social Contract. Yet again it was not possible for the two sides to agree on anything except a reference to arbitration. The arbitration award on teachers' pay was one of a crop of several awards affecting LACSAB negotiating groups in the summer of 1975. After outlining the submissions of the two sides, the arbitral body stated there were valid points in support of both sides of the argument, and considered it right to have regard not only to the Social Contract but also to other pay levels and settlements. With no more by way of justification the arbitral body made recommendations which added about 15% to the paybill, the increases weighted towards the lower end of the structure.

Although there were no problems in getting agreement on the £6 per week supplement for teachers in 1976 under the first stage of the Government's "Attack on Inflation" policy, there were difficulties in 1977 arising from the management panel's insistence that a deduction from what was due under the Stage 2 guidelines had to be made to take account of the phenomenon referred to as "incremental drift". In the event agreement was reached on 18th March 1977 on the basis of a deduction of £21 from every teachers' 1977 supplementary payment, provided no teacher received less than £132 or more than £189.

Acceptance by both sides of the Government's Stage 3 guidelines led to a relatively quick deal in the Burnham primary and secondary committee in

March 1978 on 10% increases from 1st April 1978 on top of the consolidation of the Stage 1 and 2 salary supplements. Arising from the pressure by the teacher unions to seek to maintain the levels established by the Houghton award, it was also agreed to set up a joint working party to examine the movement of salary relativities with a view to reporting before the next negotiations.

1979 began with the teachers' panel tabling a claim for increases averaging 35%, ranging from 26.3% at the bottom to 43.8% at the top. Although a main plank of the claim was the restoration of the Houghton relativities, the claim was lodged before the joint working party had reported on the movement of salary relativities. Negotiations in both Burnham committees were exceptionally protracted and complicated by the timing of the general election, with an inevitable hiatus as the change of Government took place. However a significant new option was available in the form of a reference to the independent standing commission on pay comparability chaired by Professor Clegg. All was not plain sailing and a public argument erupted (not for the first time) between the leaders of the NUT and the NAS/UWT, with the latter threatening legal action on the grounds that the Burnham committee had not fulfilled their statutory duty by failing to refer the dispute to arbitration. Agreement was nevertheless reached in the Burnham committees in May 1979 on (a) an increase of 9% from 1st April 1979; (b) reference of the teachers' claim to the standing commission; (c) payment of £6 a month pending the implementation of the committee's findings to be recouped from the first instalment of the future salary rates; and (d) increases arising from the commission's report to be in two equal stages from 1st January 1980 and 1st September 1980. The agreed terms of reference to the standing commission addressed issues on which both sides had deeply-held views. The teachers insisted on a firm reference back to the Houghton recommendations and the more recent working party report on relativities. The employers were equally insistent that teachers' terms and conditions should feature in the remit, so that there would be a hard look at the professional obligations on teachers following the recent industrial unrest in schools.

There was no great surprise when the standing commission announced on 4th January 1980 that they would not report until the end of March, and this led to protracted negotiations on an interim pay settlement pending their report. A typically marathon session of the Burnham primary and secondary committee in February 1980 lasting for eight hours finally yielded agreement at 7.5% from 1st January 1980 which provided for recoupment of the £6 monthly "advance" comparability payment.

THE "CLEGG ERROR"

Teachers' pay discussions can be confusing at the best of times, but those in the early part of 1980 were complex and bizarre by any standard. The Clegg commission's report No.7 on teachers' pay was finally published on 14th April 1980 and recommended increases costing 18.2% overall. The two Burnham committees lost little time in reaching agreements to implement the Clegg finding in two stages with effect from 1st January 1980 and 1st September 1980 as already agreed. But then the famous "Clegg error" came to light and an amended report was issued reducing the increases from 18.2% to 14.5% overall. The management panel immediately sought to reopen the 18.2% agreements; the teachers firmly refused; and the independent chairman ruled that he would begin the process of making the agreements binding under the Remuneration of Teachers Act. This left the management panel with the difficult task of trying to recoup the error in the negotiations on the annual pay rise due on 1st April 1980, but they had already made a 13% offer (see next chapter).

Professor Hugh Clegg.

There was also resort to arbitration in 1976 on 1975 London weighting for schoolteachers which was one of three concurrent arbitrations on 1975 London weighting. The arbitral body supported the major thrust of the management panel's case by reaffirming the principle of cost compensation as adumbrated by the Pay Board in their 1974 report. The arbitral body awarded a total "kitty" of £27.31m, the distribution of which was to be decided by the Burnham committee which it then proceeded to negotiate. As this negotiation was in progress, arithmetical errors were discovered in the published award. Hasty telephone calls to the arbitration chairman resulted in the errors being immediately rectified and agreement being reached on the distribution of a revised "kitty" of £28.27m. The management panel did not succeed in clawing back any of the 1974 excess although an arbitration body meeting at about the same time with the same chairman and employer member agreed in the case of APT&C staffs to reduce the excess to 70% of its 1974 value.

A flavour of the esoteric nature of the Burnham committee discussions is obtained by reference to the proceedings of the October 1977 meeting and the operation of Burnham's celebrated "opposite sex rule". This stipulated that the post of second master or mistress in a mixed secondary school must be filled by a teacher of the opposite sex to that of the deputy head. But an industrial tribunal had ruled in a case brought by a Surrey teacher that the authority had unfairly discriminated against her by refusing to consider her application for a post as second mistress. It was necessary in consequence to amend the offending section to allow in future for the appointment of either men or women to these posts despite the original intention of the provision to increase the number of women to more senior posts!

Two important constitutional developments occurred. First in 1976 the Burnham farm institutes committee and the Pelham committee were merged into an enlarged Burnham further education committee which would then negotiate pay for all teachers in further and higher education outside the universities. Second, at the beginning of 1980 a new national joint council was established for the negotiation of conditions of service for further education teachers, replacing the earlier national forum under the auspices of the Council of Local Education Authorities (CLEA).

STAFFING AND PEOPLE

The considerable strengthening of the LACSAB secretariat in 1974 made it imperative to secure additional premises. Early in 1974 a small office suite was rented in Grays Inn Road, but the location was far from convenient and the accommodation inadequate. Later in 1974 the lease was obtained for 23

Chesham Street which was only a few minutes away from Belgrave Square, and this was much more suitable in size and location. In 1978 No. 38 Belgrave Square came on the market and the lease was eventually secured by LACSAB in 1979 – but on far less advantageous terms than 41 Belgrave Square – and 23 Chesham Street was vacated.

There was not only a rapid influx of staff in this period but also a continuous stream in and out as young people found it convenient to work in central London for a few years acquiring valuable experience at LACSAB before looking for career opportunities elsewhere. There were many changes in the more senior posts in 1974: Frank Walton was redesignated deputy secretary; Ken Woods was appointed as additional deputy secretary; Ron Hayward resigned as assistant secretary and Geoff Kelly was promoted to succeed him; and Geoff Roberts and Chris Curson (who left for British Gas in 1978) were appointed as additional assistant secretaries.

In 1976 Harry Rae retired after almost 30 years' service at LACSAB, having been Edward Bishop's first appointment to the LACSAB secretariat in 1947. Harry had practised law as a solicitor for Glasgow Corporation until 1939. He had then a distinguished war-time career with the RAF being awarded the Croix de Guerre in 1944 and mentioned in despatches in 1945; and immediately prior to joining LACSAB he was Scottish district officer and solicitor for NALGO. As right-hand man to Edward Bishop, Reginald Griffiths and Brian Rusbridge, Harry Rae had been involved at various times in the work of virtually every negotiating group, but he will be particularly remembered for his long and sustained leading role on manual workers. One of Harry's main interests was public relations. He established "News Summary", edited it for many years from its inception, and he thus in fact provided much of the source material for this book. A vigorous untiring Scot with a lively sense of humour, Harry was always accessible and prepared to tackle any problem through to solution.

Alun Gronow was appointed assistant secretary in 1978 from Surrey and promoted under secretary in 1979 concentrating on education. He left LACSAB in 1981 for the AMA where he achieved rapid promotion, eventually to secretary, before his untimely sudden death in October 1989.

1979 saw the departure of another LACSAB deputy secretary when Frank Walton had to retire early on ill-health grounds. Prior to joining LACSAB in 1970 as assistant secretary, Frank had been in the Civil Service with the Customs and Excise and the Home Office. He was promoted senior assistant secretary in 1973 and then deputy secretary in 1974. Frank for many years led at LACSAB in the Burnham and allied committees for teachers and took over on manual workers in 1976 on the retirement of Harry Rae, as well as being involved in other negotiating groups. But Frank will most be remembered for his tremendously valuable work in the area of employment legislation, being virtually entirely responsible for the compilation of many of the LACSAB booklets which were recognised universally for their authoritative and reliable advice and which gave LACSAB such a high reputation in this field.

Two veterans of earlier years died in 1975. First Colonel S.P.Dawson who died on 19th April 1975 had been a founder-member of LACSAB and vice-chairman at its inception. But he was probably best known as chairman of the APT&C employers from 1946 (when the original APT&C "charter" was negotiated) through to 1967. The "Colonel", as he was affectionately known, had been awarded the CBE, the Military Medal and the Territorial Decoration, represented the Association of Municipal Corporations and had been Lord Mayor of Manchester.

The other veteran to die in 1975 was Edward Bishop, the first LACSAB secretary and who was widely regarded as the main architect of Whitleyism in local government, who died on 2nd August 1975 at the age of 82.

Party politics came into the proceedings of the LACSAB Board with a vengeance in 1977 when Sir Leo Schultz was ousted from the chair by a majority political vote and John Lovill was appointed to the chair. Sir Leo, who had been LACSAB chairman since 1973, had served on many national and provincial bodies for many years and had been a member of Hull City Council since 1926 and Lord Mayor in 1942, was particularly well known for his work as chairman of the Yorkshire and Humberside provincial councils and predecessor bodies. John Lovill had been a member of East Sussex County Council since 1967 and its leader from 1973 to 1977, and represented the Association of County Councils (ACC) on LACSAB. Sid Dennett, representing the APT&C employers of which he was chairman, continued as vice-chairman, having been on the LACSAB Board since 1969 and LACSAB vice-chairman from 1973 right through to 1989, when he was appointed LACSAB chairman.

Margaret Thatcher at a careers convention prior to her election to Prime Minister in 1980.

8 THATCHER POWER

"Rather like a worm chopped in two, Burnham just carried on wriggling its erratic and painfully slow course through July..."

(David Brindle of the "Financial Times" in Local Government Manpower of August 1985)

This is a period marked by the political will of central government headed by Margaret Thatcher as Prime Minister to bring local government within its firm grasp and control. All earlier periods can be seen to have had their "ups and downs", but this one is notable for the relentless manner in which central government exerted its will, and by 1987 a much weaker and emaciated local government resulted, with even more measures to curb local authorities' powers yet to come.

LACSAB was in the thick of all this. Central government's influence was felt on pay levels not by formal pay policies but rather, and in the long term much more effectively, by their attitude towards the funding of public services, and in particular through the rate support grant and cash limit mechanisms applicable to local government. This was a far from easy period for LACSAB, given the Thatcher government's criticism of local government's staffing levels; its opposition to national pay bargaining; and its general hard line with the trade union movement.

Yet the national negotiating bodies continued to produce workable agreements acceptable to most of their constituents with however one sad exception. The Burnham primary and secondary committee, by far the most cumbersome and unproductive negotiating mechanism possible, was eventually brought to an end after many tortuous months of desperate discussions.

This period closes in 1987 with the Thatcher government confirmed in office for a further period and proceeding forthwith to curtail much more drastically in many ways the remaining powers of local authorities. And at LACSAB Brian Rusbridge relinquished the job of LACSAB secretary after 15 years, handing over to David Thomas as LACSAB began a search for a new negotiating strategy to fit the changing context.

POLITICAL AND ECONOMIC CONTEXT

Given the Government's decision not to declare guidelines in the public sector for the current pay round, their proposals announced on 16th November 1979 by Michael Heseltine, the Environment Secretary, for the rate support grant for 1980/1981, together with the increase orders for 1978/1979, 1979/1980 and 1980/1981, were of critical importance in setting the financial constraints for future pay negotiations in local government. The Government insisted that the published increase orders were "final" and intended there should be no further adjustment to them, whatever the levels of pay settlements which might be reached. In calculating the 1979/1980 increase order, account was taken of pay settlements but there would be a £310m abatement for rate support grant purposes from the total calculated.

Although the Government related the 1980/1981 increase order to new pay and price changes affecting local authorities of 13%, subsequently the AMA calculated that only between 9% and 10% had been allowed for the 1979/1980 pay round (which included settlements across the board at much higher levels), meaning that the cost of settlements over and above 9% would have to be met in full by local authorities or by manpower reductions. Geoffrey Drain of NALGO reflected the thoughts of other trade union leaders in greeting with dismay the "unsatisfactory low level of cash limits". As these had to cover the cost of comparability awards, "it seems that the Government is trying to introduce by the backdoor a wages policy for local government employees". These Government decisions were in the context of evidence of continual cost pressures throughout 1980, with estimates of increased earnings ranging from 14 to 18%, and prices from 13 to 15%. The Government saw it as their responsibility to educate people on what they considered to be the economic facts of life, and to insist that any pay settlements not justified by profitability or productivity must be paid for by lost jobs.

By May 1980 increases in average earnings and in prices had reached 21% and unemployment had soared to 1.5m, the highest May figure since the war.

The Government's proposals for the rate support grant for 1981/1982 and the increase orders for 1979/1980 and 1980/1981 were announced by Michael Heseltine on 16th December 1980. Sir Gervais Walker of the ACC described the settlement as "tough but fair" whilst Jack Smart of the AMA with his "the most unjust settlement I have known" came to the opposite conclusion - an indication of the extent of political polarisation which was taking place in the local authority associations.

Two major features of the 1981/1982 settlement were (a) the volume of local government current expenditure for RSG purposes was 3.1% below the figure for 1980/1981, and (b) the aggregate Exchequer contribution to relevant expenditure was reduced from 61% to 60%. The cash limit on grant would provide for increases in total earnings arising from annual pay settlements of 65% which, because of the overlap between "pay rounds" and the financial year would apply to the pay rounds both for 1980/1981 and 1981/1982. This had to be seen in the context of increases in average earnings and in prices at the end of 1980 running at just over 15%. The 6% tough Government policy did nevertheless meet with relative success as local government groups struck deals in the 1980/1981 pay round at about 7.5% – as compared with the nationalised industries who, not faced with the same cash limit pressures as local and central government, were reaching settlements at about the level of inflation in the 12 to 15% region. Local government employment figures continued to fall, with the joint manpower watch for December 1980 recording a 2.3% decrease in general service employment over the preceding year. The impact on employment in the economy generally was even more marked with unemployment figures soaring to 2 millions by the end of 1980 and to nearly 2.5 millions by mid-1981. It seemed that the Government's economic education of the electorate would be effective as by June 1981 increases in average earnings had dropped to 11.8%, with evidence that pay settlements in the 1980/1981 pay round were into single figures, plus a substantial drop in days lost through industrial disputes.

The 1982/1983 rate support grant settlement announced on 21st December 1981 showed no signs of seasonal generosity and continued the Government's measures to reduce local government current expenditure. It was only 2% more in cash terms than local authorities were budgeted to spend in 1981/1982; it allowed 4% for pay and 9% for prices; and aggregate Exchequer grant was reduced to 56% of relevant expenditure. In the preceding year there had been the largest total drop in local government manpower recorded in one year, and the total of 1.9 million full-time equivalent employees was the lowest recorded since the joint manpower system had been introduced, thus effectively eliminating all the manpower growth which had taken place since the 1974 reorganisation.

An important indicator of the Government's attitude towards any degree of flexibility in interpreting their 4% cash limit in the public services was provided in the first few months of 1982 when it accepted the award of the Civil Service Arbitration Tribunal giving increases averaging 5.9%. Most local government settlements were within that range of flexibility, but this was no easy task as LACSAB strove with some success to put a fence round the manual 6.9% deal of December 1981. Increases in prices had by mid-1982 fallen to just over 9%, increases in average earnings still remained in double figures at 10.3%, and unemployment had surged up to 2.8 millions with gross domestic product still falling.

There was much earlier notice of the Government's expenditure targets for local authorities for the year 1983/1984 which came on 27th July 1982. A main feature was that there would be no special cash factors for pay and prices as hitherto; an increase of only 2.5% in cash terms of relevant current expenditure over the expected final out-turn for 1982/1983; and a decrease in Government financing of relevant current expenditure from 56 to 53%. The Government was also going to withhold £312m. of grant from authorities who had exceeded their targets. The targets set for individual authorities varied according to how they kept their budgeted expenditure in 1982/1983 within the Government's targets. The 1983/1984 rate support grant settlement announced on 16th December 1982 confirmed much of what had already been said in the July statement and also provided much detail on the penalties to be imposed for overspending – which were to be very severe for high spending authorities. The December 1982 issue of LGM was able to comment that the rate of increase of average earnings had been falling steadily through the year, then standing at an underlying rate of 8.75%, rather higher than the rate of price increases (which eventually fell below 6% by the end of 1982), while the CBI could report that the majority of settlements so far reported to them for the pay round 1982/1983 were within the 5 to 8% range.

The rate of price increases continued to fall in 1983, dropping to 3.7% by May, but increases in average earnings did not respond as planned and by May were at 8.45%, although the underlying increase had fallen to 7.25%. Unemployment figures continued to increase and by May stood at 2,857,500 – 12.3% of the total available workforce.

The rate support grant settlement for 1984/1985 announced in August 1983 exerted further firmer downward pressures on local government spending. The 3% cash increase was expected to necessitate a substantial fall in the real level of resources available to local authorities and, if inflation increased by 5%, this was expected to lead to a 7% volume reduction. A publication – "Local Government: The Facts"" – by the Society of Local Authority Chief Executives (SOLACE) in 1983 produced evidence to refute the Government view concerning "excessive" expenditure levels. It showed (a) that in the period 1977/1978 to 1982/1983 local authority capital and current expenditure declined in real terms by 3% while central government spending grew by 17%; and (b) in the period 1974/1975 to 1980/1981 local government's share in the gross domestic product, a measure of the nation's wealth, had fallen from 15.9% to 13.5% whilst central government's share had risen from 33.3% to 35.3%. Central government's contribution to local government in the form of grants had shrunk from 66.5% of relevant expenditure in 1975/1976 to 52.8% in 1983/1984. Despite tough financial targets set by central government, local authorities had achieved planned expenditure levels whilst keeping rate increases within the general level of inflation. One important reason for this was the relatively modest level of increase in earnings amongst local government employees and general adherence to Government pay policies. In addition, between 1976 and 1982, local government had shed 4% of its labour force. Manual employment had declined most rapidly, by 11.8% in the four years to June 1983, with non-manual figures taking a varied course.

In their now annual meeting with Ministers on 24th October 1983 LACSAB members assured them there were greater pressures than ever for moderate pay settlements in local government in the coming year, as local authorities' tight financial position meant that the ability to pay was severely curtailed. But there would be a stiffening of resistance to this by negotiating groups as they saw their relative pay position continuing to fall away. If this went too far there was the risk of an explosion and an eventual solution usually more expensive than negotiated settlements. The index-linked pay arrangements for police and fire demonstrated that the level of settlements elsewhere was markedly higher than for local government.

Patrick Jenkin, now Environment Secretary, announced on 24th July 1984 the Government's proposals for local government expenditure in 1985/1986, providing a maximum cash increase of 4.25%, although many authorities would be allocated smaller increases. Penalties for exceeding the Government's targets would be made much tougher, and the Exchequer grant would be reduced from 51.9% to 48.8% of expenditure eligible for grant.

In the annual meeting with Ministers on 22nd October 1984, LACSAB members stressed that local government pay settlements had been modest, but these had been most difficult to achieve because of much higher settlements in the private sector. There was appreciation on the Government side of the very firm line taken by local government employers, as well as an awareness of the considerable difficulties presented by the current manual workers' claim.

During 1984 price increases had mainly hovered around 5% while increases in average earnings had been more erratic, although the rate of underlying increase had dropped marginally from 7.75% to 7.5%.

Commentators referred to an unmistakable pre-election flavour in the Government's announcement in 1985 on public spending for 1986/1987 which was to be held broadly flat in real inflation-adjusted terms. The new Environment Secretary, Kenneth Baker, made no secret of his belief that the old system of targets had become unworkable and unfair. Local authority expenditure would be higher than previously planned and the Government increased provision for the 1986/1987 financial year by 4.4% in cash terms. Aggregate Exchequer grant would be reduced to 46.6% of total relevant expenditure. Expenditure targets were no longer to be used, and tough block grant mechanisms would be used to encourage restraint in expenditure.

The annual meeting on 21st November 1985 between Ministers and LACSAB showed less rapport than for many years past. Ministers made it known they were unhappy about the "high" settlement for manual workers recently struck, which LACSAB members defended, with both sides eventually agreeing piously that this should not be taken as a going rate for other groups. LACSAB members argued that the amount allowed for pay settlements in the rate support grant was unrealistic and unfair, but Ministers made it very clear there would be no relaxation of the Government's tight control over local authorities' expenditure.

During 1985 price increases had crept up from 5.4% to 7% in May before dropping to 5.7% at the close, while the underlying increase in average earnings had remained virtually constant at 7.5%.

Chancellor of the Exchequer, Nigel Lawson's autumn 1986 economic statement was seen to make an important shift in the direction of Government policy on public expenditure. Having come to office in 1979 with a promise to reduce public spending in real terms, they adjusted their objective in the early 1980s to keeping spending constant in real terms, hoping that the economy would grow and reduce the public sector's share of overall national income. The significance of the autumn 1986 statement was that the Chancellor dropped the revised objective of holding spending constant and announced plans for an average growth in spending of about 1.25% a year.

Nicholas Ridley, the new Environment Secretary, confirmed his 1987/1988 rate support grant settlement on 13th January 1987. Among the main aspects in a tough settlement were an increase of 4.1% over 1986/1987 budgets, Exchequer grant kept at 46.4% of relevant expenditure, and an increase from 12 to 20 in the number of authorities to be ratecapped.

The Government had succeeded in pulling back increases in prices to 2.4% in July 1986, but this had crept up again to 3.7% in December 1986, whilst the underlying increase in average earnings remained at 7.5% throughout 1986.

Another important development in the autumn of 1986 was the start of a ministerial campaign against nationally agreed pay deals, with Nicholas Ridley urging local authorities to opt out of national agreements.

EMPLOYMENT LEGISLATION

The Thatcher Government's first Employment Bill published on 7th December 1979 included clauses on picketing and the closed shop, thus going some way to achieve the Government's objective to reduce the power of the trade unions. Schedule 11 of the Employment Protection Act 1975 was repealed and thus brought to an end the provision for arbitration awards against employers who failed to provide "recognised terms and conditions". These changes, together with revised maternity provisions, were eventually enacted in the Employment Act 1980.

Following the publication of a green paper in January 1981 on "Trade Union Immunities", the Government subsequently early in 1982 published their

Employment Bill which in due course became enacted as the Employment Act 1982. The provisions largely related to union membership and closed shops, introducing punitive levels of compensation for non-union members unfairly dismissed from a closed shop.

In what appeared to be becoming a two-year cycle, trade union powers were further curtailed under the Trade Union Act 1984. These measures were already in place when the coal miners' strike erupted in 1984/1985 and helped in the eventual collapse of that strike.

Early in 1985 the Equal Pay Act 1970 was amended to allow claims for equal pay for work of equal value to be brought, an aspect on which UK law was regarded as deficient relative to the 1975 European Commission Directive on equal pay. Fears that the effect could be damaging to existing collective agreements were to some extent allayed because of the complex and time-consuming procedures.

OTHER RELEVANT LEGISLATION

Government legislation which had profound implications for local government in general and for pay bargaining in particular were those directed towards compulsory competitive tendering, beginning with the Planning and Land Act 1981. This led to much thought and comment by LACSAB on the future of direct labour organisations and the impact on them of national agreements, especially those affecting manual and craft employees. The lengths to which the Government would go to pursue their policies was by no means fully appreciated at the outset. Local government unions were amazed by Patrick Jenkin's disclosure during the Queen's Speech debate late in 1983 that the Government were considering compelling local authorities to put their services out to competitive tendering. John Edmunds of the GMBU was quoted in 1984 as saying – "I don't take it seriously...I don't think he'll be able to do it and I think the opposition from his own party will be enormous. I don't think they will swallow it any more". The Government, having achieved their objectives for compulsory competitive tendering, were not content to leave it at that, and as this period 1980 to 1987 drew to a close, the revived Local Government Bill referred to in the Queen's Speech in July 1987 was proposing yet more draconian measures to reduce still further the powers of local authorities.

The Government's proposal in 1984 to abolish the Greater London Council and the six metropolitan county councils placed LACSAB in a dilemma. This proposal was so politically controversial that for many months LACSAB officers were not allowed to take any steps towards the usual arrangements for the protection of staff interests in such a statutory reorganisation. When eventually the political clearance was given, much had to be done in haste after the enactment of the Local Government Act 1985 which gave effect to the Government's proposals. A feature of this reorganisation was the creation of a multitude of joint bodies for specific functions, raising a number of new issues on the scope and representation of existing negotiating bodies.

OVERALL LACSAB ACTIVITIES

The minutes of the LACSAB Board in this period 1980 to 1987 indicate much activity on a wide variety of issues, some more political than others.

The views of LACSAB were quickly sought by the new Government as it developed proposals for future industrial relations legislation to fulfill their manifesto commitments, but there were considerable doubts whether LACSAB could respond because of the high political content. Ultimately it was decided on a majority vote that the Board's chairman and vice-chairman should confer with association chairmen on the draft of a suitable reply.

It was particularly important for the LACSAB Board, which includes many leading members of the local authority associations involved in RSG negotiations, to monitor closely the pay negotiating scene as central government utilised to an ever greater degree their funding mechanisms of rate support grant and cash limits to impose their will on the level of pay settlements. Very useful developments in this process were the series of annual meetings which took place between LACSAB members and Government ministers, and also separately with leading members of the Confederation of British Industry (CBI). The meetings with Ministers assessed the extent to which local government pay settlements eventually conformed to the Government's targets, and it was usually possible to demonstrate that local government employers had achieved results closer to targets than other employers in the public and private sectors, including the example set by the Government themselves as employers. The earlier meetings with the CBI were notable for much criticism by them of the allegedly high level of local authority pay settlements, and this was in no small measure due to the 1979/1980 round of comparability deals initiated by the Callaghan government. As these meetings continued it was increasingly the case that LACSAB were able to produce evidence as to the moderate pay increases awarded in local government as compared with other sectors in the economy. Readily available measuring tools were the index-linked pay arrangements for police and fire, the high level of which local government employers had to justify to other negotiating groups because they were based on the increases in earnings elsewhere in the economy.

As local government pay negotiators adjusted to the new situation in which the Government funding mechanisms became of fundamental importance in determining the levels of pay increases, the LACSAB Board recognised this and agreed in January 1981 that employer negotiators should be supplied with information about the amounts available from rate support grant and cash limit settlements and be advised to negotiate within the limits these imposed.

As the Government moved towards financial targets for individual authorities this inevitably raised questions about the future of centralised national pay bargaining. At their meeting in January 1981 LACSAB endorsed the concept of central bargaining as opposed to any move to unrestricted local bargaining, but in so doing this they recognised the need to reflect the wishes of local authorities and the advantages of national "framework" agreements to meet local conditions rather than rigid set standards.

London weighting continued to occupy the attention of the LACSAB Board throughout this period. After a debate over many months they decided in January 1981 against undertaking a fundamental review, and opted for a policy of seeing London weighting increases in the context of the size of the overall pay package. Later that year they decided to ignore the Department of Employment index updating the Pay Board's 1974 cost compensation formula before the

Government dropped the index themselves. October 1984 was an occasion for the Board again to have a comprehensive look at London weighting when they settled on the policy of "leaving well alone" and against a fundamental review, whilst reaching the conclusion that Fringe area allowances could no longer be justified. But when they met in July 1986 and examined the then current scene, the LACSAB Board concluded that the whole position "had become somewhat ragged"; that serious recruitment and retention problems were emerging; and that the time was ripe for a fundamental review of the basis of London allowances and whether they were still appropriate. At their October 1986 meeting the Board decided against a re-examination of the cost compensation basis for London weighting and opted instead for a review based on the labour market approach. This inevitably skewed the review towards a thorough examination of recruitment and retention problems in London as compared with the rest of local government and the rest of the economy. The preliminary report of this survey was made in time for the LACSAB Board meeting in Edinburgh in August 1987 (the final report, a weighty tome of four volumes was eventually published later in 1987). The report suggested that there was little overall cause for concern, although there were particular pockets of recruitment and retention problems affecting a limited number of occupational groups, especially clustered in London and the South East. It discussed the reasons for the staff shortages revealed; noted that local authorities had adopted a wide range of measures to combat these problems; concluded that London weighting was only a partial answer to this; and suggested appropriate advice to negotiating bodies and local authorities.

Another issue preoccupying the minds of LACSAB members in the earlier part of this period was the attitude to be adopted towards arbitration. Central government was much exercised that the use of unilateral reference to arbitration by the unions could seriously undermine their pay strategy and circumvent the "ability to pay" argument, and they were taking a very strong line on this in their discussions on civil service pay. The Government were able to impose their decision in respect of the statutory provisions governing teachers' pay so that in future reference to arbitration had to be by the agreement of both sides. The LACSAB Board had considerable reservations about adopting such a dogmatic attitude, noting at their July 1981 meeting that there were times when it was to the employers' advantage to initiate a reference to arbitration; and at their July 1982 meeting they decided against giving general advice. By this time the APT&C employers had twice exercised their right to initiate arbitration in 1981 on maternity provisions and in 1982 on that year's pay negotiations, and the issue thus appeared to resolve itself for many years in the local government context.

Over this period 1980 to 1987 the LACSAB Board had on occasion to concern themselves with the negotiations for specific negotiating groups. Successive Government pay policies in the previous two decades had stultified pay negotiations so that it was normally little more than the employers reacting to trade union claims. So in July 1981 the LACSAB Board noted with approval that the APT&C employers had begun to take the initiative in pay negotiations and to state in advance their terms for arriving at settlements. There was then an inexplicable timelag before the LACSAB Board decided at their October 1984 meeting that the time was ripe for change and for the employers to gain the initiative and break the mould of always responding defensively to trade union claims.

Although this was a period in which party political views were frequently polarised, there was no doubt that LACSAB chairman, Tony Prendergast, reflected the general consensus view of local government in exchanges of correspondence with the Prime Minister in July and August 1985 when he said that everyone present at the LACSAB Board meeting in July 1985 felt let down by the Government's decision to implement the huge increases for top civil servants and others recommended by the Top Salaries Review Body in their Report No.10. The Board registered their concern both about the levels of increases accepted and also the underlying principles which seemed to have been accepted in justification for them; and were very bothered about the serious implications for local government pay negotiations. This had come at a particularly awkward moment just after NALGO had settled quickly and moderately, but with large claims from the chief executives and the chief officers still outstanding. As was becoming increasingly usual local government's protestations were of no avail.

But the two negotiating areas which engaged much attention by the LACSAB Board for much of this period were manual workers and teachers. In the earlier stages the manual worker negotiations tended to start off the annual pay round with attention concentrated on them as the pacesetters. When it was necessary to reach a settlement because of their special circumstances, especially low pay (such as in 1982 and 1984) – much would be piously said that the manual worker increases were not to set the standard for other groups, frequently with very little effect. The manual pay deal of January 1985 led to the in-depth examination of the pay structure and service conditions and to an immensely heavy workload for the LACSAB secretariat for the next few years. The acute difficulties on teachers' pay and negotiating machinery covered a period similar to the manual workers' major review and led to interminable discussions driving members and officers alike to new levels of exhaustion. But whereas the manual workers' negotiating machinery resolved their own problems, the difficulties on teachers' pay – especially the unco-operative attitude and lack of cohesion of the teachers' unions – eventually resulted in the dismantling of the Burnham apparatus and the cessation of collective bargaining.

LACSAB initiated a debate on the longer-term implications of the reduction and reorganisation of working time in the paper published in October 1983 – "Working Time – A Preliminary Step in a Major Debate". It was felt essential for the short-term issues of trade union pressure for a reduced working week to be set against longer-term needs and philosophies, thinking beyond the traditional pattern of working life. The meagre response to this paper perhaps showed how difficult it was for those overwhelmed by immediate problems to carve out sufficient time to address longer-time issues.

Nevertheless the LACSAB Board recognised at their meeting in July 1986 the need for an overall local government pay strategy spanning a number of years, and requested LACSAB secretary, Brian Rusbridge, to prepare a paper on the topic.

After some preliminary discussions LACSAB decided in August 1987 that the debate should go beyond the issues of pay and conditions of service and to examine the main principles and philosophies to guide the employer approach for the future. The wider review thus became the vehicle by which the LACSAB secretary designate, David Thomas, could initiate and encourage a wide debate as to LACSAB's future from within, rather than allow the pressure for change to build up externally.

In October 1986 LACSAB took over from the ACC the responsibility for the United Kingdom Steering Committee on Local Government Superannuation (UKSC), thus entering the very specialised field of pensions work of which previously they had experience only through committee E of the Police Negotiating Board.

This period saw a welcome strengthening of LACSAB's advisory service and the formation of what became the Personnel and Industrial Relations Advisory Team (PIRAT) headed by Tim Rothwell. One particular development was the publication of a new series of LACSAB Employer guides. The first of these was produced in September 1982 and twelve (plus a general update) had been published by January 1986 covering a wide variety of topics, especially those arising from new employment legislation. This was in addition to the series of regular LACSAB advisory bulletins and the in-depth advisory service to employers' sides of negotiating bodies, provincial employers' organisations and individual local authorities, including an increasing demand for LACSAB officers to speak at local and regional seminars.

There was no easement in the work of LACSAB's research and information division in this period 1980 to 1987. One major piece of research work recognised as of great value was that undertaken on behalf of the local authority associations on the effects of central government initiatives (CGIs). One strand in the continuing debate with central government on the levels of local government staffing as measured by the joint manpower watch conducted by LACSAB was the extent to which increases in staffing arose because of legislation and other measures imposed on local authorities by central government. Whilst employment levels had fallen in local government by 6% between 1979 and 1982, they had begun to increase slightly in late 1982. Government ministers expressed concern at this at the July 1983 meeting of the consultative council for local government finance (CCLGF) when local government representatives maintained that CGIs were an important contributory factor, which LACSAB was then asked to investigate. The major report prepared by LACSAB and published in October 1984 concluded that CGIs had added almost 1% to local authority employment in England and Wales between June 1979 and December 1983, compared with the overall reduction of 5.5%, and that they were equivalent to all the upward movement in numbers between 1982 and 1983. A further LACSAB survey for the period September 1984 to September 1985 showed a net total of 4,335 additional full-time equivalent posts were attributed to CGIs. Another survey for the period September 1985 to March 1986 attributed a net total of 2,281 posts to CGIs.

The other major research report produced in this period was that on London weighting and recruitment and retention (see above under "Overall LACSAB Activities").

One interesting report followed a number of questions as to why when local government employment was falling most rapidly in the early 1980s manual workers were hit most hardly. This "Chiefs versus Indians" debate was met by a report to the LACSAB Board in January 1983 which showed that manual worker numbers had decreased more than white-collar numbers for a variety of apparently respectable reasons. It still left hardened LACSAB cynics believing that the manual worker was least able to answer back and defend his or her job when razor gangs were abroad.

The usual regular annual survey work on joint manpower watch and for specific negotiating groups continued and was revised and developed to meet the changing situation, while special surveys were devised and conducted as necessary. Survey work was also conducted on behalf of other organisations, notably the Local Government Training Board (LGTB).

MANUAL WORKERS

The 1979/1980 pay round for manual workers began with the trade unions submitting a claim at the meeting of the NJC in late October 1979 for a substantial increase and other improvements, including a 35-hour week, together with an updating of the Clegg Commission's recommendations by some form of indexing. The heavy restrictions from rate support grant and cash limits seemed to indicate a single figure offer from the employers and the likelihood of a long-drawn out struggle. But the employers at a meeting in November 1979 made a 13% offer, including basic rate increases of 11.9% and substantial holiday improvements, which was finally accepted by the unions at the meeting on 17th January 1980. Although there was relief at the agreement, there was a feeling that a number of problems were being stored up for subsequent resolution, notably on the reduction in the working week where there had been a significant concession in the water supply industry.

Council building workers

The annual pay negotiations for manual workers for 1980/1981 seem to have attracted little attention. At a meeting of the NJC in December 1980 the employers made an offer of an increase of £4.60 to basic rates as from 4th November 1980 together with an extra day's holiday for employees with not less than twelve months' but not more than five years' service. The percentage increases ranged from 8.4% to 6.7%; the package was estimated to cost 7.5% overall; the trade unions agreed strongly to recommend it to their members; and they were able to come back to the NJC meeting on 27th January 1981 to clinch a deal on that basis.

Discussions within the TUC in 1981 were moving towards a co-ordinated campaign based on a common strategy collectively to resist the Government's intentions in the 1981/1982 pay round more effectively than in the 1980/1981 round. The claim submitted by the manual trade unions in October 1981 was identical to that already submitted for water and sewage workers, and the teachers and APT&C staffs were expected to follow shortly afterwards well in advance of their usual dates with claims which included the same core element for a cost of living pay increase. The manual claim also called for a reduction in the working week without loss of pay and for improved holiday entitlements. Fears of difficult and protracted negotiations were allayed with a quick settlement following an offer made by the employers at the NJC meeting on 10th December 1981. "Local Government Manpower" of January 1982 blandly reports an offer made which the trade unions accepted having consulted their members. Reference to the LACSAB Board minutes of January 1982 sheds much more light on the events. The meeting of LACSAB scheduled for 18th January 1982 was brought forward to 7th January at the request of the ADC and the ACC because of their concern at the level of the manual offer and the hasty way it had been made. The debate at the LACSAB Board meeting revealed that the final offer was eventually tabled after nine hours of talks during which the employers had weighed carefully the advantages of an early offer to avoid a protracted dispute in which other local government groups, co-ordinated by the TUC, could become involved. On 10th December the employers had started with an offer of 4% and had finished up with a recommended settlement at 6.9% overall. The employers had also made it clear that a settlement at the level offered must involve further savings by authorities by cuts in manpower or services or by greater efficiency. In consequence all local authorities were advised that "the manual offer had many features which were peculiar to manual workers and that in no way should it be regarded as setting a going rate or standard for any offers to be made to other local government groups". LACSAB also requested that if any national employers saw a need to go beyond a 4% offer it should consider the implications for other groups (the fence erected by LACSAB round the 6.9% manual deal held reasonably firmly with APT&C and teachers finishing up at arbitration at 5.7% and 6.0% respectively). One aspect of the manual 1981 deal was a commitment to a 39-hour week – the first reduction in manual workers' hours since 1966 – from the forward date of 1st November 1982, not to be costed against the 1982 settlement provided both sides would work together to introduce the shorter working week without further loss of jobs. Later in 1982 the NJC concluded a framework agreement on arrangements for the implementation of the 39-hour week which it was felt provided authorities with the means to achieve this as economically as possible.

The 1982/1983 pay round began with the manual trade unions tabling their annual claim at the meeting of the NJC on 29th October 1982 at Weston-Super-Mare. This claim was for a substantial flat rate pay increase, a shorter working week without loss of pay, and increased annual leave. By the time of the NJC meeting on 9th December negotiations on NHS ancillaries were at a critical stage and there was mutual anxiety that local government should not rock the boat, so no great exception was taken by the unions to the employers' moderately pitched opening offer of 3%. The subsequent NJC meeting in January 1983 was described by LGM that month as "a long day of detailed negotiations which included some acrimonious debate on school meals, school caretakers and bonus schemes". The employers eventually made an offer which would increase each basic rate by £3.25 per week and add 4.5% to the total paybill. In pitching their offer at this level and at this stage the employers once again were mindful of the possibility of co-ordinated action by the manual workers and other local government groups if they failed to make such a move. They made it clear this was the best offer they could achieve and in the lengthy discussions they attempted strenuously to obtain a quid pro quo, concentrating on securing savings on the school meals service, the bonus calculator and one feature of the school caretakers' agreement. Despite the continued loss of manual worker jobs there was no softening of the unions' line and they adamantly refused to accept any conditions attached to the pay offer as pressed by the employers which they insisted would make it impossible for their members to accept the offer. There was much hope at the time that the union members would accept the 4.5% offer pitched at the same level as the April 1983 increase for NHS ancillaries which had become the unions' minimum target. But these hopes were dashed by a subsequent extravagant pay deal in the water industry following a dispute. Eventually at a meeting of the NJC on 28th February 1985 there was a settlement increasing basic rates by between 4.8% and 5.1% at an overall cost of 4.87%. Councillor Tony Whitmore, the employers' chairman (who most unfortunately died suddenly a few months later), commented that this settlement had "jerked us back from the water workers' settlement to a realistic figure" - in fact it was the lowest manual deal for more than ten years. Charlie Donnet, the chief union negotiator about to retire in April 1983 (and who subsequently died in October 1986), was obviously pleased to have secured an improved offer with the union position fragmented and knowing the local government manual workers did not have the industrial muscle of their counterparts in the water industry. He summed it up - "I was asked to make bricks from straw here today and I think I have done rather well".

The fears of the employers of previous years of TUC co-ordinated pay campaigns were banished when the manual workers' pay claim for the 1983/1984 pay round was tabled at the NJC meeting at Portsmouth on 19th October 1983. For it was in effect arguing for manuals to be treated as a special case, and the manual unions were thus distancing themselves from other local government groups. This was the first claim presented by the new trade unions' side secretary, John Edmunds of the GMBATU, and his presentation was most impressive. The claim was for a substantial wage increase as a major step towards the target of two-thirds of national average earnings; a reduction in the working week to 35 hours, with alignment with APT&C staffs as the first step; increases in holidays and shift allowances, and a paternity leave provision. In support of the claim John Edmunds pointed out that manual average earnings were at their lowest compared to all the economy since 1970; that 10% of manual jobs had disappeared over the last four years while there had not been significant APT&C job losses; the size of manual pay settlements had been consistently over-estimated by the employers over the last four years; and that manual workers were discriminated against by comparison with white-collar staff on service conditions and status. He recognised the financial difficulties confronting local authorities and suggested the staging of awards.

The NJC meeting on 23rd January 1984 extended over "a very long day" in which there were lengthy exploratory discussions between the leaders of the two sides to identify where a settlement might be reached. The outcome was that the employers offered to increase each basic rate by £2.25 per week from 4th November 1983 which would add 3% to the paybill, but this was firmly rejected by the trade unions. Although it became evident that an offer of £3 per week plus additional payments targetted on the full-time lower paid might be accepted by the unions, the employers were not prepared to move without gauging opinion further among local authorities. Two means of giving more money to the lower paid full-timers had emerged: a minimum bonus payment and a minimum earnings guarantee. The NJC meeting on 21st February 1984 did result in a settlement on the single approach of a flat rate increase to all basic rates of £3.40 to apply from 4th November 1983, adding 4.5% to the paybill. Both sides were disappointed at the failure to achieve any radical change, especially the trade unions who had set themselves ambitious targets at the outset. The improved pay offer was made by the employers and accepted by the unions on the clear understanding that it reflected the very special circumstances of manual workers which did not apply to other groups in local government.

The unions' claim for 1984/1985 presented at the NJC meeting on 15th October 1984 was in most respects a replica of their 1983/1984 claim, and was again well argued by John Edmunds who concentrated on the low-pay position of manual workers. He was able to point out that, although the 4.5% 1983/1984 deal was supposed to reflect the very special circumstances of manual workers, it had nevertheless subsequently set the baseline for other local government groups, most of whom had managed to better it. An important and interesting feature of this claim was the unions' pressure to move the settlement date away from the November date which they regarded as disadvantageous in that it placed the manual employers in the position of having to negotiate the "going rate" not only for the rest of local government, but also for much of the public sector. John Edmunds put it forcefully – "the manual workers' negotiations should cease to be the annual battleground for the Government's public sector pay policy... our people have had enough of being the cannon fodder in other people's wars".

By the time LACSAB pronounced on 22nd October 1984 that employers should gain the initiative and break the defensive mould, the manual employers were already well advanced in their preparation for a comprehensive consultation exercise with local authorities. The full text of John Edmunds's submission was circulated and with it went an employers' discussion paper – "Manual Workers – The Autumn Round 1984" – which initiated examination of a range of areas ripe for change. The employers' objectives were identified as

(a) a pay settlement within the financial means of authorities;
(b) changes in out-dated national agreements;
(c) greater flexibility at local level; and
(d) a manual pay settlement fair by comparison with other groups.

Four longer-term issues of grading; productivity bargaining; working time; and negotiating date were discussed in detail.

Joint discussions resumed with NJC meetings on 18th December 1984 and 9th January 1985 centred on the unions' pressure to move the settlement date which the employers could see no advantage in conceding. The employers tabled a 4% offer in December which they improved to 4.5% on 9th January. At a further meeting on 25th January talks broke down after the unions had rejected a revised offer of 4.75% – £3.70 on each basic rate. Although there had been no agreement on the size of the pay increase or the settlement date, there had however been willingness on both sides for some form of commitment to review the grading structure and the issue of working time. Agreement was eventually reached when the union members voted by a small majority to accept an improved offer made by the employers at a meeting of the NJC on 1st March 1985. The agreement increased all basic rates by £4 per week from 4th November 1984, giving percentage increases ranging from 5.7% to 4.7%. There was also agreement to move the next annual settlement date to 1st September 1985 in the hope this would be seen as the end, rather than the beginning, of the annual pay round. This meant that the duration of the 1984/1985 deal was only ten months. The agreement also included what were to become historic decisions to examine the totality of grading and manpower utilisation by September 1985 and to establish a working party to look at the broad area of working time for report by September 1986. For the employers this opened up the opportunity for a fundamental and wide- ranging review of many aspects of the national agreement hitherto regarded as "out of bounds", in particular for a radical reform of the grading structure last reviewed in 1969.

The revised settlement date of 1st September 1985 meant an earlier start to the manual workers' 1985/1986 pay talks with John Edmunds presenting the trade unions' 1985 claim at a meeting of the NJC on 17th July 1985. The claim set out eight main items for negotiation, including a substantial wage increase towards their target of two-thirds of national average earnings; revision of the grading structure; a 35- hour week; a minimum bonus guarantee; and consolidation of bonus into basic pay. The outcome of the next NJC meeting on 16th September was that the unions agreed to take away a package proposed by the employers for consideration by their members. The four elements of the package were:-

(a) existing groups A, B and C to merge into current group C to form a new general grade;

(b) all basic rates of pay to be increased by £6 per week from 1st September 1985;

(c) commitment to the review of the grading structure using job evaluation techniques; and

(d) review of working arrangements and practices, grading criteria and service conditions in conjunction with the job evaluation exercise.

The £6 per week had become the "bottom line" for the manual trade unions negotiators after APT&C had settled for a £6 per week minimum for adults from 1st July 1985. It was felt that the merging of the three lowest groups would ease some of the immediate trade union pressure while the job evaluation exercise proceeded. It was hoped this exercise could be completed within twelve months although the earlier 1969 exercise had taken two years to complete. Most of the main areas for the simultaneous review of working arrangements, etc. had been identified by various specialist officer groups set up by the employers to look at different jobs and services.

So began what was to become the mammoth task of the manual workers' job evaluation exercise. The employers' thinking was that the use of job evaluation techniques was more likely to produce a structure which met current needs and was also capable of being adapted to meet future trends. The recent "equal pay for equal value" regulations also presented a real challenge to many preconceptions about the worth of a range of jobs traditionally regarded as "women's work". A very tight timetable was set for completion of the whole exercise by July 1986 to inform the September 1986 pay negotiations. LAMSAC were engaged to visit 67 authorities by Christmas 1985 to collect job descriptions for the seven jobs in the pilot exercise. Initial evaluations would be carried out by ten panels, who would also evaluate the main body of jobs in April 1986. Recommendations to the NJC on a revised grading structure would come from a central co-ordinating panel. Many people at local, provincial and national level from the employers' network, together with trade unionists, were brought together for this huge task.

The April 1986 issue of LGM reported that the job evaluation study hit a major snag when LAMSAC, engaged to carry out job interviews and complete job descriptions, pulled out of the exercise, asking to be allowed to withdraw due to resource problems and other commitments. The pilot exercise had been set to use job descriptions prepared by LAMSAC and LGM's bland report that "much has been learned about problems with the scheme design and the collection of information for the main study" obscured the fundamental nature of the difficulties and unsatisfactory data which led to LAMSAC being obliged to withdraw. This hiatus meant that the target date of July 1986 was clearly no longer achievable and left the NJC with the question of who was to replace LAMSAC. This was resolved by the appointment of a team of 50 job analysts from universities and other institutions headed by Professor Sidney Kessler of the City University, London, with more emphasis now on quality control. The NJC in April 1986 decided on a revised timetable which set a new target for completion of the exercise by March or April 1987 and also that there would be advantage in reaching an early and straightforward agreement on pay for September 1986. Meanwhile the parallel review proceeded of working arrangements, grading criteria and service conditions, taking aboard views of authorities arising from employer consultations.

It was one thing for the NJC to agree in principle on an early pay settlement for September 1986, but a much more difficult thing for them to achieve in practice, and NJC meetings in April and May 1986 failed to produce a pay deal. Eventually the trade unions (Donald Macgregor leading them on the elevation of John Edmunds to the general secretaryship of GMBATU) submitted a full pay claim of the traditional basket variety at the meeting of the NJC on 17th July 1986. Settlement was nevertheless reached after a long day's negotiations at the meeting of the NJC on 16th September when the employers finally made an offer of an increase of £6 per week on all basic rates with effect from 1st September 1986. The offer was made on condition that the trade unions would recommend it to their membership and included a statement recognising the desirability of harmonising certain service conditions as between manual workers and other comparable local government groups. There had been considerable difficulties on the employers' side in agreeing to pitch the offer as high as £6 per week (7.2% to 6.3% in percentage terms): the meeting on 16th September had been preceded by a meeting between Government ministers and employers' representatives when ministers expressed their concern that increases in pay should more closely match inflation (then currently at 2.4%).

LGM of December 1986 was able to report on the job evaluation front that the ten evaluation panels had completed their evaluation of the main group of job descriptions. A measure of the scale of the exercise was that a total of 800 sets of scores were to be considered by the co-ordinating panel.

Meanwhile in November 1986 the employers set out for all local authorities the direction of their thinking on the overall review of the grading structure, service conditions and working arrangements. The employers' criteria were modernisation of the national agreement, greater flexibility for authorities, and a change in the balance between what was determined nationally and locally. The most controversial ideas were radical changes suggested on working time, moving away from the concept of a working week towards a working year.

LGM of April 1987 was pleased to report that "the most detailed study of manual worker jobs ever undertaken has been successfully completed". After employers and unions had worked closely together for nearly 18 months without disagreement, both sides of the NJC accepted unanimously the results which produced a new rank order of manual worker jobs. The rank order showed considerable changes in the pecking order because equal value considerations were now taken into account. In general terms the jobs which moved up had a significant "caring" element or combined responsibility of resources with a fair degree of skill, whilst jobs without these features stayed still or went down in the ranking. Much negotiations still lay ahead including fitting the rankings into a new grading structure and deciding how many grades there would be. On other matters under review, whilst authorities were generally in favour of moving to the concept of a working year, they recognised the unions' quid pro quo was a reduction in hours which was costly and thus unpopular with them.

After two days of negotiations in April 1987 and a further two days in May the employers eventually made a comprehensive detailed package offer which covered all the areas under separate reviews. This contained a pay offer with an overall cost of 10.6% to run from 1st July 1987 right through to September 1988 and allocated all the manual jobs into six new grades according to their points ratings. The unions said that parts of the offer were unacceptable but took it away for consideration: the chief stumbling blocks for them in the offer were in the area of working time, particularly a clause which would give more flexibility on working patterns and which would enable payments for weekend premium payments to be determined by the local authority.

After two further days of negotiations at the end of July 1987 the employers formally tabled a package of proposals which the unions undertook to take back to their members. It was not however until the meeting of the NJC on 29th October, just over two years after the decision to launch the review, that the trade unions were in a position formally to accept the employers' offer. The essential difference between the employers' original offer of May and their revised July offer was on the thorny issue of working patterns and weekend premium payments where the new clause stated that, unless and until both sides locally agreed to variations, the existing provisions continued to apply. At the same time as the trade union leaders were being castigated for having sold the pass on this issue, a number of authorities were criticising the employers for failing to deliver sufficient change. The ultimate test of the effects of the agreement lay in future at local level as authorities faced such pressures as competitive compulsory tendering. Of all the many personalities involved in the long-running saga, Derek Lodge, the LACSAB assistant secretary for manual and craft negotiations, clearly stood out both as author of the job evaluation scheme and at the helm throughout.

One other issue in respect of manual worker negotiations worthy of comment in this period 1980 to 1987 was the dispute on the grading of home helps which eventually had to be resolved by arbitration. The employers initially offered a plus rate to those undertaking wider tasks but this found favour neither with the authorities nor with the unions who sought the same level as for care assistants and would not agree to the employers' improved offer of group E grading. The ACAS board of arbitration in their award of July 1985 awarded that home helps should receive the same grade of pay as care assistants with effect from 1st April 1986, preceded by an interim payment of £2 per week from 1st April 1985 which would cease when the award came into full effect.

CRAFT WORKERS

In the earlier years of this period the position of craft workers could be summed up as "the same deal as manuals". But difficulties were nevertheless mounting up as local authority craftsmen in direct labour organisations were much affected by competitive compulsory tendering. This came to a head in the JNC for building and civil engineering craftsmen when the trade union side's 1983/1984 claim for a substantial pay increase, a 35-hour week and improved annual leave was eventually referred in January 1984 to arbitration. Award 84/10 of the central arbitration committee in May 1984 was that basic rates should be increased by 4% from 4th November 1983; the higher bonus calculator to be increased by 4%; bonus consolidation to cease; and no award on hours or sick pay. Problems arose from the arbitrators' recommendation for the introduction of a national grading structure for supervisors which finally resulted in a reference back to them in February 1985. The Central Arbitration Committee (CAC) resolved the matter in a letter of 29th April 1985 ruling that chargehands and trade foremen would be covered by their recommendation as being within the scope of the JNC, but not general foremen who might be in the scope of the NJC for APT&C staffs.

An important feature of the 1986/1987 settlement in the JNC for building and civil engineering craftsmen was the joint commitment to a review within the next year of the then current ways earnings packages were derived at local level and a study of possible alternatives for the future. Many concerns had led to this, especially the ability to compete in local labour markets in the context of compulsory competitive tendering.

MUNICIPAL AIRPORTS

The agreements of the municipal airports panel of the NJC for manual workers in the early 1980s usually reflected those made in the parent body, although the trade union side repeatedly sought restoration of relativities with British Airways and the British Airports Authority established by the Clegg comparability report in 1980.

An important development which had a major impact on the negotiating machinery for airports was the publication in June 1985 of a Government white paper on airports policy which proposed – inter alia – that existing municipal airports with an annual turnover of £1m. or more should in future be constituted as companies under the Companies Act. Following the publication early in 1986 of the Airports Bill which would give effect to this proposal by 1st April 1987, it was agreed to set up a new National Council for Airports from 1st April 1986 to undertake negotiations both for those airports which would become public limited companies and for those which would remain municipal airports. A subsequent development early in 1987 was the setting up of another National Council for Airports to cover non-manual staff with the same employers' side as for the national councils for manual and craft employees.

APT&C STAFFS

There was no one big issue in the period 1980 to 1987 for the NJC for APT&C staffs of quite the same magnitude as for manual workers and teachers. The staff side seemed more prepared to resort to arbitration in the earlier years, but less so in latter years which included two ballots in NALGO for industrial action in furtherance of annual pay claims neither of which gained a majority vote. The largest single issue was the largely unexpected residential staffs dispute which erupted quite suddenly in 1983 and led to the Residential Staffs Inquiry of 1984.

The Radar room, air traffic control at Luton airport.

After the debacle in March 1980 on the outcome of the comparability study, the APT&C employers were very sensitive to the needs for thorough consultations with local authorities and addressed themselves to this when they met at Swansea in April 1980 prior to the NJC meeting. The staff side claim soon followed seeking a general increase of 20%; a minimum wage at age 18 of £70 per week; 25 days minimum holiday entitlement; and a 35-hour week. The employers were clearly influenced by local authorities' ability to pay in the light of the rate support grant settlement for 1980/1981, and at two NJC meetings they stuck at an offer of 13%, insisting this was their absolute limit. When the NJC met again in September 1980 the staff side asked for arbitration and the employers reluctantly agreed (the issue of arbitration versus ability to pay was then becoming a popular Government theme). The CAC's award of November 1980 confirmed the employers' offer of 13% from 1st July 1980 but awarded a further 2% from 1st April 1981. Their award of a minimum annual leave entitlement of 20 days (25 days if five years consecutive service) came as a surprise as there had been scant mention of annual leave during the arbitration hearing.

Early in 1981 the APT&C employers reviewed their aims and objectives with a view to adopting a more positive approach in developing negotiating policies to meet the needs of constituent authorities. This new approach was forthwith put into effect for, as the staff side tabled in April 1981 their claim for improved pay and conditions, so the employers at the same time submitted their proposals for restructuring the lower end of the salary structure. After an initial offer of 6%, the employers finally moved to an overall offer of 7.5% from 1st July 1981,

A librarian at work.

insisting that the changes they sought at the lower end of the structure must form part of the package. The resultant 7.5% agreement included the major change of amalgamating into one division the existing grading provisions for all basic clerical, administrative and secretarial jobs, with two distinct and separate scales within it, thus liberating about 150,000 posts from nationally prescribed occupational gradings.

Relationships between the two sides of the NJC became very strained in the latter half of 1981, with NALGO taking industrial action on three fronts. The first was a prolonged and bitter dispute at Liverpool where 500 typists and other staff had taken strike action for improved gradings. The national employers decided to take a full part in seeking to find a solution and raised the issue with the staff side at the NJC meeting on 20th October 1981. LGM of November 1981 pithily reports – "The national employers' pressure brought the meeting to a precipitate close". The second dispute involving industrial action affected registration officers in support of their grading claim which had been rejected in NJC discussions. Their "work to rule" received publicity by their refusal to conduct weddings on Saturdays, but otherwise did not have great impact on local authorities. Eventually the industrial action ceased when the staff side sought reference of the grading dispute to arbitration. The subsequent CAC award in January 1983 gave significant grading improvements to registration officers. Whilst this caused some immediate employer concern, it did at least close the issue for some years to come. The third dispute involved another national "work to rule", this time by meat inspectors in support of their grading claim following limited improvements proposed by the employers. NALGO did not appear to have considered sufficiently the isolation of their meat inspector members who work in abattoirs alongside slaughtermen. The combined efforts of the employer network and the meat trade to stifle quickly any attempts at local deals and to stress the risk of job losses in the industry meant that the industrial action had much less impact than NALGO had hoped. Attempts by NALGO to persuade their members to escalate the action failed and the dispute petered out by the end of 1981 as meat inspectors continued or resumed normal working.

When in 1981 the staff side rejected the employer proposals to bring maternity provisions into line with the Government's 1980 Act, the employers resorted to arbitration and the staff side retaliated by referring their claim to arbitration also. This led to difficulties in agreeing terms of reference and, even when these were resolved, the arbitration outcome in November 1981 was inconclusive as the CAC suggested further joint discussion of all the issues referred to them. It was no surprise that joint discussion in December 1981 failed to find any solution, and so the issues went back to arbitration. It was not until April 1982 that the NJC finally received the arbitrators' report which made no award in respect of the employers' claim and awarded in favour of one small aspect of the staff side's package claim, thereby essentially confirming the status quo ante bellum.

In concert with other local government groups and in line with policy co-ordinated by the TUC local government committee, the APT&C staff side tabled their 1982 claim three months earlier than usual at the NJC meeting in January 1982. Following discussions in April and May the employers eventually offered a three-part package consisting of a reduction in the working week to 39 hours for the minority still conditioned to a 40-hour week; proposals to revise and simplify the salary structure (arising from extensive "road show" consultations with authorities); and a total offer of 5.25%, of which about 5% would be available for general pay increases. A temporary difficulty was largely overcome in subsequent meetings after the employers had initially refused to increase the salaries of chief officers and their deputies until new negotiating machinery had been established. But more fundamental stumbling blocks to a negotiated settlement were the size of the overall package and the employers' radical lower-end structural proposals. This time it was the employers who took the initiative to seek resolution by arbitration, believing that settlement was unlikely whilst the unions were closely watching developments elsewhere in the public sector. When the CAC's award was announced on 25th October, Mike Blick, the staff side leader, expressed "bitter disappointment" at the 5.7% increase awarded. The employers noted that their aspirations for changes in the salary structure had not been met and resolved to continue to pursue them in the next pay round.

The winter of 1982/1983 was marked by intensive discussions within the APT&C NJC on two service conditions issues, namely motor car allowances and travelling and subsistence allowances. The latter was eventually resolved in March 1983 and resulted in major changes following a review instigated by the employers. But negotiations broke down in January 1983 on motor car allowances when the employers had not been prepared to moderate their proposals to simplify the scheme and reduce the costs. By the time discussions resumed in March the employers were confronted with strong pressure from local authorities to settle the matter very quickly as local pressure exerted by NALGO had also caused a dozen authorities to make local deals - with others threatening to do so. The employers had to abandon their objective of simplifying the structure of allowances but achieved some success in their other objective of reducing significantly the costs falling on local authorities.

The decision of the APT&C staff side to submit their 1983 pay claim in January 1983 and to seek an earlier operative date of 1st April 1983 arose from further efforts at improving trade union co-ordination in pressing their claims, and was also aimed at NALGO exerting a greater influence than had hitherto been possible at the tail end of each pay round. The employers responded earlier than usual with a total offer of 4.4% plus structural proposals, the main feature of which was the merging of the separate clerical, administrative/ professional and technical divisions into a single grading structure. The employers' dropping of their provocative 1982 lower-end proposals had a beneficial effect on the climate of the 1983 negotiations as agreement was reached on 18th May on a package which the staff side recommended their members to accept. Varying percentage increases were agreed at different levels in the structure and the overall package, which included the employers' structural changes, added 4.894% to the total paybill. The staff side leaders received much criticism at the NALGO conference on 13th June but eventually delegates adopted the schizophrenic approach of endorsing the offer recommended by their leaders, and at the same time censuring them for recommending it!

1983 RESIDENTIAL DISPUTE

Meanwhile the most bitter dispute in the APT&C field in this period was coming to the boil. A staff side claim for reduced hours and premium payments for residential staffs had been repeatedly rejected earlier in 1983 by the employers as local authorities were not prepared to concede any point of the claim. NALGO eventually balloted their residential members and claimed this showed a majority in favour of industrial action, but they were not prepared to release any details when challenged to do so. So at the beginning of September 1983 NALGO instructed their residential members to refuse to work overtime and to ban admission to homes. Despite earlier warnings of troubles looming, it was a surprise to many authorities that their residential staffs should for the first time resort to industrial action and place old people and children at risk. Monitoring by the employers revealed that the response to the NALGO instructions was patchy and that the majority of authorities were managing to maintain services without undue difficulty. Given the volatile political dimension to social services it was surprising there was virtually no breach of the employer line. Efforts were made in discussions in the NJC in September and October to find a means of bringing the dispute to a conclusion. The employers maintained that much of the staff side claim was wrongly based and saw no reason for changing their stance that the claim should be rejected. But they made it clear they would continue to search for solutions and to ask authorities whether in a wider context there were changes in the work done by residential officers which could be recognised, thus launching a review to consider the longer-term needs of the residential service. NALGO however vigorously pursued their claim and sought to escalate the industrial action, but this did not appear to have much effect. In November NALGO decided on a further ballot on a proposal for "office hours only" working, thus banning shift work, night work and weekend working as well as overtime. Meanwhile NUPE requested ACAS to intervene in "a really unpleasant dispute" and ACAS called the two parties in for discussions. By this time NALGO were anxious to end the industrial action, especially because the ballot was not going to support escalation. The employers at their December meeting were encouraged by the thoughtful and constructive responses received from authorities to their long-term review; decided to move to the next stage of the review; and again invited the staff side to join with them and end the dispute. After many hours of talks at St. James's Square ACAS produced a conciliation report on 14th December 1983 recommending a joint inquiry with an independent chairman. This was eventually accepted by both sides and the first meeting of the joint inquiry took place on 16th January 1984 chaired by Ian Buchanan of the University of Dundee.

There was a nasty hiccough when the employers learned at the NJC meeting on 25th January that NALGO branches in the North East were not following the ACAS recommendation of a return to work "without recriminations" and were disciplining members who had not fully supported the industrial action. The employers walked out of the meeting in protest but the matter was eventually resolved at a special meeting of the NJC on 13th February. The joint inquiry proceeded seeking detailed information and visiting residential homes in eight selected authorities. The employers wanted to complete quickly their review already well in hand (with the main 1984 pay review in mind) and when they produced their own report in May this led to angry protests by the staff side that this pre-empted the joint inquiry which was by then seriously delayed by an internal dispute at NALGO.

Meanwhile the staff side tabled their main 1984 APT&C pay claim in March which sought a general increase of 7%, bottom-end restructuring - and, surprisingly, grading improvements for nursery staffs in schools and classes (the normal staff side stance was to insist that consideration of the grading claims on specific groups took place outwith the main annual pay negotiations). The employers responded in May with a 4% offer, rejecting other aspects of the claim, and the staff side said this was unacceptable. These main pay negotiations were also then delayed by the internal NALGO dispute.

When a meeting could eventually take place on 13th August the employers put forward a carefully constructed improved package adding 4.5% to the total paybill, giving most APT&C staffs increases close to that figure, enabling many lower paid staff to get at least 5%, and including improvements for nursery staffs in schools and classes. This was rejected by the staff side and NALGO were instructed by their members to seek an improved offer and plan industrial action. When the staff side came back to negotiations on 21st September the employers were unanimous in sticking to their 4.5% offer from 1st July 1984. When the NJC met again on 31st October the staff side tried to "move the goalposts" by seeking arbitration on the main pay issue, but excluding the nursery staffs. The employers insisted that the nursery staffs were an integral part of the staff side claim and an indivisible part of their offer: the whole issue had to go to arbitration, not just a part of it.

At this stage the issues of 1984 APT&C pay and the residential dispute/inquiry became interwoven as the NJC on 31st October also received a preliminary report of the residential inquiry identifying areas of agreement, based on which the employers made an offer for residential staffs effective also from 1st July 1984 which would add 5.16% to the residential paybill and 0.32% to the total APT&C paybill. Although the preliminary report also identified areas of disagreement, the staff side did not register a failure to agree but wished to postpone a decision on this - thus keeping the two issues apart for arbitration.

When the CAC hearings took place on 7th and 9th January 1985 the first matter to be decided was the scope of the arbitration, which they resolved by hearing the case on nursery staffs, but on a different day. The eventual award marginally improved the employers' offer on main pay and essentially endorsed their offer on nursery staffs, thus bringing to a close a most lengthy process seriously delayed by the staff side's internal problems and tactics.

At a meeting of the residential staffs joint inquiry on 21st December 1984 agreement was reached on a final report, and at a meeting of the NJC on 24th January 1985 the staff side accepted the employers' offer of improvements based on the joint inquiry report. The staff side did not make any immediate decision on pursuing their original claim for reduced hours and premium payments which in fact were to lay dormant for several years. Whilst it is difficult to be sure of the reasons why this trade union campaign spluttered to such an inconclusive end, their pressure for premium payments was seen by many to be contrary to the ethos of the residential service and in contrast to the developing trend for more flexible working patterns.

Having taken so long to gain so little in 1984 the APT&C staff side were understandably under strong pressure to reach a speedy settlement in 1985. Their claim was for a £15 per week increase for all staff plus bottom-end restructuring. One again however negotiations were delayed and meetings cancelled in May 1985 because of a strike by NALGO staff. When eventually serious negotiations took place in early July, two meetings led to an employers' offer of a 5.25% general increase plus an underpinning increase of £6 per week, costing 5.35% overall, which the staff side agreed to recommend to their membership who in turn endorsed the deal.

Another issue on the APT&C front meanwhile was fringe area allowances for 1984 which finished up with an arbitration award in September 1985. This gave a clear decision on the inner fringe (i.e. to follow the outer London pattern), but a less clear-cut recommendation on the outer fringe which was eventually resolved by sticking to the status quo.

Amongst a variety of issues tackled by the APT&C NJC between the 1985 and 1986 main pay reviews, those arising from the abolition of the GLC and metropolitan county councils as from 1st April 1986 were the most controversial. The issue of disturbance and travelling allowances had to be resolved by arbitration; and the employers by settling in negotiations on procedures for the handling of grievance and grading appeals incurred the wrath of receiving authorities who had already made their own arrangements. Also in 1985 the employers embarked on extensive consultations with authorities on the possibility of introducing an element of performance related pay into the APT&C salary provisions, but there was insufficient support for such a move which had evoked hostile reactions from NALGO.

The 1986 staff side claim for APT&C staffs sought an increase of 12% or £900 whichever was the greater, together with the deletion of the miscellaneous grades, and NALGO mounted a large campaign in support of this, canvassing members of all authorities, as they were most concerned that APT&C staffs had fared less well in 1985 than other local government groups, notably chief executives and chief officers who had benefited from the spin-off from the Government's top salaries awards announced just after the APT&C 1985 deal. The employers' offer on 2nd June was an all-round increase of 5.96% from 1st July 1986 plus the absorption of miscellaneous grades (except grade M1/M2) into the main salary scales. The staff side totally rejected this and returned to the NJC meeting on 10th July pressing strongly for an improved offer, but the employers refused to improve on their 5.96% offer. This led to NALGO balloting all their local government members on a rolling programme of short all-out strikes, but only 45.2% voted for strike action. When discussions resumed at the NJC meeting on 10th September, the staff side surprisingly argued that the ballot result showed widespread dissatisfaction and attempted to reopen negotiations, but the employers firmly adhered to their 5.96% offer and agreement was then reached on that basis.

Given the backcloth of the previous two or three years, the 1987 APT&C pay negotiations were felt likely to be particularly fraught with difficulty. That feeling was reinforced when in January 1987 the staff side submitted their 1987 claim in identical terms to their 1986 claim, a tactic which would make it relatively easy to convert the 45% 1986 vote into a majority for industrial action. The employers in their consultations with authorities starkly set out the problems likely to be confronted in the 1987 negotiations, and leading national members toured the country meeting members from most local authorities. The outcome of this activity was (after an "opening offer of 5% on 30th April) a quick realistic employers' offer at the NJC meeting on 14th May which on the following day the NALGO negotiators recommended their members to accept. The offer was in two stages: the first stage gave increases averaging 5% from 1st July 1987; the second stage gave increases averaging 2.5% from 1st February 1988; each stage included weighted increases at the lower end of the structure; the one remaining miscellaneous grade 1/2 was deleted; and the overall cost was within 6% in the negotiating year, although the full-year cost subsequently would be 7.5%. The NALGO local government group meeting accepted the offer by a 2:1 vote on 8th June after a lively debate.

A common feature of many other decisions reached by the APT&C NJC in this period 1980 to 1987 was the deletion of many "purple book" provisions, moving from national to local determination especially on grading issues. Agreements on service condition issues such as continuous service and maternity provisions were largely based on employers' counter-proposals following consultations with authorities.

There was less continuity in terms of the political leadership as the employers' chairmanship changed hands several times. David Chatfield who had taken over from Sid Dennett was deposed in his own group by Margaret Shaw, and she then lost her seat when political control changed to Labour with Arthur Steventon as chairman. He in turn lost his seat in local elections and Harold White took over as chairman.

TOP POSTS

For many years the employers had been exasperated because of the division of chief officers and their deputies between two negotiating bodies (JNC for chief officers and APT&C NJC) and their objective of having one negotiating body for all of them had been thwarted by the two staff sides being unable to accommodate each other in one body. In the summer of 1981 the employers tried to bring matters to a head by declaring publicly what new machinery they would like and what its scope should be, saying it was up to the chief officers themselves to say who should represent them. They set a time limit of six months for all parties to agree on a new body for all chief officers and deputies. (It was also in 1981 that the local authority association secretaries relinquished their roles as joint employers' secretaries on the JNCs for chief executives and chief officers, leaving Brian Rusbridge, the LACSAB secretary, as sole employers' secretary). A helpful move was made in November 1981 when a NALGO delegate meeting reversed previous NALGO policy which had favoured all negotiations within the framework of the APT&C NJC, and this was closely followed by the APT&C staff side agreeing in principle to a new negotiating body covering all chief officers and deputies. The employers tried to exert pressure for rapid progress by refusing to negotiate 1982 pay for chief officers and deputies until the negotiating machinery change could be agreed, but eventually had to relent on this because of the delay to negotiations for APT&C staffs generally. In the event the two staff sides agreed at meetings on 30th June 1982 to a new negotiating body being set up as soon as possible and for the staff side representation to be settled by ACAS balloting chief officers and deputies themselves choosing between the Federation of Professional Officers' Associations (FPOA) and NALGO.

The employers' general "slip-stream" approach of awarding chief officers and chief executives increases similar to those agreed for APT&C staffs ran into difficulties in 1982 when the chief officers rejected the 5% offer; refused to await the outcome of the impending APT&C arbitration, and sought arbitration themselves. The outcome was a 5.7% award which was the same as the award made to APT&C staffs.

The ballot of chief officers and deputies had resulted in FPOA securing 23 seats on the staff side of the new negotiating body as compared with NALGO's three seats, and at meetings on 6th April 1983 the former JNC for chief officers was disbanded and the new JNC established.

Neither the chief executives nor the chief officers were prepared to settle in line with APT&C staffs in 1983 when employers' offers of 4.9% were rejected. The employers coupled these offers to a proposal for a fundamental review of chief executives and chief officers' pay which the staff sides agreed to, whilst insisting this was quite separate from the 1983 pay negotiations which had reached an impasse. The arbitration awards published in November 1983 gave increases of 4.9% to chief executives and chief officers from 1st July 1983 and extra increments for those on the higher population bands, providing overall increases of 5.27% for chief executives and 5.54% for chief officers. The arbitrators also made clear their view that a structure review was needed, but by this time the employers were already consulting authorities, putting to them two main options for change - either simply widen the local discretion available to local authorities, or introduce the concept of job evaluation. There was not an entirely clear answer, with 38% wanting simple widening of discretion, 33% favouring the use of job evaluation in some way; and 19% preferring no change.

These consultation responses nevertheless added to the momentum for fundamental change, and intensive negotiations led to deals being struck early in July 1984 providing the most significant structural changes for over a decade. The three-part agreements provided for all-round increases of 4.5% from 1st July 1984; new salary structures dropping the fulcrum point devise with ranges of salaries based on population which provided more headroom at the top and more local discretion; and making a modified version of the Hay job evaluation scheme available to authorities.

1985 pay negotiations for chief executives and chief officers were profoundly affected by the Government's acceptance in July 1985 of the recommendations for massive increases for senior civil servants and others in Report No. 10 of the Top Salaries Review Body (TSRB). With a moderate deal for APT&C staffs just about clinched and hopes that this would set the pattern for other groups, Tony Prendergast, LACSAB chairman and employers' chairman of these two JNCs, had written to the Prime Minister early in July asking her when considering the TSRB report to bear in mind the effects elsewhere, particularly in local government. His representations went unheeded, and this meant that some account had to be taken of the huge TSRB increases in subsequent negotiations. Agreement was eventually reached in September 1985 providing a 5% increase for chief executives and chief officers from 1st July 1985 and then further increases ranging between 1% and 4.2% from 1st April 1986 as the structure was pulled out "concertina fashion" in favour of the larger authorities.

The professional officers' associations on the JNC for chief officers finally united in 1986 into one union as the Federated Union of Managerial and Professional Officers with the delightful acronym of FUMPO. For quite different reasons however a difficult period ensued in negotiations with chief officers, and in 1986 moderate settlements with APT&C staffs and chief executives contrasted sharply with the attitude of the chief officers who insisted on pursuing an omnibus claim riddled with flawed arguments to arbitration. It was not entirely a surprise that the Central Arbitration Committee's award of 31st March 1987 went no further than to confirm the employers' offer of 5.5% from 1st July 1986.

Part of the 1986 agreement for chief executives had been a commitment to review their pay with similar jobs in the public sector and Hay management consultants were engaged for this using their job evaluation system. The information flowing from this review led to intensive negotiations which culminated in a settlement on 4th September 1987 providing a general salary increase of 7% with delayed effect from 1st September 1987 (broadly the same effect as the APT&C two-stage deal); and a radically revised salary structure from the same date reducing the population bands from 35 to 16, providing separate (and higher) salary ranges for metropolitan districts and London boroughs, reflecting the findings of the review (and their post-1986 reorganisation responsibilities). A settlement was clinched the same day for chief officers for the same general pay increase and a similarly revised salary structure.

FIRE BRIGADES

It might have been thought that the existence of the index-linked pay arrangement in operation since the 1977 dispute would have reduced the scope for disputes within the fire brigades NJC, but this period shows that this negotiating body continued to find one issue or another to fall out about. First it was the 1980 negotiations on fire service pay which ran into serious difficulties, with the Association of County Councils (ACC) particularly most concerned about funding and ability to pay. Their concern went to great lengths and to the point when their regular representatives on the employers' side were at one critical stage unceremoniously replaced by their policy barons. Their tough line in negotiations was not supported by the AMA and COSLA and was matched by an equally strong reaction from the FBU, who eventually held on to keep their hard-won index-linking. The final settlement in December 1980 gave a 13% increase from 7th November 1980 and a further 5.8% from 1st April 1981, covering both lower ranks and officers. The employers gave notice of seeking to reduce costs by staff economies and that they could not guarantee the pay formula in future years. LGM of January 1981 acidly comments – "The response of the unions.....was predictably terse."

The next meeting of the fire brigades NJC in February 1981 was a mini-marathon lasting two days. Battle lines had been pitched with the employers raising five items related to economies and a sixth on the pay formula, matched by the employees tabling a total of twelve claims for improved conditions. The employers' economies package was given a preliminary hearing, but the temperature of the meeting rose sharply when the employers announced their decision to withdraw from the pay formula. The employees side reacted passionately and vehemently, making it clear their next claim would be based on the pay formula and that meanwhile they would be mounting a press and

Firemen at the scene of an incident.

publicity campaign. The lack of much comment in LGM about the subsequent 1981 agreement based on the pay formula indicates that the FBU campaign one way or the other gained its desired effect.

Teachers' negotiations did not have an entire monopoly of inter-union strife in this period as the fire service had two major problems of this ilk in the early 1980s. The first was the claim of the Retained Firefighters Union (RFU) representing 17,000 part-time (retained) members of fire brigades for negotiating rights, pressed first at national level and then pursued with individual fire authorities with little success. The RFU then proceeded with claims to ACAS under Section 11 of the Employment Protection Act, but after long delays decided in 1980 to drop these rather than risk a decision against them in the last days before Section 11 was repealed. Following this the NJC agreed to process one test case through its disputes procedure but there was no agreement on the key issue of local consultative rights, and eventually the dispute was resolved by referring it to ACAS for arbitration.

It was however the dispute between the FBU and NAFO over representation on the NJC's autonomous officers' committee, smouldering for some years previously, which erupted on the national scene early in 1982. There had been an uneasy coexistence in earlier years with NAFO having the majority of seats and the FBU seeking parity refused by NAFO. The 1979 FBU annual conference resolved on industrial action if their claim for parity was not met. The employers, dismayed at the prospect of being drawn into an inter-union conflict, suggested outside mediation. Norman Singleton, a deputy chairman of the Central Arbitration Committee, was invited to chair a working party which in 1980 produced an interim arrangement for co-operation between the two unions. In Spring 1981 the detente fell apart when NAFO withdrew from the interim arrangement. The FBU's response was to put forward proposals in the NJC which achieved parity in the officers' committee but the employers would not grant the FBU equal representation against NAFO's wishes. So the employers suggested an ACAS enquiry which the FBU agreed, but NAFO did not, and NAFO moreover took out writs against both the FBU and the local authorities associations alleging that the NJC decision to take away their veto was unconstitutional. The employers were faced with an intolerable impasse and all their many attempts to resolve the dispute were frustrated as the situation deteriorated and working relationships were disrupted at national and local level. So finally early in 1982 the employers felt compelled to dissolve the existing machinery by withdrawing from it in order to create the conditions for new machinery.

The employers then took the initiative during the course of 1982 to resolve the impasse. They commissioned an independent inquiry into the numbers of fire officers in fire brigades and to ascertain the union membership amongst them, inviting both unions to co-operate. As NAFO refused to co- operate, the report was limited to FBU membership and showed that 49% were FBU members. The employers then drew up proposals for new negotiating machinery which were then put to the two unions. Agreement quickly followed and the inaugural meeting of the new NJC for fire brigades took place on 4th October 1982. There were three main changes from previous machinery: the new officers' committee would deal only with issues solely concerned with officers' terms; there would be equal representation on it for the FBU and NAFO; and a mechanism was provided for periodic reviews of employees' representation.

The new NJC went quickly into action by agreeing 7.5% increases from 7th November 1982 based on the pay formula, but a major impact on firemen's remuneration that year was the Government's decision to increase the firemen's pension contribution from 6.75% to 10.75% of pay. An outstanding issue outstanding from the old NJC on annual leave was resolved by an arbitration award accepted by the newly formed Lower Ranks Committee giving two extra days' leave from 1983 and a further two days from 1985.

One change in unions' spheres of influence was effected relatively peacefully in 1983 when the three recognised unions with membership of assistant chief fire officers (ACOs) agreed that ACOs should be transferred from the main NJC to the NJC for chief fire officers, where the sole staff side organisation was the Chief and Assistant Chief Fire Officers Association (CACFOA). A major change in the pay formula was agreed to operate from the 1983 pay review because the New Earnings Survey data on firemen's earnings were inadequate. This was overcome by the use of a much larger 20% sample directly surveyed in a joint exercise, showing a surprisingly low incidence of overtime. This resulted in a 7.8% increase from 7th November 1983, but the cost to authorities was less because of increased pension contributions.

Application of the pay formula helped towards rapid pay settlements in the NJC for fire brigades in 1984 and 1985, in both years giving a 6.9% increase in earnings. In 1985 negotiations foundered however on the relatively minor issue of the service conditions of fire personnel attending residential training courses ("beer money") and it needed the help of ACAS in a series of conciliation meetings to produce an agreement ratified at the NJC meeting on 7th November 1986.

The fire brigades NJC failed to agree on two issues in 1986 which were then settled by arbitration. The first issue was long service payments which hitherto were limited to basic rank firemen and fire control operators with 15 years' service. The employees side had submitted a claim for the payments to be made after 10 years' service and to be extended to leading firemen and their fire control counterparts. The single ACAS arbitrator awarded in favour of extending the long service payments to the additional grades as claimed, but against any reduction of the 15 years' requirement. The issue did not end there as subsequently the fire officers claimed that the long service payment should apply to all officer ranks and pursued this through to arbitration with an award in favour of the claim in February 1987.

The other dispute settled by arbitration in 1986 was in respect of the Northern Ireland allowance, a special payment which recognised the extra responsibilities of firemen in Northern Ireland and which had existed before the Fire Authority for Northern Ireland (FANI) had been formed by a merger in 1973. The original payment of £2 per week had been doubled by an arbitration award in 1976. After FBU claims to FANI for a further increase had been refused the issue came to the NJC in February 1986 when there was a failure to agree. The arbitration panel heard the dispute in Northern Ireland and awarded an increase in the allowance to £12 per week from 1st February 1986, with the rider that the continuance of the allowance should be subject to annual review in the light of the general recognition that at some future date the allowance would no longer be required.

There appears to have been little difficulty in reaching agreements in November 1986 on 7.3% increases in pay rates from 7th November 1986 by the application of the index-linking pay formula, improving average earnings by just under 7%.

This period saw the retirement at the end of 1981 of Terry Parry, general secretary of the FBU since 1964, and before that union president from 1959 to 1964. He had been chairman of the TUC in 1979/1980. Even at the time of the most bitter disputes such as in 1977, Terry and Brian Rusbridge, the LACSAB secretary, maintained a friendly working relationship which became very useful in helping the warring parties eventually to face each other. Terry unfortunately died in April 1982 soon after his retirement. He was succeeded as FBU general secretary by Ken Cameron who had been a national officer of the FBU since 1978.

POLICE

The setting up of the Police Negotiating Board in 1979 together with the adoption of the Edmund-Davies recommendations on index-linking brought a period of relative tranquillity to police pay negotiations in the early 1980s with annual pay agreements in 1980 and 1981. As in the case of the fire service, the existence of an index-linking formula for police pay meant that the question of a comparability study for them did not arise. The first pebble to disturb this tranquil scene came from the official side when, in agreeing in July 1981 on a 13.2% increase from 1st September 1981, they gave notice of their intention to examine certain aspects of the pay formula with a view to bringing proposals forward for the 1982 annual pay review.

The contentious issue which arose in the 1982 pay review did not stem from the official side's review of the pay formula (which was not then completed), but on the quite separate issues of central government funding and police pension contributions. The 1982 pay agreement provided increases of 10.3% from 1st September 1982 but the representatives of the AMA and COSLA disassociated themselves from the official side's majority decision to settle without comprehensive financial guarantees from central government. This was the subject of continuing representations by all the local authority associations until a satisfactory answer was finally given by the Government. The other issue of police pensions highlights one important distinction between the police negotiating machinery and other negotiating bodies in that they alone cover pensions, but with no scope to resort to arbitration on pensions issues. In the light of an evaluation by the Government actuary the official side urged the staff side to accept increases in pensions contributions also from 1st September 1982 – from 7 to 11% of pay for men, and from 5 to 8% for women. The staff side were prepared for a higher contribution but not so great as proposed. Without the facility to settle by arbitration, the official side after prolonged and unfruitful discussions requested the Home Secretary to make regulations increasing police pension contributions in line with their proposals, which he did.

The early part of 1983 was the busiest phase so far of the Police Negotiating Board (PNB) since its establishment in 1979 – with much activity in three of its four standing committees. In committees A and B reviews were underway on the pay of chief police officers and the superintending ranks respectively; in committee C the staff side were pursuing claims on annual leave and overtime with the vice-chairman of the PNB conciliating in the hope of averting arbitration as sought by the staff side; and in committee D negotiations were starting on the official side's controversial proposals to change the system for calculating police rent allowances, expecting difficult and protracted negotiations.

A Sikh community policeman in Cardiff.

In reaching agreement in the PNB in July 1983 for increases from 1st September 1983 of 8.4% for federated ranks and 7.7% for superintending ranks the official side were fully aware of the extent and depth of outside concern over the (high) levels of police pay and they accordingly proposed a joint review to compare police pay levels with those outside. The staff side of committee C for federated ranks declined to participate, indicating they would be willing to consider any specific official side proposals.

The issue of police rent allowances came to a head in the course of 1983 when after many months of meetings it was reported to PNB committee D there appeared to be no scope for any agreement. The essence of the official side's proposals was that a new system should be introduced based on average council house rents for 3-bedroom post-war houses, abated by 30% to reflect capital acquisition, etc., and including an element for rates paid and tax paid on the allowance. Again the services of the PNB vice-chairman, Professor Hunter, were invoked as conciliator in December 1983 and he put forward confidential proposals aimed at breaking the negotiating impasse. This conciliation did not succeed and eventually the issue went to the Police Arbitration Tribunal (PAT) which heard submissions from the parties on 30th August 1984. The proceedings at the hearing worried the official side representatives because of the extent of the tribunal's questioning concentrated on the Edmund-Davies report and changes since then. Disappointing as it was to the official side, the award in the staff side's favour did not therefore come as a total surprise, with the PAT accepting the staff side's view that, because Edmund-Davies took account of the allowance, it could not be changed except through an overall review of police pay.

The official side's proposals made in the summer of 1982 for a review of police pay began to bear fruit early in 1983 when there were agreements for a national job evaluation exercise for chief police officers and superintending ranks. The evaluation was to use the Hay factor plan and Hay management consultants would also provide information on outside comparators, with the intention of the results informing the negotiators who would take account of other factors. The Police Federation could not be persuaded to agree to a similar exercise for the federated ranks although agreement was reached with them to undertake a less in-depth review.

The LGM report of October 1984 on police pay negotiations that summer refers to some of the most bemusing negotiations of recent years. The review of the workings of the pay formula had been undertaken by a joint working party which reported back in July 1984 with a mass of evidence but with diametrically opposed interpretations of it. The official side's interpretation would have led to considerably lower increases than expected and they thus felt it would be fair to continue on the existing basis in 1984, leaving negotiations on the review for 1985. The official side thus made an offer of 4.8% on 24th July, believing this would lead to a quick settlement as the staff side claim was for 4.8% too. The staff side insisted that the review must be dealt with in 1984 or not at all, believing that they had a favourable climate in which to defend the status quo as they had been policing the bitter and protracted miners' strike. When discussions resumed on 28th August they claimed that there was no need to change the pay formula and that the review revealed a need for extra increases for them. The official side's reply was that the review justified technical changes to the formula resulting in a general rise of 3.34% for 1984 with lesser increases at the bottom of the constables' scales, making it very clear this was not their final position. The staff side did not wish to pursue any possibility of an improved offer and registered a failure to agree which automatically triggered conciliation. Following the usual exploratory talks the conciliator, Professor Hunter, suggested a package to resolve the dispute which both sides accepted on 26th September. This included changes to the pay formula which went some way to achieving the official side's objectives; a pay rise of 5.45% from 1st September 1984 except that the bottom two points of the constables' scale were frozen; provision for a further review of the pay arrangements after the 1987 settlement; and a package of overtime changes to apply from April 1985.

The delay in reaching the 1985 police pay settlement of 7.5% did not arise because of difficulties between the two sides of PNB committee C but because the official side felt they first needed to secure adequate Government commitment on funding it.

Difficulties arose too in 1985 in settling the pay increases for chief police officers and these were eventually resolved following conciliation by Professor Hunter by agreement for 8% increases from 1st September 1985.

An issue which could not be settled by negotiation in 1985 and had to be determined by arbitration was that of the police London allowances paid in addition to London weighting to overcome manpower shortages. When the arbitration hearing eventually took place in the summer of 1986 the official side's case that there was no case for increases because of improvements in police manpower in London was upheld by the PAT.

The 1986 police pay negotiations in PNB committee C for the federated ranks were not quite a re-run of the previous year's although the problem was again about funding. This time the official side did not delay the 7.5% increase for September 1986 but made the agreement under protest because they had not received satisfactory assurances from the Government on funding.

Memories of the heavy police involvement in the bitter miners' strike of 1984/1985 were rekindled as a dispute on an esoteric issue dragged on well into 1986 about the allowances paid to a support unit drafted into a coalfield during the miners' dispute. The agreement provided that, when police officers were held in reserve away from their normal place of duty and required to sleep in a specific location, all hours except eight out of every 24 were counted as duty hours provided proper sleeping accommodation was provided and the officers were stood down: when either or both of these provisos were not met all hours in the "sleeping period" were paid at overtime rates. The argument which could not be resolved was about the definition of "proper sleeping accommodation": the staff side strongly contested that conditions in a gymnasium of a military camp were far from "proper"; whilst the official side focussed on the not inconsiderable sums of money at stake – the officers were already receiving payments of between £70 and £104 per day for 16 hours duty time, and concession would lead to additional payments of £40 to £60 per day. This was resolved neither in negotiation nor by conciliation and went to arbitration. The PAT evidently found this a particularly difficult issue. They concluded that the conditions were sub-standard but did not fall outside the term "proper sleeping accommodation" and awarded accordingly. They gave guidance to apply to this case and others which had arisen which included the payment of a "hardship allowance" of about £10 per night when a second higher standard of accommodation had not been met.

1986 saw difficulties again in settling the pay of chief police officers which eventually led to a reference to arbitration. The official side offered tapered increases worth 6.8% overall whilst the staff side of PNB committee A pressed for 9%. The cases were heard on 10th December 1986 by the PAT who awarded 7.5% for all chief police officers from 1st September 1986, thus eliminating the tapering element of the official side offer.

The circumstances of the 1987 main federated pay negotiations were virtually a complete replica of the 1986 situation, with the official side agreeing to a 7.75% increase as from 1st September 1987 whilst complaining strongly to the Government about the lack of assurances on funding.

So a period which had begun in relative tranquillity in the immediate aftermath of Edmund-Davies moved into much activity by the mid-1980s with much resort to conciliation and arbitration, not limited to main pay but often on other quite esoteric issues.

PROBATION AND MAGISTRATES COURTS STAFFS

The period 1980 to 1987 started with a failure to agree in the JNC for the probation service on pay increases to apply from 1st July 1980 which was referred to arbitration. The award was a 13% increase plus an extension by one point of the main grade scale.

A series of meetings culminated in February 1983 with the issue of the first national code of conditions for probation service ancillary workers whose sub-committee of the JNC had been created in 1980.

The first strike ever in the probation service took place on 27th April 1983 in protest against the Home Office decision to reduce the pay of "probation trainees", more properly known as Home Office sponsored students. The staff side had previously tried to bring these into the scope of the JNC but this had been resisted by the employers as probation committees did not employ these students. Attempts were made informally outwith the JNC to resolve the dispute and to provide future stable arrangements.

Although generally settlements on probation pay were eventually reached in the 1980s, there was a continual clash of philosophies which had to be resolved, with the staff side pressing for flat-rating measures opposed by the employers.

These problems were accentuated in 1984 when the staff side also sought a major salary restructuring. When there was a failure to agree in September 1984 after the employers had tabled a 4.5% offer, the staff side requested arbitration. But ACAS intervened with conciliation which led to an eventual agreement in February 1985 on an overall increase of 4.6% from 1st July 1984 with an unusual compromise of additional weighting at both ends of the structure.

But in 1985 neither negotiating nor conciliation meetings produced a pay agreement to apply from 1st July 1985 and there was a reference to arbitration after rejection of an employers' offer of 5.25% which included restructuring proposals. The arbitration award on November 1985 raised the total cost to 5.835% but the employers were consoled by the endorsement of their restructuring proposals and rejection of flat-rating as claimed by the staff side.

April 1987 saw the ratification of a new salary structure for probation ancillary staff after much discussion and consultation stemming from an argument between the two sides for and against paying all ancillaries on the same scale (as claimed by the staff side). The outcome went towards more local flexibility, providing a new spinal column salary structure, from which probation committees could select a scale for each post.

Negotiations for magistrates courts staffs deviated from their normal "slipstream" course in August 1984 when both sides took a bold gamble and settled on a 4.5% increase well in advance of the outcome on APT&C pay which traditionally was their pacesetter.

NEW TOWNS AND INDUSTRIAL ESTATES STAFFS

The longer-term consequences of the arbitration on new towns pay in the autumn of 1981 did not stem so much from the award of 7.5% increases but from what the arbitrators declined to do. Part of the issues put to them related to restructuring and their wisdom was that "an infinitely better job of restructuring can be made by the whitley council than could be made by (us)." It was not however until November 1982 that the whitley council reached agreement on limited restructuring when they also struck a deal on general pay increases from July 1982.

A further more radical restructuring took place for new towns staffs in the summer of 1987 based on a spinal column system in which scales for each individual job would be chosen from a range for each level of job, providing a much more flexible system for the future. At the same time it was agreed to stop all grading appeals at local level, rescinding the right of national appeal – an achievement from the employers' perspective which the employers' sides of many other negotiating bodies gazed on with no little envy!

In 1982 in the whitley council for industrial estates and development agencies the staff side asked for arbitration and the eventual outcome in October 1982 was a 6% increase. It was however the award then of a reduction in the working week from 37 to 36 hours which gave rise to much subsequent trouble as the sponsoring Government department raised the question as to whether this would cause additional cost and eventually insisted this must be taken into account in the 1983 pay round. The scope of this negotiating body was reduced and its title changed in September 1986 following the withdrawal of the English Industrial Estates Corporation.

TEACHERS

It is a daunting and depressing task to attempt a brief narrative of all the contortions on teachers' pay "negotiations" in this period 1980 to 1987 on which millions of words have been written. Those who have had the misfortune to witness the proceedings of the Burnham committees could not be totally shocked to see the ending of the classic example of how not to conduct serious pay negotiations. The courses of the negotiations for schoolteachers and those for the further education sector were quite different and are separated to seek to bring some clarity to confusing sagas.

The period began with the management panels of both Burnham committees, having failed to correct the famous "Clegg" error in the negotiations arising from the comparability study, seeking the correction by means of adjusting the normal pay increase due at 1st April 1980. They had already tabled offers of 13% so in June 1980 they replaced these offers with a 9.2% proposal which not surprisingly was rejected, and the issue went to arbitration for hearings early in July. The employers were disappointed that the arbitration award did not fully recoup the "Clegg" error but were slightly relieved to learn of the arbitrators' intentions to keep the amount of new money within the 13/14% region. The award was for a 12% increase from 1st April 1980 and extra increases from 1st September 1980 (in addition to the second stage of the comparability award due on that date) of 2.5% to 4%.

At the end of 1980 the conditions of service working party set up in 1979 by the employers reported an impasse after 17 meetings. Education authorities had been concerned because teachers took industrial action without losing pay as they claimed to be withdrawing only from voluntary duties, so the employers wanted teachers' contracts to clarify what they were required to do and their entitlements. The price the teachers wanted for this was new benefits. Lack of progress was in part due to a boycott by the NAS/UWT inducing a "fear of agreeing" by the NUT.

With a teachers' claim for 15% and a "safe" opening offer of 4% by the management panel in February 1981, teachers' pay negotiations for 1981 seemed to be heading towards the usual impasse. But by the next meeting on 2nd March there were several developments elsewhere, notably a 7.5% deal for Scottish teachers, and by the end of the day a realistic settlement was reached at 7.5% to apply from 1st April 1981. The teachers' panel had by this time been changed to bring in the Professional Association of Teachers (another PAT) and to give the NAS/UWT an additional seat.

It might be said that the long saga of the 1980s on teachers' pay began by the formulation by the Burnham management panel in the autumn of 1980 of proposals for a fundamental reform of the salary structure. Their main aim was to ensure that the payment system should contribute to the attainment of educational objectives with the work done in the classroom as its basis. A key factor in this was the concept of a relatively long main professional grade (MPG) on which teachers would be placed when they had reached a satisfactory standard after service in a relatively short entry grade.

The 1982 pay round began when on 8th December 1981 the teachers presented their claim for increases from April 1982 to maintain purchasing power, the index of retail prices then showing an annual increase of 11.7% as against the Government's plans for 4% increases in pay in local government as well as for a reduction in the teaching force. Meetings on 16th February and 3rd March produced a management panel offer of 3.4% which was not improved and which the teachers (who had by now quantified their claim at 12%) found unsatisfactory. The teachers sought a reference to arbitration but the management panel felt this was premature and suggested a further meeting. To bring pressure to bear in support of a reference to arbitration, three teacher unions embarked on action called "withdrawal of goodwill". This disruption of the education service was mainly directed at county authorities as the AMA had announced their support for a reference to arbitration. Against a background of threatened escalation by half-day strikes the Burnham management panel met again on 25th March and after seven hours of deliberations agreed to the teachers' request for arbitration. In June the arbitrators awarded a 6% increase without giving any clue as to how they had reached that conclusion. They did however note the "absence of any sustained serious collective bargaining" and that the parties had "got out of the habit" thus leading them to recommend a "serious joint effort to review the negotiating procedures". Another recommendation was to improve the data basis for negotiations to make them "more meaningful".

Arbitrators settled the 1981 London allowances at about the same time, adopting a cost compensation approach. London allowances for 1982 again went to an arbitration hearing in January 1983 with the teachers seeking a cost compensation approach; the management panel offering less, i.e. 10% in London and nothing for the fringe area; and the Government having stopped the London weighting indexation measured by the Department of Employment. The arbitrators' award for 1982 was significant in registering a departure from their 1981 ruling and in stating their view that in the future London allowance should not be a separate issue but rather part of the annual pay negotiations.

The main 1983 pay negotiations began in February 1983 when the teachers sought an early agreement for a substantial increase in salaries from 1st April 1983, staged restoration of Houghton levels, structure changes, and the setting up of joint machinery to acquire and analyse data on pay levels elsewhere. The negotiating atmosphere for the next meeting on 10th March 1983 was described in the March edition of LGM as "one of the most satisfactory in living memory", with the teachers at one stage taking the unprecedented step of saying they were prepared to move away from their 15% claim. The management panel had by this stage made an offer of 3.5% in line with rate support grant funding, and the surprising flexibility shown by the teachers caused them to say they would review their position. At the next meeting on 25th March the management panel nudged their offer up to 4% but at that stage the teachers were unable to show any signs of closing the gap when challenged to do so. Settlement was reached at the meeting on 15th April on a general increase of 4.975% plus agreement to establish a working party to examine data on the pay of teachers and other comparable occupations. The management panel had originally rejected the idea of a joint examination of pay data as they feared it would arouse expectations which could not be fulfilled, and it was their relenting on this which was an important factor leading to the settlement. This meant no move on the restoration of Houghton levels in 1983 and it was noted that the joint working party on structure was continuing its work. The pay data working party completed its initial task by early 1984 when a weighty report was produced covering statistics of teacher employment, general economic indicators, remuneration in occupations, and financial resources of local education authorities.

The intention that the pay data working party's findings should inform, rather than influence, negotiations was demonstrated in the series of meetings early in 1984 when, in response to the teachers' claim for a substantial increase from 1st April 1984 to begin the process of restoring teachers' pay to the levels established by Houghton, the management panel made it clear that they did not regard either the Houghton or Clegg reports as having any continued relevance. The low level of the management panel's 3% offer on 16th March was due in no small part to the Secretary of State's decision to impose on English and Welsh authorities a 1.05% increase in teachers' superannuation contributions – a consideration which did not apply in Scotland where there was already 4.5% on offer to their teachers. The management panel also strongly pressed the need to make progress on the reform of the teachers' salary structure. The management panel requisitioned a meeting on 30th April and improved their offer to 4.5%. This was immediately rejected by the teachers who requested arbitration which was refused by the management panel on the grounds that they could not abdicate to arbitrators their responsibility on behalf of the authorities for determining the level of service provision. The teachers' unions responded by embarking on widespread industrial action with the aim of persuading the management panel either to increase the offer to 7.5% in line with average earnings or to agree to arbitration. In its usual coy style LGM at that time does not refer to the impact of the teachers' industrial action. Suffice to say that after a further two months the management panel reversed their decision and agreed to arbitration at a meeting on 22nd June with the caveat that this should exclude structural issues. At arbitration the teachers stressed the loss of relative earnings, whilst the management panel presented a formidable case based on the constraints on local authority expenditure. As the teachers had pointed to a 6% median for private sector non-manual pay increases and the management panel had referred to other local government groups settling at 4.5%, the arbitrators' award of 5.1% came as no great surprise to seasoned observers, although it apparently was a shock to the teachers' leaders.

Meanwhile the employers became more and more frustrated by the lack of progress in joint talks on structural reform which they had started way back in 1980. This led to their publicising in November 1984 a complete set of proposals in a document hailed as "one of the most important in education since 1944". To achieve their objective of hastening reform the employers not only set out the details of a new structure and the principles underlying their proposals, but they also attached specific money values to them. A main professional grade (MPG) recognised the central importance of the classroom teacher, defined contractual duties and responsibilities, and introduced a new system of performance appraisal and review. New entrants would be placed on a short entry scale, new principal teacher and assistant head posts would be established; and a new system for heads' salaries was proposed, as well as a new scheme of teacher fellowships. The employers recognised additional financial resources would be needed from the Government, and the Secretary of State obviously first wished to know – as did the employers – whether the teaching profession was prepared to back the employers. The teachers' unions, who had opposed earlier proposals, agreed to take the document away for consideration, having a few days earlier presented a detailed claim embodying major structural changes and seeking massive increases from 1st April 1985, including a maximum of £15,250 for a basic professional scale in contrast to the employers' £11,800 for the MPG maximum.

The response of the teachers' unions to the structure reform package was however very hostile and the NUT walked out of talks on 5th December because they objected to the employers' philosophy, in particular the linking of pay and performance assessment. The employers stressed that they wanted to develop and enhance the professional role and performance of teachers: they were open to detailed negotiation, but reform must be comprehensive, not piecemeal, including service conditions (not a Burnham function) as well as pay.

A marathon Burnham meeting took place on 28th January 1985 when, after carefully considering the claim and authorities' resources, the employers offered 4%. The teachers rejected this out of hand without even withdrawing to consider it. The employers then quickly offered arbitration – in sharp contrast to their stance the previous year. This time the teachers said they wanted more talks first. The employers finally retired at 11.30pm that night, feeling very frustrated, especially because their repeated efforts to persuade the teachers back into structure talks had so far failed. No progress was made either on structure reform or main pay at a Burnham meeting on 11th February which eventually finished at 1.20am the following morning, with the employers sticking at 4.5% and the teachers rejecting arbitration. The employers pressed that teachers' pay and conditions had to be discussed in one forum but the teachers again suggested the idea of concurrent discussions which had failed previously following the Clegg comparability report.

In the battle for public opinion which ensued the employers quickly lost ground when on 19th February Sir Keith Joseph, the Secretary of State, made it plain that the additional 7% required to meet the full first year cost of the employers' proposals was out of reach. This was compounded by the leak of the minutes of a meeting held on 14th October 1984 between the Secretary of State and employer representatives which revealed that Sir Keith did not like many aspects of the employers' proposals and believed the cost implications were very difficult. This leak was in fact much ado about nothing as the teachers' unions had been told the following day, 15th October, that Sir Keith had not endorsed the package or granted additional resources – only that there was a prospect (extinguished by the teachers' walk out on 5th December) that the package was negotiable. Faced with accusations of bad faith which they felt were quite unjustified, the consequent lack of goodwill, and teachers' morale very low for a variety of reasons, the employers on 27th February took the initiative of proposing conciliation and ACAS were called in, with exploratory conciliation discussions taking place at a series of meetings in March.

Adherence to the 1965 concordat between the local authority associations and the Secretary of State which begins by affirming that "the management panel will speak with one voice throughout the negotiations and any arbitration.."

seemed to have been totally ignored by the Secretary of State when on 21st May 1985 he wrote publicly to the employers' leaders suggesting what changes he would like to see in teachers' contracts before he would provide any more money. The Government would not make available any additional resource for teachers' pay in 1985/1986 but offered more money for 1986/1987 "if and only if an acceptable and firm agreement in principle could be reached by October 1985 which would ensure progress towards the Government's objectives".

An NUT Special Conference in 1986.

At a Burnham meeting two days' later the employers raised their offer for an increase from 1st April 1985 to 5%. This was immediately rejected by the teachers, whereupon the employers suggested conciliation or arbitration. The teachers declared that arbitration was unacceptable as a solution and re-embarked on a summer of industrial action and disruption.

A political change of major significance to the continuing teachers' pay saga took place following the county council elections in May 1985 which resulted in a swing to Labour. At a management panel meeting on 3rd July Philip Merridale (ACC) was replaced by Nicky Harrison (AMA) as chairman with John Pearman (AMA) as new vice-chairman. The employers sought throughout that day to agree on a constructive way forward to resolve the dispute. The following day the education committees of both the ACC and the AMA voted unanimously to give notice of their intention to withdraw from the 1965 concordat between them and the Secretary of State. The employers engaged in intensive discussions in the next few days internally and with the teachers to seek to break the impasse. At meetings on 11th and 16th July (with a marathon Burnham further education committee intervening on 15th July into the early hours of 16th July) the employers informally discussed with the teachers a set of proposals – with the twin objectives of achieving a 1985/1986 settlement and a resumption of long-term discussions on structure reform and related issues – with a view to meeting the Secretary of State's deadline for financial support. The employers on 16th July (now led by their acting chairman, the indefatigable John Pearman) modified their original proposals for 1985/1986 so as to give all teachers 7% by the end of 1985 and stressed throughout the 13.5 hours of talks their flexibility and desire to settle. But the teachers would not move from their original claim seeking Houghton restoration, so the eventual formal outcome was an offer of 5% and an employers' proposal for arbitration which the teachers refused to consider despite the independent chairman, Sir John Wordie, commending this course of action. This sorry state of affairs was aptly described by David Brindle of the "Financial Times" when he wrote in LGM of August 1985 – "Rather like a worm chopped in two, Burnham just carried on wriggling its erratic and painfully slow course through July...".

Although the political leadership change had resulted in a greater emphasis to find accommodation with the teachers, the resolution at a meeting of the Council of Local Education Authorities (CLEA) on 18th July showed no signs whatsoever of inter-party strife. John Pearman proposed and Philip Merridale seconded a motion carried unanimously which - inter alia - commended the employers' efforts to secure equitable settlements in 1985; referred to the attitude of the Secretary of State and policies of the Government as making the employers' task "monumentally difficult"; and called upon the teachers' unions to reconsider their refusal to settle.

The usual August break in teachers' pay negotiations was abruptly interrupted by two statements by the Secretary of State. The first on 5th August was of most significance when he announced how much cash would be available for pay structure reform in 1986/1987 and over the following three years. £200m. was to be available in 1986/1987, rising in broadly equal steps to a maximum of up to £450m. in 1989/1990, amounting to £1.25b. over the four years. The strings attached to this were (a) agreement by 11th October which secured satisfactory progress towards the Government's objectives; (b) an end to the disruption in schools with 1985 pay levels to be negotiated with no extra cash beyond the 3% in the RSG formula; and (c) 53% of the £200m. in 1986/1987 to be found by the local authorities under the RSG formula. Two broad objectives on structural reform were set by the Secretary of State: a clear definition of the range of teachers' duties linked to their contracts of employment (excluding midday supervision of pupils) plus a structure with more promotional opportunities for the better teachers combined with promotion arrangements and differentials designed to recruit, retain and motivate teachers of the right quality throughout the structure.

The LACSAB secretariat and their officer advisers faced and accomplished a daunting task to produce revised structural proposals which would meet the approval of the Secretary of State in time for a side meeting on 20th August and which were then put to the teachers on 12th September at a Burnham meeting. LGM of October 1985 records that the teachers took a mere 20 minutes before returning to announce their rejection because the 1985/1986 pay increase was too low and without examining the important structure reform proposals. At this stage the Burnham proceedings became even more bizarre than normal as, when the teachers were reluctant to enter into informal discussions "behind the chair", the independent chairman, Sir John Wordie, endeavoured to keep the discussions from total collapse by putting a series of questions to the representatives of both panels who returned with their response, usually in the form of another question. The employers were determined not to disaggregate their package proposals, but said the package was negotiable even although the cost exceeded the Secretary of State's £200m. The teachers were asked whether they would discuss the whole package if it were increased to provide 6.9% during the current year, gave every teacher 7%, and had a full year effect of 7.43%, but the eventual question to this hypothetical question was negative. As it was evident that the teachers were not seriously considering the structure reform proposals, the employers indicated their view that negotiations had broken down, no further meeting was arranged and, with a NUT conference decision blocking the route to arbitration, they approached ACAS to see if they could assist. Also in August the Secretary of State announced his proposal (justified by teacher association membership returns) to reconstitute the membership of the teachers' panel, reducing by three the seats held by the NUT, thus depriving them of their overall majority. At the conclusion of the Burnham meeting on 12th September prospects looked especially bleak as the major teachers' unions resumed industrial action, but there was a faint ray of hope that the changes in the teachers' panel to be effected in November might possibly help in some way.

No joint meetings took place for some time although the two panels met separately to explore areas for a settlement. Expectations that the newly constituted teachers' panel would on 11th November decide on a new initiative were dashed as the discussions were inconclusive. The position improved slightly when the teachers' panel met again on 5th December after the lecturers' union (NATFHE) had been finally removed and by a majority vote agreed on a "new approach", dropping the immediate commitment to restoration of Houghton levels, but making it clear the last informal offer of 6.9% end-loaded to 7.5% was not enough to end the 1985 dispute. A period of intense activity and informal talks ensued in December with a better atmosphere but with no means being found to bridge the gap. Eventually the employers asked the teachers to consider a fresh approach to ACAS, who with great alacrity invited both panels for informal exploratory discussions which took place quickly on 7th and 8th January 1986, with the NUT insisting on separate representation. The ACAS discussions were fruitful and led to a joint meeting on 14th January, special conferences of the NUT and NAS/UWT on 18th January, and further protracted joint talks at ACAS on 24th January when eventually agreement was reached in the form of a lengthy memorandum of agreement signed by the employers and five out of the six teacher unions, NUT dissenting. The memorandum was in five clauses setting out (i) introduction and objectives, including commitment to negotiate on salary levels and structure; (ii) the 1985 settlement on the basis of a 6.9% increase from 1st April 1985 and an additional 1.6% from 31st March 1985; (iii) future procedure including the appointment by ACAS of an independent and impartial panel to guide, advise and assist the negotiating parties; (iv) cessation of all industrial action; and (v) ratification and adoption.

Despite serious misgivings about the financial implications and absence of endorsement by the NUT, a well-attended meeting of representatives from all education authorities ratified the agreement. The next hurdle was ratification by the NAS/UWT who balloted their members and on 26th February announced a result of nearly 70% in favour of the agreement. But a serious problem arose on the clause relating to cessation of industrial action, a key issue being letters issued by 70% of authorities expressing a view on the contractual duties of teachers. This led to further discussions at ACAS on 26th, 27th and 28th February (the latter ending at 3.0am and with the NUT absent). The drama continued at a Burnham meeting on 28th February with the problem still unresolved, but at a subsequent Burnham meeting on 3rd March agreement was finally registered but leaving much to be sorted out at local level.

Meanwhile the farce continued as the ACAS agreement of 24th January had to be ratified in respect of matters not within the scope of Burnham by the non-statutory CLEA/ST where the NUT used their majority position to block the adoption of the ACAS agreement. This was however neatly sidestepped by the chairman asking just the parties to the agreement to adopt it as was required.

So the way was now clear for the first meeting under the auspices of ACAS and this took place on 7th March with the ACAS-appointed panel chaired by Sir John

A teacher giving piano lessons.

Wood. Yet another hurdle had to be surmounted as ACAS had invited the NUT. The employers welcomed the NUT but said it was essential they should signify their assent to the ACAS agreement before taking part. This the NUT refused to do, so everybody else involved decided to carry on without them, setting up four working groups to consider each area. The NUT then set about gaining entry to the talks by a number of routes. First they applied unsuccessfully to the High Court, and then on appeal to the Court of Appeal, to subject to judicial review the decision to proceed without them. Secondly they held a series of meetings with employer representatives to test alternative arrangements for them to participate. Thirdly they threatened sustained strike action in 21 areas represented by national employer members.

When all this had failed the NUT requisitioned a Burnham meeting to consider their claim for an immediate 1986 pay increase and this took place on 9th May. There was a surprisingly encouraging response when the employers first sought assurances on cessation of industrial strife and co-operation in the ACAS talks before any talks could begin on any pay increases from 1st April 1986. Assurances were given by all the teacher unions including the NUT and a pay deal was quickly struck giving increases of £519 or 5.5% whichever was the greater, costing 5.73% overall.

After the four working groups had completed their tasks and cleared the ground, the talks under ACAS auspices moved into higher gear at a residential meeting held at Coventry at the end of July with detailed negotiations designed to establish a secure framework for the future. The employers had prepared an outline package with four objectives: (i) definition of teachers' duties into a contractually binding agreement; (ii) streamlining of grade structure with new levels emphasising the crucial importance of the classroom teacher; (iii) an appraisal system; and (iv) reform of negotiating machinery to combine consideration of pay and other conditions. The centrepiece was a main professional grade (MPG) of £9,600 to £14,000 over 12 years. The Coventry talks certainly set new LACSAB records for the longest meeting (four and a half days) and the longest night (4.30am). The inordinate time taken was due in no small measure to the uniquely competitive structure of teacher unionism, as well as "dishevelled negotiators struggling to improve on Roget well past the witching hour" (LGM of October 1986). These Herculean efforts were rewarded by the "heads of agreement" outcome representing a framework of agreement in principle covering duties; working time, non- contact time and maximum class sizes; midday supervision; grade and salary structure (with MPG of £9,600 to £14,500); entry grade assessment and performance appraisal; and negotiating machinery. The employers had secured agreement but not without concessions which added much extra cost: LACSAB estimated the extra cost in 1986/1987 would be £364.2m. (Government target £200m.) with a cumulative cost by 1989/1990 of £1,748.6m. (Government target £1,250m.) Many outstanding issues remained to be settled, including a final list of teachers' contractual duties, the number of working hours per year, maximum class size, amount of non-teaching periods, and new negotiating machinery. At the beginning of August the full employers' side endorsed the Coventry agreement by 22 votes to one on condition the remaining issues would be dealt with satisfactorily. Much then depended on central government providing adequate new money as employer leaders met Kenneth Baker, the new Secretary of State, on 12th September. But Kenneth Baker did not see himself merely in a paymaster role, did not like the shape of the agreed salary structure, and was concerned about career opportunities for teachers. So his response was to publish at the end of October his detailed proposals based closely on the Main report recommendations for Scotland (within a cost envelope of 16.4%) and to issue an ultimatum that the negotiators should agree a deal on this basis or he would impose it. This led to marathon discussions between the employers and the teachers at Nottingham breaking all records and lasting seven days (and nights) in a last attempt to reach a freely negotiated agreement covering all outstanding issues in the belief that this was preferable to a solution imposed by the Secretary of State against the wish of the teachers. Among many detailed decisions in the agreement eventually reached on 15th November the MPG was now to be a 13-point scale from £9,970 to £15,508 after staging, and a new national joint council would be established to negotiate pay and conditions, with the role of the Secretary of State in it to be discussed with him. The ACAS-led talks were reconvened on 21st November back in London to register final agreement subject to ratification.

Another objection of Kenneth Baker was to the proposals for a national joint council which he believed would simply perpetuate old problems. So late in 1986 he took the dramatic step to introduce the Teachers' Pay and Conditions Bill to repeal the Remuneration of Teachers Act 1965 and to empower him to determine teachers' pay and service conditions without the direct participation of employers or unions (although there would be provision for consultation with an interim advisory committee). This brief but draconian Bill provoked the obvious hostile reaction from the teachers' unions; aroused concerted opposition from the employers irrespective of party colour; but was nevertheless rushed through the House of Commons. The employers at meetings on 2nd and 19th December reaffirmed their commitment to a negotiated (not imposed) solution and to machinery that would allow collective bargaining. They also agreed modifications to the agreement to overcome reservations about superstructure expressed by two smaller teacher unions. With the Secretary of State in a very strong position the employers and unions did not despair and the ACAS agreement was ratified on 7th January 1987 at meetings of the Burnham committee and CLEA/ST subject to appropriate funding by the Government.

After 50 hours of debate in both houses, the Teachers' Pay and Conditions Act 1987 entered the statute book on 2nd March, largely unaltered except for some cosmetic textual changes. And so the Burnham committees ceased to exist: whilst this could not be entirely unexpected, it so happened there was much frustration in both the employer and teacher camps that much frantic effort over many months had come to nothing. Also on 2nd March Kenneth Baker published revised proposals on pay and conditions in the form of a draft Order and differing only slightly from his October 1986 package. These proposals would be introduced by stages on 1st January 1987 and 1st October 1987 and included extending the basic scale by two points to £7,600 to £13,300, introducing five levels of incentive allowances and spot salaries for heads and deputies, and incorporating provisions relating to duties and hours into teachers' contracts. A short period of consultation resulted in minimal textual changes. The first Order under the new 1987 Act was laid before Parliament on

9th April and came into force on 30th April 1987. The major teacher unions embarked on industrial action and the Easter conferences saw the unusual spectacle of a rapprochement between the NUT and the NAS/UWT as they united to request a meeting with the Prime Minister (which she declined) to seek restoration of negotiating rights in return for a cessation of all industrial action.

The period came to a close with the industrial action petering out after the June 1987 general election with the employers and unions sorting out details of a national joint council for schoolteachers, conscious that central government would have to be involved, and Kenneth Baker promising to publish a Green Paper in the autumn of 1987 on teachers' pay machinery. But as LGM for August 1987 put it – "For once the great pay and conditions soap opera has been upstaged" as attention turned towards the Great Education Reform Bill (otherwise known as "Gerbil") to be presented in the autumn.

FURTHER EDUCATION

The proceedings in the Burnham further education committee in the period 1980 to 1987 were also not without their moments of farce, especially after the Secretary of State late in 1981 awarded a seat on it to the Association of Polytechnic Teachers (APT) in the teeth of opposition from all sides. At the meeting in February 1982 when the APT took their seat NATFHE and the other unions displayed their strength of feeling by walking out, leaving the employers facing the solitary APT representative. The employers made an offer of 2.5% to the APT representative who rejected it. The other unions did not comment on it when it was brought to their notice afterwards, but NATFHE took some limited industrial action in some areas in protest. However agreement was reached at the next meeting on increases from 1st April 1982 at an overall cost of 5.8%, including a general increase of 5% plus £69. By this time the other unions had acquiesced in APT having a representative in the joint body but refused to allow him into their side meetings. As all the detailed discussion had taken place "behind the chair", it was only in the final brief formal session that the APT representative could express his views against the settlement. It was much the same scene when settlement was reached on 6th May 1983 for increases all round of 4.5% plus £51 from 1st April 1983, adding another 4.95% to the paybill.

There was a change of tack by the unions when in 1984 they decided against the usual plethora of claims and concentrated on seeking a combination of lecturers' grades 1 and 2. The initial response of the employers was to suggest a wide-ranging review of structure and conditions in which this could be considered, and to offer a general 3% increase which was rejected. A further meeting resulted in a provisional settlement giving a general increase of 4% from 1st April 1984 and a lump sum of £330 at the maximum of lecturer grade 1, within a total cost of 4.45%. It was a bold move to settle in advance of schoolteachers and it did not come as a great surprise when on 22nd May NATFHE's national council rejected the provisional settlement and sent their negotiators back to do better. At a meeting on 8th June an unquantified higher offer was sought and industrial action was threatened, and on 11th June a redistribution of the 4.5% package was offered and rejected. The employers proposed arbitration, this was agreed, and the industrial action was called off. When the issue got to arbitration in August the arbitrators fell out between themselves and the chairman acted as umpire by giving a ruling decision. The outcome was an award amounting to 5.1% overall, comprising 4.6% throughout and the £330 lump sum on the grade 1 maximum as in the provisional settlement.

The 1985 round began with the lecturers lodging a claim for 40% increases based on restoration of Houghton levels at a Burnham meeting on 23rd November 1984. The initial employer response was a speech by their leader, John Pearman, stressing the vital need for a radical review of pay and conditions. Thirteen hours of intensive negotiations on 21st March 1985 failed to produce a settlement after the employers had made an offer of 4% which was rejected. Developments in schoolteachers' pay negotiations and county council elections were factors which caused a suspension of talks during which there was some sporadic industrial action by NATFHE members. Two days of prolonged negotiations led to a deal being struck just before midnight on 15th July which would add 5.82% to the year's paybill. The basic increase was 5% from 1st April 1985 with a further 2% to follow from 1st December 1985, the latter increase conditional on progress on structure reform and conditions, together with feasibility and quantification of economies. It was not until well after the summer break on 30th September that the NATFHE national council ratified the agreement on a close vote. This delay caused some panic when it was realised that a change in national insurance rules affected all earnings after 6th October 1985, eventually resolved by LACSAB advice for "on account" payments in the September pay packets.

Although the 1985 two-stage settlement had been conditional upon progress on structure reform, little was achieved in the subsequent talks, much to the regret of the employers. So when the lecturers put in a claim in 1986 for a 20.5% increase from 1st April 1986 the employers renewed their efforts to achieve structure reform. Much work eventually resulted in a joint statement which outlined the matters to be negotiated to produce by that October meaningful reforms which would increase the flexibility and responsiveness of the service. This statement was agreed after a lengthy meeting of the NJC for further education teachers which established the acceptance in principle by both sides of the statement and a pay award. A meeting of the Burnham F.E. committee then followed immediately formally to agree a "without prejudice" pay increase of 5.5% or £519 whichever was the greater. A series of working groups was set up for detailed joint talks to culminate in a residential meeting on 18th to 20th October. Meanwhile a pamphlet was issued to all local education authorities giving good practice guidance on managing the further education service. The advice in it had been prepared by LACSAB officers and advisers and, for example, drew attention to the degree of flexibility already allowed in the scheme of conditions of service. Difficulties were however encountered in November in the structure reform talks when the unions refused to discuss employer proposals on reform of service conditions but pressed to move the talks on to pay structure. The lecturers had balked at an employer proposal for a new maximum of class contact time which they suspected would become a "norm" and thus lead to redundancies which the employers did not believe would occur. This led to a "pause" in the negotiations in which NATFHE balloted members on an overtime ban to take effect from 1st January 1987 to bring the employers back to the negotiating table with a "fresh attitude". The ballot result was in favour of industrial action and LACSAB issued advice to minimise its effects which in the event proved to be patchy.

A series of meetings early in 1987 led to the employers offering at an NJC meeting on 27th March a pay rise which would increase the paybill by 9.3% costing 7.1% in the year 1987/1988. This offer was linked to a package of service conditions reforms, and the employers asked for a suspension of industrial action while talks continued. No real progress was made by the time the NJC met on 23rd July with the likelihood looming of escalation of the NATFHE industrial action in September. But the employers were determined not to release the "carrot" of an attractive 1987 pay increase without the "quid pro quo" of agreed reform, and they then proceeded to publicise widely details of their proposals which they believed had not been fully understood in the further education service.

SOULBURY COMMITTEE AND YOUTH AND COMMUNITY WORKERS

Events of significance in this period 1980 to 1987 in the Soulbury Committee (which straddles the teacher/administrator divide) included agreement on a new salary structure for school meals organisers in 1985. Severe problems were faced in 1987 after the Government had imposed the 16.4% for schoolteachers. The employers eventually succeeded in September 1987 after acrimonious negotiations and ACAS conciliation – not in fact until December 1987 in respect of education psychologists – in severing their pay link with schoolteachers. This they also achieved, but again not without many difficulties, in May 1987 in the JNC for youth and community workers with agreement on revised pay scales and the introduction of a job and grade structure review.

STAFFING AND PEOPLE

In many respects this period 1980 to 1987 was relatively stable in terms of staffing at LACSAB. Although there was a steady stream of people appointed and departing for a variety of reasons, there was not the flood proportions experienced in the 1970s – this change no doubt reflecting the employment market situation generally. The accommodation position too had settled down with the advantage of operating from adjacent premises at 41 and 38 Belgrave Square.

However there was a serious setback to the programme of reconstruction and refurbishment of 41 Belgrave Square when on Friday 16th January 1987 the early starters at LACSAB arrived to find the building devastated by gallons of water gushing from a fractured (and previously frozen) pipe on the third floor. Because of "the flood" all staff working at No.41 had to be evacuated to temporary accommodation in Greycoat Place SW1 for several months.

J.K.(Ken) Woods left early in 1981 after eight years as deputy secretary for a post in industry in the USA. His main negotiating roles had been on the white-collar side, but he may be most remembered for his major contribution to pay and manpower information systems. He brought much breadth and depth of vision to LACSAB, exemplified in the major studies in social services and environmental health. David Thomas who was appointed to succeed him as deputy secretary and took up his duties in September 1981, had extensive experience of local government manpower matters, having been previously at LACSAB between 1963 and 1968, and subsequently county personnel officer at Surrey and under secretary (manpower) at the AMA.

Tim Rothwell joined LACSAB as assistant secretary in March 1982 and took over responsibility for leading LACSAB's personnel and industrial relations advisory service which had languished for some while since the departure of Frank Walton. January 1984 saw the retirement of the veteran LACSAB stalwart, Alisdair Campbell, after 19 years at Belgrave Square, mostly in the thick of manual workers' negotiations in close association with his fellow Scot, Harry Rae. Another familiar figure left the LACSAB negotiating scene as Steve Rouse took up a post in charge of university pay negotiations in April 1986. Steve had been at LACSAB since 1966, had experience in many negotiating spheres, and in latter years as assistant secretary for education had pioneered the development of a radically new approach to teachers' pay. Charles Nolda moved over from the Home Office section to lead the education section in place of Steve Rouse and Marcia Barton was promoted from the APT&C section as assistant secretary in charge of the Home Office section. The untimely death occurred in March 1986 of LACSAB staff member, Richard Giles, aged 38, familiar to many as "father of the chapel", i.e. chairman of the LACSAB branch of NALGO.

But the big event which brings this period to a close was the retirement in September 1987 of Brian Rusbridge after 15 years as LACSAB secretary. In his period of office he had experienced and survived many turbulences originating from a wide variety of sources – in marked contrast to the relatively tranquil times hitherto. The 1974 reorganisation of local government saw the emergence of the county policy barons and other likeminded local politicians with their very strong views on the funding of pay settlements, fuelled by the Government's relentless pressure through rate support grant and cash limit mechanisms. Brian's style was very different to that of his predecessor, Reginald Griffiths, and it took time for his LACSAB colleagues and his trade union counterparts to adjust to it, but he very quickly sensed the political pulse of elected members. He was always very sensitive to the needs and feelings of his LACSAB staff. He did much to bring openness to negotiations through the sharing of all pay and manpower data: he could see no sense in endless arguments on the accuracy of figures which should be agreed in advance. It was he who built up enormously the LACSAB capability on manpower and pay information and in the personnel and industrial relations advisory services. Allied to a durable toughness Brian had a good sense of humour as well as the nerves for such a daunting job, being able to switch off from his work totally and swiftly (although his habit of switching back on again by retrieving his memory in front of those assembled could be infuriating). Tony Prendergast, the LACSAB chairman, called Brian "Squirrel Nutkin" – "a tribute to his ability to find money in cocoa tins buried in the Square...as he balanced the books and scratched around to keep the ship afloat". There many were tributes to Brian – who was awarded the CBE in 1984 – from leading members, trade union leaders and LACSAB colleagues as he "relinquished his responsibilities". David Thomas, who had been LACSAB deputy secretary since 1981 and who had extensive experience in local government at local and national level, was appointed to succeed Brian Rusbridge.

Brian Rusbridge hands over to David Thomas who became Secretary of the Board in 1987, having been Deputy for the previous six years

As to elected members, the most important event occurred in April 1983 when John Lovill stood down after five and a half years as LACSAB chairman. Although John Lovill had assumed office as LACSAB chairman through a political coup in October 1977, he earned the respect of members of all political groups and of leading trade unionists as he exercised his skills as chairman in pulling divergent and polarised threads together to bring meetings to successful conclusions. There were many problems in his stint in negotiations with the unions and in endless trips to Whitehall when he was prepared to speak out on behalf of local government. He was awarded the CBE in 1983 and subsequently there much pleasure when he was knighted in 1987.

John Lovill was succeeded as LACSAB chairman by Councillor C.A.(Tony) Prendergast CBE who had been a member of Westminster City Council since 1959 and was also a member of the AMA policy committee and manpower sub-committee, as well as serving on the employers' side of the NJC for manual workers since 1978.

1983 saw the retirement from the LACSAB board at the ripe old age of 83 of Sir Leo Schultz who had been a LACSAB member since 1957 and chairman from 1973 to 1978. His colleagues at their meeting in July 1983 presented Sir Leo with a vellom scroll on which it said – "his invaluable contribution has been vital to the inauguration and development of a national bargaining system which had brought stability and order to the industrial relations of local authorities throughout the land".

A Council surveyor.

9 ALL CHANGE!

"An experienced colleague, momentarily lost for words to sum up the Government's plans for local government in the Queen's Speech, suddenly smiled. 'Gotcha', he said. As the full impact of what promises to be the most wide-ranging incursion into local powers this century began to sink in, there were many in local government who feared that after years of heavy shelling from the Government they had finally been holed below the water line."

(Douglas Broom, Press Association, in LGM of August 1987 on the Queen's Speech and local government)

This period begins with the confirmation in power of the Thatcher government in the 1987 general election heralding an extensive range of proposals which would reduce still further the powers of local government. Many of these impacted a great deal on the work of LACSAB, particularly in the education sector. As the period came to an end, John Major replaced Margaret Thatcher as Prime Minister amidst speculation as to whether changes in Government policies would impact on local government and the work of LACSAB.

David Thomas, the new LACSAB secretary, sought to ensure that LACSAB could influence and shape its own destiny by initiating extensive consultations on future employer strategy, accepting the challenge to face up to change. But then "review fever" set in. First a review body set up to look at LACSAB's funding saw a strong future for LACSAB whilst proposing some radical changes. This was quickly followed by another review body set up under the same mechanism to review the funding of the LGTB taking a fundamentally different course and recommending that the LGTB, LACSAB and LAMSAC should all be swept away and replaced by a Local Government Management Board(LGMB).

The creation of the new Local Government Management Board was not without difficulties. At the heart of much squabbling about representation was the issue of the future role of the provincial organisations and how much influence they could wield in respect of national pay negotiations. As Alan Hoskins, the Yorkshire and Humberside provincial employers' secretary put it in their 50th anniversary report in 1990 – "Déjàvu or plus ca change".

So the day-to-day work at Belgrave Square had to continue to be carried out by apprehensive officers in the context of a rapidly changing local government, a reduction in the scope and influence of national pay bargaining, and in the throes of contradictory proposals for the radical reform of local government's national organisations, which eventually led in April 1991 to the demise of LACSAB as a separate entity after over 40 years' existence – but its work transferred to the newly formed LGMB.

POLITICAL AND ECONOMIC CONTEXT

The second half of 1987 was noticeable for a sharp increase in the gross national product, rising to 5.3% at the end of 1987 (compared with 3.9% a year earlier) and up still further to 6.3% in the first quarter of 1988 before falling to 5.0% in the third quarter of 1988. This generally buoyant economic situation (for which Chancellor of the Exchequer, Nigel Lawson, was much criticised subsequently) was reflected in other indices, notably unemployment figures which continued to drop and had by the end of 1988 fallen below two millions for the first time for many years. This buoyancy was also shown in increases in average earnings with the underlying annual percentage increase rising from 8.25% in mid-1987 up to 9.25% in August 1988 before shading off slightly to 8.75% towards the end of 1988. Retail price increases reached a temporary plateau of 4.4% in mid-1987, fell to 3.3% at the beginning of 1988, and then crept inexorably upwards to reach 6.8% by the close of 1988, the highest increase for many years.

In 1989 increases in the underlying average earnings hovered around 9% throughout the year, well ahead of price increases which ranged between 7.5% and 8.3%. But by August 1990 price increases overtook underlying increases in average earnings which at July 1990 stood at 10.0%. The trend for pay exceeding prices had been set by the motor industry, notably Fords, whose 1989 two-year deal broke the psychologically important 10% barrier and was worth 10.2% in the first year while the second stage turned out to be worth 13.4% as it was pegged to the October 1990 price index (10.9%) plus 2.5%.

One of the longest industrial disputes ever began in September 1989 when ambulance crews in the National Health Service started limited industrial action on their claim for a pay index similar to that for firemen. The employers stuck to their 6.5% offer while senior civil servants gained 8.7%, and the unions escalated the ambulance dispute as qualified ambulance crews refused to carry out non-emergency work. The Government refused to budge and relentlessly insisted that union claims could be defeated and settled below the level of inflation, even when public opinion was substantially with the ambulancemen. The six-month dispute ended in March 1990 as the unions accepted a complex two-year agreement which they reckoned was worth 17.6% over the period, whilst the employers stressed it added only 13.3% to the paybill. Of more importance ultimately was the fact that the settlement did not contain a pay formula mechanism which had been one of the unions' central demands.

A movement of some significance occurred in 1989 when in the engineering industry there were several local settlements for the phased introduction of a 37-hour week as the unions singled out one employer after another in their campaign of industrial action.

1990 was marked by a large number of high pay settlements in the retail sector and, under the threat of claims for equal pay for equal value, many of the high street chain stores instituted job evaluation exercises, mainly to see how the jobs of sales staff compared with those of warehouse workers.

During this period from 1987 onwards the strong hand of central government in influencing pay levels in local government through the rate support grant and cash limit mechanisms was proving very effective, taken very much for granted, and not causing the furore of earlier years. For example there is scant reference to the rate support grant settlement for the year 1988/1989 in the minutes of the

LACSAB Board or in LGE. However the secretary's report to the LACSAB Board in January 1988 makes the assumption that RSG for 1988/1989 would be 4%, and it was then agreed that the attention of chairmen of employers' sides be drawn to the continuing difficult financial position of local authorities. At the previous meeting in October 1987 the LACSAB Board had been told that the Secretary of State for the Environment, Nicholas Ridley, did not wish to revive the traditional annual meeting between LACSAB representatives and ministers, preferring instead smaller meetings on specific topics as they arose.

A meeting did take place on 11th May 1989 between representatives of LACSAB and the Environment Secretary at LACSAB's request arising from concern about an adverse negotiating position outside their control. The RSG allowance was only 4.8% but price increases were running at 7.9% and average earnings were stuck at 9.25%. Elsewhere in the public sector there were settlements of the order of 7% and 7.5%. In particular the APT&C negotiations were not going well and the employers had hardly been helped by the Civil Service increases amounting to about 9% overall. The Secretary of State acknowledged the problems; restated the Government's view that it was essential to the economy that pay increases be kept to the minimum; and stressed there would be no adjustment to RSG.

LACSAB took the opportunity of this meeting to question the Government's attitude to pay bargaining and were told by the Environment Secretary that the Government remained of the view that the emphasis in pay bargaining should be shifted from national to local level. The position on the ground was that a number of small authorities had decided to settle pay locally, usually by adjusting national agreements to suit their local circumstances, but in January 1990 the LACSAB Board were informed of the first example of a major local authority (Kent County Coucil) introducing its own pay arrangements with the prospect of withdrawing altogether from the national agreements.

The effects of the Government's measures to constrain the finances of local authorities could be seen in the quarterly joint staffing watch figures which showed a gradual decrease in staffing levels, falling to below 1,900,000 staff from June 1989 onwards.

EMPLOYMENT LEGISLATION

The Employment Bill introduced in Parliament in the autumn of 1987 represented the Government's fourth bid to rein in the unions in their step-by-step approach through the Employment Acts of 1980 and 1982 and the 1984 Trade Union Act. The consequent Employment Act 1988 received royal assent in July 1988 and covered the regulation of trade unions and their relationships with their members, although dealing too with employment and training. The provisions affecting trade unions included rights of trade union members; use of trade union funds; removal of statutory protection for closed shops; amended provisions on ballots and trade union elections; and the creation of a new Commissioner for the rights of trade union members. The LACSAB Advisory Division produced detailed advice to local authorities on this new legislation. The 1988 Act was quickly followed by a draft code of practice on trade union industrial action balloting. The Government's step-by-step approach continued unabated with the publication at the beginning of 1989 of another Employment

Bill proposing the repealing or amending of employment protection legislation which in their view acted as a barrier to employment growth generally. This was passed in Parliament and so the Employment Act 1989 received royal assent on 16th November 1989.

As widely predicted following the summer's disputes on the public sector transport system, the Government later in 1989 issued their proposals to limit unofficial industrial action in their Green Paper – "Unofficial action and the law: proposals to reform the law affecting unofficial industrial action". Behind these proposals lay the Government's view that unofficial industrial action was a major and longstanding problem which was disproportionately damaging to businesses and jobs because of its unpredictable and disruptive nature.

In the Queen's Speech on 21st November 1989 the Government proposed a further Employment Bill to enact the March 1989 Green Paper proposals to introduce measures to end the pre-entry closed shop and the further Green Paper on unofficial action. LGE reported in October 1990 that this Bill had not yet received royal assent and was to return to the House of Commons that month for its final stages. This would be the Government's sixth piece of legislation in their continuing approach to the reform of industrial relations. Also a new Social Security Bill would introduce proposals to provide protection for members of occupational pension schemes.

LOCAL GOVERNMENT CONTEXT

The extensive range of proposals in the Queen's Speech after the 1987 general election continued unabated the Thatcher government's approach of changing drastically the powers and duties of local authorities. Quite apart from the controversial community charge proposals, the Government intended to offer six million council tenants the right to choose a different landlord and to revive the Local Government Bill which fell because of the election, its key elements being the requirement to go out to private tender in six new services, together with curbs on publicity and on "contract compliance" (which had nevertheless worked successfully for over 20 years in the USA). In education the proposal to allow schools to opt out of local authority control would further reduce local government's role.

The Local Government Act 1988 was eventually enacted in May 1988 bringing in compulsory competitive tendering in the six specified services in phases beginning on 1st August 1989. This and other legislation led to many requests to the LACSAB Advisory Division for advice on the employment law implications of reorganisations and transfers, and a new LACSAB Employer Guide – No. 13 in the series – was produced to cover these topics.

In many ways the biggest blockbuster in the Government's programme affecting local government was the Education Reform Bill eventually published on 20th November 1987. The objective of the Government's proposals was to concentrate more power at the centre and in the hands of head teachers and governing bodies – in both directions at the expense of the local education authorities (LEAs). This package proposed the most extensive shake-up of the education system since the 1944 Act. Individual schools would be able to opt out of LEA control; financial management would have to be devolved to school level (except for the smaller primary schools); and there would be a national core curriculum. Boroughs could also opt out of the Inner London Education Authority (ILEA) but this was overtaken by the abolition of ILEA from 1st April 1990. Many aspects of these wide-ranging proposals directly impinged on the work of LACSAB, with the most curious paradox emerging in the Government's attitude to LEAs as employers. Whilst they confirmed LEAs would be the employers of staffs in schools not opting out of LEA control, they proposed that LEAs should have no powers of appointment of schools staffs, other than in the smallest schools. The Education Reform Act duly received Royal Assent on 29th July 1988, leaving LEAs only until 30th September 1989 to prepare their schemes to implement financial delegation. LACSAB had expressed major reservations related to the employment implications of the proposed legislation, and extensive advice was made available to LEAs to enable them to prepare for the many changes ahead of them.

LACSAB was involved in giving advice on the personnel management implications of the provisions of the Local Government and Housing Bill published early in 1989 which would restrict the political activities of employees in "politically restricted posts", including the prohibition of "twintracking" - whereby a local authority employee is also an elected member of another local authority. Despite difficulties in the House of Lords the Local Government and Housing Act 1989 received Royal Assent on 16th November 1989. Following this the Secretary of State issued regulations prescribing the type of political activities in which politically restricted postholders would be restricted from engaging, as well as defining which would become "sensitive posts". The LACSAB Advisory Division gave much detailed advice to authorities on various aspects of the Act, especially as the Local Government Officers (Political Restrictions) Regulations 1990 made under the 1989 Act came into force on 1st May 1990. This Act had some implications for pay bargaining as the effect of Section 12 was to prevent local government employees or officials of local government trade unions from serving on the employers' sides of any body at local, provincial or national level responsible for negotiating the terms and conditions of employment of local government staff.

The Government's legislation on competitive compulsory tendering (CCT) under the Local Government Act 1988 continued to occupy much attention throughout local government and attracted several articles in LGE. The unions got their act together to produce in 1988 a joint guide - "Who Cares Wins" - and then subsequently further booklets for each of the "defined" services. LGE of June 1989 reported that the NJC for manual workers agreed to publish a document entitled - "Changing Employment Practices" - commenting on the changes to local authority practice brought about by the introduction of CCT, arguably the most important issue affecting manual workers in the history of the NJC. February 1990 saw the re-launch of the Competitive Tendering Information Service by LACSAB on behalf of the LGTB specifically for the benefit of local authorities. The service, based on information from authorities, was commissioned by the local authority associations who fully supported the project which involved a database as a central contact point through which local authorities could obtain information necessary for the tendering process.

LGE of April 1989 reported a significant development in the local government trade union sphere in that a joint committee of NALGO and NUPE had been set up to hold exploratory discussions on the possible merger of the two unions. At this stage NALGO already supported the merger, but no firm proposals were to be agreed before 1990. These discussions appeared to be progressing satisfactorily as 1990 drew to a close, with another union, COHSE, being drawn into the talks, so that the merger could produce the largest union in the UK with around 1.6 million members.

OVERALL LACSAB ACTIVITIES

It was off to a good start at the first meeting of the LACSAB Board in October 1987 after the Rusbridge/Thomas handover with agreement on a consultation document on future employer strategy which it was agreed should be widely circulated throughout local government. There was relief at Belgrave Square that the consultation exercise would be conducted by LACSAB – rather than by the local authority associations - and local views were to be fed back by February 1988. The consultation document attracted a great deal of attention, and at the next LACSAB Board meeting in January 1988 it was reported that 6,000 copies had been distributed. Arrangements were agreed for the feedback to be collated and analysed and to be considered at a conference of about 90 senior local government representatives on 25th April 1988.

This "Lords" conference (held at the Lords cricket ground) did not produce much in the way of excitement or revolution. David Thomas was able to comment in LGE of June 1988 that "what emerged was consensus, common sense and a realistic agenda for the future". The conference discussed seven draft resolutions prepared by the LACSAB secretary which were all adopted subject to minor changes and one further resolution proposed by the AMA was also adopted. The eight resolutions carried and subsequently adopted by the LACSAB Board at their meeting in July –

(1) Overwhelmingly supported collective bargaining, recognised the need for change, and recommended (a) arrangements should ensure employer representatives could negotiate with employee representatives; (b) both parties should honour joint agreements and resolve problems peacefully by negotiation; and (c) procedures for conciliation and arbitration.

(2) Recommended retention of joint negotiating machinery at national level for all negotiating groups as there was virtually no support for abandoning national negotiating arrangements.

(3) Accepted the strong desire for the main national agreements to be simpler, more consistent with each other, and reduced to provide more local flexibility; and called for proposals from LACSAB on how these objectives could be achieved.

(4) Called for a report from LACSAB on how improved co-ordination between the separate employers' sides could be achieved (including reducing the number of employers' sides).

(5) Recommended that criticism that communications needed to be improved between LACSAB and local authorities should be drawn to the attention of all national employers' sides; and whilst taking the view that other measures recommended should ease these problems, recommended LACSAB to consider later whether fundamental changes were needed.

(6) Noted the general wish for more employer advice from national and

provincial level; asked LACSAB and provincial employers' organisations to work together on this; and for LACSAB to report in due course.

(7) Had regard to different views on a more strategic across-the-board approach to pay bargaining and a more systematic method of determining pay, recommending further consideration of this by LACSAB; and recommended the main strategy in the short term should be to seek streamlining of main national agreements, closer co-ordination and improved communications.

(8) Supported views that local government should continue to be a "good employer", with particular reference to equal opportunities, low pay, single status and the merit principle; and endorsed the need for all national agreements to reflect the "good employer" role.

The LACSAB Board at their July 1988 meeting considered in depth two key issues arising from the "Lords" conference - streamlining national agreements and employer co-ordination. On the issue of simplification of the main national agreements (i.e. those covering groups employed in all types of authorities) it was noted that there had been different emphases placed on the need for greater flexibility which seemed to be about the method and timescale for achieving this and which subjects should be retained in the national agreement. The Board agreed in principle that the "core" conditions which should apply to all groups should cover (a) the principles that should govern the local determination of policies on such matters as procedures for local negotiation, consultation and grievances; (b) the main conditions to be laid down nationally, i.e. public holidays and annual leave, maternity leave and pay; and (c) the disputes procedures (whether national or local). Each negotiating body should then be left to determine its own approaches on matters outside the core, deciding which should remain inside the national agreement, e.g. national pay structures and basic hours, and which ideally should be phased out or capable of variation by local agreement.

The desire to improve co-ordination between national employers' sides and to reduce their number had been strongly expressed but this raised potentially controversial and complex issues. Steps would be taken immediately to improve co-ordination between existing employers' sides and to seek to reduce by five the number of employers' sides through the merging of some small bodies. The concept of a single employers' organisation for APT&C, manual and craft employees was agreed in principle and extensive consultations would now proceed as this raised two fundamental and sensitive issues: whether the provincial employers' organisations should continue to be represented; and whether the present balance between the local authority associations needed reviewing. This challenged the traditional theory of the need for "checks and balances" between the views of various types of authority and of different regions.

The LACSAB Board had been advised at their meeting in January 1988 of the intention of the local authority associations to set up a review panel to look at the funding of LACSAB under Section 56(9) of the Local Government Planning and Land Act 1980 – under which the Secretary of State may deduct amounts from the aggregate block grant after consultations with the local authority associations. This "top slicing" arrangement was used to fund, at least in part, a number of bodies serving local government as a whole and at the time LACSAB got 32% of its income this way. Similar review panels were to look at the LGTB – and later other national bodies.

The review panel on LACSAB funding reported in July 1988 and saw “a strong future for LACSAB”. The report said there was “much evidence of how the negotiating work, the research and advice of LACSAB are valued by all users”. Its main recommendation was “that LACSAB should continue in being: it offers good value for money and does essential work for local government as a whole”. The review team concluded that a national employers' organisation remained a necessity but changes were needed, such as the continuing shift of emphasis and resources away from the negotiating function to advisory and research work. A review of the role of provincial employers' organisations would be timely and, whilst there must be close relationships between LACSAB and the LGTB, the panel came out against a single personnel organisation. The complexity of the LACSAB accounts made them very difficult to understand and they should be simplified to help identify how well funds were used. The panel considered the existing level of resources as about correct but looked for a shift in emphasis over the next three years in the sources of funding – away from Section 56(9) (which should be regarded as “core” funding for LACSAB work for local government as a whole) towards more income from fees, sales and certain levies which should rise gradually to 25% of the total. A most controversial recommendation was that the levy on local authorities should no longer be collected via the provincial system but directly by LACSAB which would then be more accountable, with a clearer identification of LACSAB's costs and individual authorities' contributions.

The immediate response of LACSAB secretary, David Thomas, was to congratulate the review team on a thorough and challenging report and to accept that they had made some sensible and necessary suggestions, whilst recognising that the plan for direct levying of authorities touched on a number of sensitive issues, particularly on the role of provincial employers' organisations. Action on the review body's recommendations soon followed. LACSAB agreed to freeze its grant under Section 56(9) for 1989/1990 at the cash levels for 1988/1989, to ask local authority pension funds to meet the costs of running the UKSC and to increase fee income – so as to reduce LACSAB's call on Section 56(9) funding.

The need to clarify relationships between LACSAB and the provincial employers' organisations had been a major feature both in LACSAB's own future employer strategy review and in the review of LACSAB's funding, but there were divergent views on how this should be tackled. An important step was taken when the LACSAB Board at their meeting in October 1988 accepted a suggestion by the local authority associations that discussion of the complex issues involved would best be handled by a small group representing all the interested parties (which was much to be preferred to earlier thoughts that the associations would alone consider this matter behind closed doors) but these discussions were soon overtaken by other events.

An architectural assistant on site.

When they reported in January 1989 the review panel which was supposed to be looking at the funding of the LGTB took a fundamentally different approach on important issues from that taken earlier by the LACSAB review panel. Their main proposition was that the LGTB, LACSAB and LAMSAC should be replaced in April 1991 by a single Local Government Management Board (LGMB) with members drawn solely from the local authority associations. The new board's terms of reference would incorporate the existing activities of the LGTB, LACSAB and LAMSAC revised as necessary to reflect future needs; it would have a single negotiating panel drawn solely from the associations (replacing the 450 members representing a variety of interests hitherto); and a regional network of offices would replace the existing provincial network. Quite apart from the effects of this sweeping proposal on those running the employer organisations at national and provincial levels, the trade unions would also lose their representation on the LGTB.

The LACSAB Board were able to give preliminary consideration to the LGTB review panel's findings at their meeting on 23rd January 1989 when – inter alia – they noted the report as a constructive contribution to the debate on the future of central bodies, but asked the LACSAB secretary to analyse the implications for the negotiating machinery. In his advice to the next LACSAB Board meeting on 17th April, David Thomas accepted that in principle the case for a single "manpower" body incorporating the functions of LACSAB, LGTB, LAMSAC and the provincial employers' organisations had always been persuasive; but he argued strongly that the review panel's report did not provide a sound basis for this. He drew attention to its major flaws:-

(1) **Funding.** The report advocated total reliance on RSG top slicing but this would risk undue influence from central government whereas a mixture of local authority levies, RSG top slice and fee income would enhance accountability to local authorities.

(2) **Regional Organisation and Representation.** The report advocated a small new body drawing all its members from the associations, but this would make it too remote from its customers. Membership of a new body should reflect a balance of different types of authority – through the associations – and different areas via regional organisations which were essential to ensure accountability and sensitivity to authorities' views and needs.

(3) **Functions and Scope.** The report concentrated on "strategic" training issues, but it was clear from the local authority feedback in the LACSAB strategy debate that there was a considerable and growing demand for practical, detailed advice and assistance over the entire personnel/employee relations field.

(4) **Negotiations.** The report proposed a single negotiating panel. But it was unrealistic to suppose that the existing pattern of employers' sides representing a multiplicity of employer interests could be absorbed into a small national body. The rationalisation of the numbers of employers' sides flowing from the LACSAB stategy debate should continue.

(5) **Trade Unions.** The report proposed a much reduced consultative role for the unions who would need to be reassured that the establishment of new employers' machinery would not of itself change the joint constitutions of the existing negotiating machinery nor disenfranchise them at national level on training policy.

On 19th June 1989, meeting together in the Central Bodies Advisory Group (CBAG), the local authority associations agreed to establish a Local Government Management Board (LGMB) to replace LACSAB, the LGTB and LAMSAC with effect from 1st April 1991. When their proposals were disseminated for consultation in July 1989 it was noticeable that several of the points made by the LACSAB secretary had been met. For example, although the new shadow board would be drawn only from the associations, there would be an employers' standing conference including representatives of national and provincial employers' organisations. There would also be a training forum on which the trade unions would be represented. The new board would be funded by a mix of RSG money, fee income and a national levy on local authorities. It was acknowledged that it would be difficult to resolve differences on the future role of provincial/regional organisations, their accountability and their boundaries, and a "continuing dialogue" was envisaged.

When the LACSAB Board met on 17th July 1989 they were reassured that the outline terms of reference for the new organisation fully recognised the three main areas of LACSAB's work - negotiating, research and advisory - and that it was intended that all existing functions of LACSAB were to be transferred to the new board. They noted, however, some ambiguity about the future position of employers' sides of national negotiating bodies and felt they must be free within overall Board policy to negotiate with the unions, and could not in any sense be subservient to an employers' standing conference. The LACSAB Board noted their obligation to consult the union (NALGO) representing LACSAB staff and that a group of their members had met LACSAB staff representatives earlier that day. The staff representatives had sought reassurances on continued employment and the safeguarding of terms and conditions of employment, including location, asking whether redundancies were contemplated. Leading members from the associations recognised the importance of LACSAB's work all of which would be transferred to the new organisation, and stressed that the larger existing LGTB would not be allowed in any sense to take precedence.

The LACSAB Board at their meetings in October 1989 and January 1990 received progress reports on the setting up of the new LGMB as from April 1991 and in particular took the necessary steps to consult LACSAB staff as well as to ensure adequate procedures for the transfer of responsibilities, bearing in mind LACSAB's status as a company limited by guarantee. Differing views emerged on the latter aspect and it was noted at the July 1990 meeting of the LACSAB Board that counsel's opinion was being sought. By this stage it was felt more sensible for consultation with existing LACSAB and LGTB staff to be with the chief executive of the LGMB and his management team (when appointed). At their meeting on 22nd October 1990 the LACSAB Board were told that the local authority associations had received counsel's opinion on the legal and constitutional steps needed to wind up LACSAB and LGTB to ensure the proper transfer of responsibilities, assets and liabilities to the LGMB in April 1991. It was agreed that an Extraordinary General Meeting should be called to pass the necessary special resolution to dissolve LACSAB and to transfer its responsibilities to the LGMB.

The "continuing dialogue" about the future role of provincial/regional organisations showed no signs of resolution, causing the LACSAB secretary to lament in the editorial of LGE's August 1990 edition about the very bad impression given of local government by the squabbling in public as to how many seats each faction should have at the negotiating table. Commenting that the traditional balance of representation between the associations and provincial councils had worked well in the past, David Thomas said "it is essential that the employers' side of the pay machinery is seen to be properly representative of the local authorities and that everyone feels that the system is fair". What we needed above all else was an objective appraisal of the situation in a cool atmosphere. "The issues are complex and cannot be rushed. Consensus is crucial". There were, however, few signs that the associations versus provincial employers battle for power in pay negotiations would be settled amicably as 1990 drew to a close.

When the financial accounts for the year ended 31st March 1990 were presented to the LACSAB Board at their October 1990 meeting they were pleased to note that there was an excess of actual income over budget of over £350,000. This was due in part to an increase in income received from fees and charges made for the "non-standard" services provided by the LACSAB secretariat and very much in line with one of the major recommendations of the LACSAB review team.

Meanwhile the LACSAB Board was monitoring progress on a major objective set by their employers' strategy debate in 1987 to reduce the number of employers' sides. By far the most important proposal was to form a single employers' organisation to replace the separate employers' sides for APT&C, manual and the two groups of craft employees. Although this was widely supported in principle, there was much protracted discussion on the detailed arrangements. At their meeting on 15th January 1990 the LACSAB Board reaffirmed their support in principle for the formation of a single employers' side. This was finally achieved in the Spring of 1990 at a joint meeting of the employers' sides involved with a new constitution being adopted without dissent but to be subject to review in April 1992. This successfully completed the objective of reducing the number of employers' sides from a total of 24 to 15.

During 1989 and 1990 the LACSAB Board were especially concerned about difficulties in co-ordinating employer interests on the pay of senior posts which was subject to differing and conflicting pressures, such as vertical considerations in police and fire (where subordinate staff had index-linked pay increases), external pay comparisons, internal relativities, and recruitment/retention problems (with stiffening competition from elsewhere in the public sector, e.g. crown prosecution service and the polytechnics). The LACSAB secretary was asked to examine the issue in depth and there was further consideration by the employers' side of the JNCs for chief executives and chief officers. By this time it was apparent that well over 25% of authorities were exceeding the nationally recommended maximum salaries for their senior posts despite the much greater flexibility and local discretion in recent national agreements as well as use of the LACSAB/Hay job evaluation arrangements.

At their October 1990 meeting the LACSAB Board were advised that the 1990 local government pay round was virtually completed with only the three craft groups, probation, education advisers and fire service outstanding. Settlements were in the range 9.0% to 9.75% and generally below price inflation although beyond what most authorities had budgeted for. Harmonisation of conditions of service was likely to be one of the most important issues in 1991 for the local government employers because of the commitment in the manual workers' 1990 agreement on harmonisation with APT&C.

The editorial by Charles Nolda in LGE of October 1990 put the 1990 pay round into a historical perspective as in this year local government settlements had fallen short of price inflation, although this was the exception rather than the rule in the 1980s. After the trauma of the 1989 APT&C negotiations local government needed an orderly pay round in 1990 – and achieved it. Most settlements had been at the 9.38% mark set by the APT&C deal in May. With the August price index figure at 10.6% and further price increases in prospect because of the Gulf crisis "the wisdom of the national employers in seeking an early settlement of the manual workers' claim is clear for all to see".

"The Times" leading editorial of 22nd October 1990 criticising public service pay increases and policies drew a quick response from LACSAB with the support of the local authority associations. "The Times" article referred to local government earnings going up by 11% in the year, as compared with 9.1% in the private sector and only 7% in central government. In a published letter to "The Times" the LACSAB secretary pointed out that the figures quoted related only to male manual workers, a minority of the total labour force. Use of the Government's figures for all full-time employees, male and female, manual and non-manual, revealed a very different picture. In the one year April 1989 to April 1990 average earnings in local government were 9.7% as compared with 10.1% in the private sector and 8.4% in central government. If the wider perspective of a two-year period was taken, the figures for April 1988 to April 1990 put average earnings in local government at 18.2%, well below the private sector at 21.1% and central government at 24.1%. "No evidence there, I suggest" wrote David Thomas "that current inflationary pressures in the labour market emanate from local government."

Otherwise in this period 1987 to 1991 the LACSAB Board continued to take an overview of the negotiations proceeding across the board. The shift in emphasis from the earlier concentration on the negotiating scene and more towards the research and advisory functions was reflected from October 1987 onwards as the Board received on a regular basis reports of LACSAB activities in the three separate divisions – negotiating, research and advisory.

RESEARCH DIVISION

In the research division there were of course annual pay surveys for specific negotiating groups as well as the regular joint staffing watch which showed slight increases until June 1988 but then decreases in the later half of 1988, with a grand total of 1,920,685 full-time and full-time equivalents at December 1988. The quarterly returns continued to record decreases in overall staffing numbers throughout 1989 but the March 1990 showed increases in Wales (but not in England) and then the June 1990 return gave increases in England (but not in Wales), with the grand total by then being at 1,900,460. (By this time "joint manpower watch" had been renamed "joint staffing watch" and "Local Government Manpower" had been retitled "Local Government Employment" in line with equal opportunities terminology)

The interest generated through the major research into recruitment and retention arising from the review of London weighting led to much additional activity in this field. Several regional recruitment and retention surveys were subsequently brought together in an "omnibus" report made available in 1989.

Research into the youth labour market of the 1990s was necessary as the Office of Population Censuses and Surveys estimated a sharp fall in the numbers of school leavers available for work in the early 1990s. Another major LACSAB survey was in respect of teacher wastage in 1987, the results of which cast doubt on the reliability of DES estimates. Surveys on the staffing effects of central government initiatives continued. Other major surveys were subsequently undertaken on social services employment and on various aspects affecting teachers for the IAC.

Much work was done by the research division throughout this period on performance related pay, with surveys, research papers and one-day conferences followed in January 1990 by the "LACSAB Handbook on Performance Related Pay" prepared in co-operation with management consultants, Kinsley Lord.

An important step in the light of interest on future relationships at provincial and national level was the agreement in 1988 with provincial employers' secretaries on the development of information services and advice to local authorities. Subsequently there was a great deal of effort into help for groups of authorities and provincial organisations on information on a range of important labour market issues.

The guidelines for personnel record systems in local authorities were updated in 1990 to take account of employment legislation, computerisation of personnel records and grading developments.

The extent of LACSAB research work in this period was shown by a report in July 1989 which indicated that the research division was then running 33 surveys and that its capacity was stretched to the limit.

ADVISORY DIVISION

Considerable concern was expressed at the meeting of the LACSAB Board in October 1987 that the increasing pressure of work on pension matters related to the UKSC was jeopardising the other work of the LACSAB advisory division. 1988 was the year of change for pensions as a result of the wide-sweeping changes to pensions legislation nationally following the Social Security Acts of 1985 and 1988, especially the introduction of personal pensions from April 1988 – which meant that employers could no longer insist that employees belonged to occupational schemes. All four local government schemes had to be examined carefully to ensure they complied with the new legislation. Subsequently a survey by the LACSAB secretariat showed a sharp decline in the number of employees entering the Local Government Superannuation Scheme (LGSS) and a consequent increase in employees lapsing into the Government State Earnings Related Pension Scheme. Following representations by the UKSC, Ministers relented and agreed to three proposals of the UKSC to seek to reverse these trends, the most important of which was that from 1st October 1989 whole-time local government employees became members of the LGSS unless or until they made an election to the contrary.

Quite apart from much advisory work arising from the stream of major employment legislation and that relating to the supply of local authority services, the work of the advisory division covered many other issues of the day, such as data protection, violence to staff, and access to medical reports. Of many individual cases on which in-depth advice was given, the equal pay for equal value case of Leverton versus Clwyd County Council may be mentioned: it had begun in 1983; it had serious implications for national pay bargaining as well as its equal value considerations; and eventually completed the full course through the courts with a House of Lords' decision in December 1988 which largely upheld the county council's case that the variation in pay was genuinely due to a material factor which was not a difference of sex.

A great deal of valuable advice to local education authorities was provided by the LACSAB advisory division on the personnel implications of the local management of schools, with a successful series of seminars being followed by an advisory booklet published in May 1989, and subsequently a LACSAB Employer Guide published in February 1990. The extent to which this guidance was needed and welcomed locally could be gauged by the fact that over 3,000 copies were sold of the preliminary booklet and over 4,000 copies of the later LACSAB Guide.

MANUAL WORKERS

Considerable encouragement was derived from the extent of co-operation from all sides on the implentation of the 1987 agreement which brought to a conclusion the mammoth review spanning several years. The big question to be faced however was whether the benefits accruing from it on job flexibility and working time would help local authorities and their staffs as they confronted many crucial problems in the next few years, especially in the area of compulsory competitive tendering.

With so much to be done in implementing the 1987 agreement, particularly in respect of the major grading review, a quick and straightforward 1988 pay deal was highly desirable and fortunately achieved. On the same day (19th July) as the trade union side submitted their 1988 claim, the employers proposed increases in pay which added 5.6% to the paybill and which was accepted after trade union consultations. The employers also made a concession on annual leave to bring it into line with APT&C staffs, and agreed a statement on pay protection arising from the 1987 agreement. The employers were able to secure a common percentage increase to apply to all the revised rates thus maintaining the differentials established in 1987.

LGE of August 1989 announced details of the 1989 claim from the manual workers' trade union side for a substantial flat rate increase. They also sought to ensure the value of the 1987 settlement was maintained by continuation of the protection clauses negotiated in 1988. Improved conditions were claimed through the harmonisation of service conditions in line with other local government workers, particularly a reduced working week, increased holiday entitlements and average earnings during sickness. It was clear at the NJC meeting on 12th September 1989 that both sides wanted an early settlement without protracted negotiations, as many of the negotiators had been involved in the difficult APT&C dispute. The employers had this in mind in unanimously offering increases worth 8.8% on the paybill with effect from the pay week including 1st September 1989. For their part the trade union side unanimously agreed this was clearly the best that could be achieved through negotiation in the current round and to put it to their members. During a long day most of the discussions took place informally "in the corridor", with both sides dispensing with ritual statements of position. As Ron Keating of NUPE aptly put it – "It seems to help negotiations if we do not make a lengthy formal presentation of our claim!". It was clear that the offer was beyond what many authorities could afford, but the authorities themselves recognised in consultations that the employers had little alternative but to aim at a settlement which took account of events elsewhere within and outside local government.

There seem to have been few problems in reaching settlement for manual workers' pay in 1990. The claim was for a flat- rated substantial increase to improve their standard of living and other aspects, but it was made very clear at the outset that the unions were looking for tangible progress towards harmonisation, not just a further commitment to talks. At a meeting of the NJC on 17th July 1990 the employers made an offer the overall effect of which was to improve pay rates by between 9.38% and 9.63%, adding 9.33% to the national paybill (some elements of earnings were not affected by an increase in rates). The trade union side agreed that day to recommend the offer for acceptance. An important aspect of the provisional agreement was the establishment of a joint working party on harmonisation of service conditions, with a priority to look at sick pay with a view to new arrangements applying by not later than 1st August 1991. The employers' judgement in going for an early settlement before price inflation peaked was shown after the event to be entirely correct.

A revised edition of the manual workers' handbook was published at the end of 1988 incorporating the extensive changes made to the national agreement in the 1987 and 1988 agreements. A consequence of the 1987 deal was the deletion of much of the old handbook, whilst the opportunity was taken to simplify, clarify and update as necessary.

An agreement late in 1988 for manual workers in Scotland attracted wide interest south of the border as this provided that there could be local negotiations to vary the terms of the national agreement (save basic rates of pay, annual leave entitlement and sickness provisions) but only in the context of the competitive tendering provisions of the Local Government Act 1988.

CRAFT WORKERS

The two sides of the JNC (Building and Civil Engineering) could not settle on a pay deal for 1987/1988 after three long days of discussions in the autumn of 1987: the difference was neither on the pay structure following the joint review nor so much on overall pay levels, but rather the extent to which the national agreement covered bonus earnings, with the employers seeking maximum flexibility at local level. The trade unions sought arbitration, and ACAS set up a board of mediation/arbitration chaired by Professor Sir John Wood. After two days of conciliation, arbitration took place on 22nd January 1988. Both sides likened the outcome to a curate's egg – "good in parts". The employers' offer of 7% was upheld and bonus was to be entirely a local matter from September 1988, but the price was the introduction of a guaranteed minimum bonus plus the release of frozen holiday entitlements.

The 1987/1988 deal for engineering craftsmen reached in the summer of 1988

Lambeth Council brick-layers

after four months of negotiations was of great importance in fundamentally altering the shape and nature of the national agreement and in shifting the balance on negotiation of total pay from national to local level by raising the basic rates and reducing the bonus calculator. This brought all craft groups on to the same base, loosening all the national agreements to allow more flexibility at local level.

After the drastic changes arising from the 1987/1988 arbitration and negotiations there was hope for quick craft settlements for 1988/1989 as the employers offered all three groups increases of 5.74% on basic rates. Some delay arose as each of the craft groups waited for someone else to take a lead, but eventually the electricians asked for arbitration which was heard by an ACAS board on 22nd February 1989. Their award must have made the electricians wonder whether it was worth going to arbitration as it merely confirmed the employers' offer to apply from 1st September 1988. Meanwhile in the JNC (Building and Civil Engineering) the trade unions balloted their members to seek support for the rejection of the employers' offer and to seek a better offer. The result of the UCATT ballot gave a majority in support of industrial action short of strike but against an all-out strike. Industrial action short of strike was set in motion by the unions, although in the case of UCATT the total votes cast was less than 40%. LGE of June 1989 was able to report that local government craft negotiations for 1988/1989 were finally completed following a settlement within the JNC for building and civil engineering. The agreement followed those made for engineering craftsmen and electricians, the employers having maintained their "5.74% increase on basic rates" offer constant.

With all matters relating to bonus left for local discussion, the national agreements for the craft groups had been transformed into minimum agreements allowing maximum local flexibility in devising local earnings packages to suit local circumstances.

Craft negotiations for the 1989/1990 round appear to have been in the slipstream of the 1989 APT&C dispute settlement, with LGE of December 1989 reporting 8.8% agreements for building and civil engineering, electricians and engineering craftsmen, all with effect from 1st September 1989.

The negotiations for the three craft groups in 1990/1991 ended in agreements similar to those reached for manual workers.

WORKSHOPS FOR THE BLIND

The introduction of the revised grading structure for manual workers and the disappearance of the traditional group E link in 1987 meant for once really fundamental negotiations in the NJC for workshops for the blind. The employers' offer to apply from 1st July 1987 and which was eventually accepted by the National League for the Blind early in 1989 established a substantive grade midway between the new manual grades 2 and 3, thus re-establishing the link with the manual grade structure.

MUNICIPAL AIRPORTS

The two National Councils for Airports - manual and non-manual - reached agreements on new pay structures to apply in 1988 which introduced more flexibility allowing individual airports a greater degree of autonomy. The manual deal struck in February 1989 was effective from 1st November 1988. The non-manual agreement concluded at the end of 1988 provided staged increases from 1st July 1988 and 1st April 1989 and achieved the employers' objective in establishing a new settlement date of 1st November for 1989 onwards - in line with manuals and hopefully distanced from peak periods of activity prone to industrial action.

That hope appears to have been fulfilled to some extent as there is no reference to difficulties on airports pay in 1989 and 1990.

APT&C STAFFS

The 1988 APT&C pay round began when the staff side tabled their "indivisible" claim for a general 10% increase plus the merging and restructuring of scales 1 and 2. Having initially offered 4.4% on 10th May, the employers improved this to 4.8% at the NJC meeting on 19th May after lengthy talks. These had mostly concentrated on exploring inconclusively a basis to balance the two sides' conflicting aspirations: the staff side were pressing strongly their low pay objectives, whilst the employers were looking for more flexibility in the salary structure. 6th July was a day which started off promisingly and appeared to most employer members to finish well, only for them to learn something very different the following day. The employers had made a package offer which improved the general increase to 5.4% from 1st July 1988; combined spinal column points 10 and 11; and committed both sides to joint talks on the national pay structure having regard to local needs. With both sides having read into the record their statements on their structural objectives, the staff side took the offer away for consultation, with the employers having first received the clearest possible indications that the unions would recommend it to their members. But, much to the embarrassment of the staff side leaders, the NALGO local government committee (the majority of the staff side) when it met immediately at the rising of the joint meeting, inexplicably decided on a narrow vote to recommend rejection of the offer. A reconvened NALGO local government group meeting on 26th July endorsed the rejection and decided to ballot members on a programme of industrial action. Although NALGO earlier that year had gone over the heads of the employer negotiators to leaflet all local councillors on the merits of their claim, LACSAB officers were constrained by political decisions from putting the employer case to trade union members. There was therefore some relief at Belgrave Square when the ballot result eventually announced on 3rd October was 44.5% to 55.5% against industrial action on a 60% turn-out - very similar to the 1986 NALGO ballot outcome. The relative closeness of the ballot result reflected employees' fears that the employers' approach towards more flexible pay arrangements was an attack on national bargaining. In preparation for the 1989 pay review the employers immediately began extensive consultations with local authorities on proposals for major changes to the APT&C pay structure and related issues, starting with officer-level talks in the autumn of 1988, followed by member-level consultations early in 1989.

1989 APT&C DISPUTE

All the portents were therefore of real difficulties being likely to arise in the APT&C 1989 pay negotiations. The employers' extensive consultations with authorities were well in hand when the staff side presented their 1989 claim at the NJC meeting on 28th January for increases of £1200 or 12% whichever was the greater – at an overall cost of 14%.

The employers' first offer was 6% and, when this was increased to 6.4% early in May, it was rejected out of hand and industrial action looked likely. A key meeting of the NJC took place on 17th May when the employers judged that there was an unbridgeable gap between the two sides, not only on the level of the pay increase, but also on the conditions the employers had attached to the offer at the outset. Realising that the staff side sought a conclusion to negotiations that day, the employers decided to put together their best possible offer and tabled a final offer of 7%, subject to a modified set of conditions. It was recognised this would be likely to lead to a strike ballot, but the employers hoped there would be insufficient support for prolongued industrial action. This offer too was rejected and four out of five unions balloted on strike action, with only NALGO succeeding in getting a majority in favour of a strike. The first phase of industrial action – which involved all-out strikes on six days over a period of three weeks – began on 4th July: although it was patchy in the south, it was virtually solid in the north, Scotland and Wales. The employers met on 6th July and agreed to hold firm. It was clear that the dispute was as much about the employers' conditions (the unions insisted on calling them "strings") as about pay. After extensive consultation with authorities, the employers had wanted to delete the general grades and age points from the agreement thus leaving authorities free to choose a different pattern of grades from the spinal column of salary points if they so wished; to limit grading appeals to local level; and to introduce an enabling clause allowing local negotiation on variations to the national conditions on working time and weekend premia.

NALGO's plans for the second phase of industrial action had originally envisaged an indefinite national all-out strike, but this was shelved, and instead there were indefinite strikes by small groups of key personnel receiving full pay from NALGO's £20m strike fund. By this time there had been settlements at 8.8% for British Rail and the BBC, and consequently many local authorities changed their views away from holding firm at 7.0%. The industrial action and mixed local authority reactions brought the employers back to the negotiating table, and on 31st July they said that, subject to consultation with authorities, they would settle at 8.15% (8% for most staff: 8.8% for the lowest paid), drop one of their conditions and modify the other two. This was not accepted by the staff side and conciliation at ACAS on 1st August did not bring a settlement. Urgent consultations with authorities produced a mixed response and, when the employers met again on 10th August, they felt local authority opinion was shifting fast – especially in relation to the so-called "strings" – and that the choice lay between arbitration on their 31st July offer or settling on the best terms available that day. They decided on the latter option and eventually struck a deal on an overall pay increase of 8.8% from 1st July 1989 (9.5% for the lowest paid and 8.6% for most staff) and dropped their conditions – inevitably incurring criticism from the Government and those authorities who wanted to stand firm.

The outcome of this dispute was seen to be a serious setback for the employers, not so much because of the extent of the final offer – which was below average earnings increases, well below the unions' 14% claim, and only 0.5% above price inflation, but more because of the manner in which the employers had to make their final concessions. There was a dichotomy of views on how this had arisen. Some argued that the root of the difficulties was the decision to link pay rises to changes in conditions of service, but others insisted that the "strings" were essential to preserve the effectiveness and credibility of the national machinery. There were many misgivings about the consultation process in which authorities had expressed hardline views early in the year, only for the employers to face considerably changed circumstances subsequently. The employers established a working party to review the 1989 dispute and to draw lessons for the future. The ensuing report identifying goals the employers should seek in the future was then the subject of extensive consultations with authorities by means of a series of regional meetings.

Almost before the dust had settled on the 1989 dispute, NALGO were consulting branches about their 1990 pay claim which eventually emerged at the NJC meeting in January 1990, surprisingly for a uniform £1,500 increase at all points. The employers had reckoned it would not prove possible to negotiate a settlement and aimed at an offer at 9% judged likely to be acceptable to union members in a ballot. But there was at the last minute an unexpected signal from the staff side that they would recommend an offer around the inflation rate (then 9.4%). In a carefully weighed decision the employers opted for a higher offer coupled to a firm union recommendation to accept it. So in contrast to the traumas of 1989 there was a quick settlement in advance of the 1st July 1990 operative date at an overall cost of 9.38% on the paybill, with most staffs receiving 9.25%, whilst those at the upper end of Scale 1 and on Scale 2 fared better. An early settlement was a welcome relief, but it was nevertheless higher than many authorities had wished – meaning a loss of jobs in some authorities as well as a rebuke from Michael Portillo, the Minister for Local Government.

London weighting was an especially sensitive issue for APT&C in 1987. It began with one of the most extravagant claims ever made by the staff side: a uniform London allowance of £2,500; a single Fringe area payment of £1,250; and a joint working party to consider a "South East" allowance. By this time the employers had before them LACSAB's major survey on recruitment and retention which suggested that such problems as existed could largely be solved by means other than London weighting. The employers' initial response in September was a 7% offer from 1st September 1987 and this was rejected. It became clear during lengthy talks at the October meeting that there was a prospect of the staff side accepting a moderate deal if linked to some commitment to a joint examination of factors affecting London and fringe area payments. The joint secretaries were sent away to explore possibilities, and came back with a proposition which led to an agreement on a 7.5% increase in allowances from 1st July 1987 coupled to a joint examination to be conducted on a "without commitment" basis.

A clerical worker.

After the ballot outcome against strike action on the main 1988 APT&C pay review, the staff side at the October 1988 meeting were in their "let's clear everything up" mood and one end-product of this was a very quick settlement on London and fringe allowances. This was in line with the 5.6% overall cost of the main pay award and operated from 1st July 1988. The examination of the London weighting system agreed in 1987 was still continuing.

The 1989 London weighting agreement for APT&C staffs was also in line with the main pay settlement for that year.

An important grading issue in 1988 was in respect of 20,000 nursery staffs in schools. The staff side, having been most displeased with the arbitration outcome in 1984, mounted a campaign to gain public and political support to exert strong pressure on a limited number of authorities. The employers early in 1988 sought to wrest the initiative by proposing a joint review of the jobs of nursery staffs and then of their gradings. This was agreed and the main part of the joint review was a series of visits throughout the country to see the jobs in many different settings. A potentially explosive situation was narrowly averted on 7th July 1988 when negotiations were expected to start in earnest as a lively and colourful crowd of nursery staffs demonstrated outside in Belgrave Square. As the employers met that morning they learned that the deal they thought they had struck late the previous evening on 1988 APT&C pay had been undone through the NALGO position turning round overnight. After a delicate manoeuvre that day, discussions on nursery staffs went on to the "back burner" for three months until 1988 APT&C pay was resolved. A lengthy meeting of the NJC's grading committee then produced a recommended settlement which led, after consultations by both sides, to a deal being struck in December 1988. The agreement gave a scale for a standard contribution outlined and left the grading for other levels of contribution to local discretion.

SOCIAL WORKERS AND RESIDENTIAL STAFFS

A staff side claim in the mid-1980s for improved grading of social workers and welfare assistants had led to abortive discussions and an employers' offer of marginal improvements being left on the table. Fresh discussions proceeded for some time in the NJC's grading committee on a new staff side claim presented in 1988. Employer consultations early in 1989 produced much support for (1) a single main scale for qualified social workers; (2) deletion of the prescribed scales for unqualified social workers; and (3) no rigid prescription on senior practitioners. Early in 1989 the staff side rejected an offer of a two-increment increase at the top of the scale for qualified social workers and discontinuation of other national scales. Negotiations were interrupted by the main 1989 APT&C dispute and, when these resumed in November, the employers improved their offer to a three-increment increase at the top of the scale for qualified social workers. NALGO recommended a delegate conference to reject the offer and ballot for strikes. The conference rejected

A social worker visiting an elderly client at home.

the offer but could not agree on what action to take. So NALGO came back to the negotiating table early in 1990 when the employers revised their offer and agreement was reached on a detailed package in which many of the employers' objectives were eventually achieved without any breakdown in the machinery despite union expectations running high at times.

Towards the end of 1990 the staff side put forward a claim for the deletion of the national agreement for residential staffs. Although on the face of it, this appeared to suit employer policy, the effect would be greatly to increase costs and to concede the issues at the heart of the 1983/ 1984 dispute – hours and work outside the standard week.

In 1989 and 1990 there was a resurgence of interest in job evaluation for white-collar staffs. The model joint scheme in the APT&C "purple book" was becoming outdated and suspect in terms of equal pay for equal value and the NJC agreed to its deletion. So LACSAB developed a new scheme "in house", tested it in several assignments for APT&C staffs in local authorities, and in his report to the LACSAB Board meeting in October 1990 the secretary reported that a launch of LACSAB's new scheme was in hand in co-operation with provincial employers' organisations.

TOP POSTS

After relatively straightforward settlements in 1988, agreements for senior groups proved very difficult to negotiate in 1989 as local authorities faced increasing problems of recruitment and retention at the top levels and as pay increases outside local government went up substantially. The employers' approach was co-ordinated by the LACSAB Board and a special working party of the JNC for chief officers made the running. A whole range of options was considered, ranging at one extreme to withdrawing from national negotiations entirely to, at the other extreme, engaging in a comprehensive evaluation of all senior local government posts. Despite continuing differences of emphasis between the two sides, joint agreement was eventually reached on four main points of principle. Both sides agreed they wanted to retain the national agreement. It was also common ground that the existing policy should be maintained of providing a national framework (based on the type and size of authority) but allowing individual authorities flexibility to choose appropriate scales from within the ranges. Thirdly it was also generally agreed that the existing ranges needed to be expanded to reflect movements elsewhere as well as the salaries actually being paid by local authorities if the national agreement was to retain credibility. Lastly there was a general view that the time had come for some general reference to be made in the national agreements to performance related pay so long as authorities retained discretion in this matter.

Based on these points of agreement settlements then followed for general increases of 9.38% with effect from 1st July 1990 for chief executives, chief officers and chief fire officers, and that in addition the salary ranges should be further extended by 10% at range maxima to give local authorities even more discretion. At about the same time the Home Secretary accepted – at the third time of asking – a recommendation of the PNB that chief constables should, on top of their increase of 9.75%, receive an extra increment worth 2.5% after three years' service in the rank.

A home help visiting a client in sheltered housing.

FIRE BRIGADES

The established "upper quartile" formula led to agreements on 4th November 1987 for 7.3% increases in the NJC's lower ranks and officers' committees. The formula was again the basis for agreements a year later on 2nd November 1988 in these two committees, this time for increases of 8.6%. The increase of 8.6% for all ranks from 7th November 1989 flowing from the formula was lower than had been widely anticipated, but still markedly greater than the 6.5% then on offer in the ambulance dispute where the unions were seeking a similar index-linked formula. The NJC meeting on 7th November 1990 produced another pay agreement based on the formula, this time providing for increases of 9.5%.

Following the Audit Commission's paper – "Value for money in the fire service" – a small group of employers looked at manning systems, and joint talks in the NJC ensued. When subsequently early in 1988 the Home Secretary suggested the NJC should set up a working party to review pay and conditions having regard to the Audit Commission's intentions, both sides of the NJC agreed in August 1988 to inform him they were not persuaded that a further working party was in fact necessary, although they were always willing to meet him if he so desired. This continued to be the object of much interest by Home Office ministers who exerted pressure to induce joint discussions on it, including whether the fire service pay formula was "the best way ahead for the future". In April 1989 the employers proposed the setting up of an ad-hoc working party, jointly with the Home Office, to report back to the parties, including the NJC. After much discussion, especially at the FBU annual conference in May, this was agreed at the NJC meeting on 19th June 1989.

The joint Home Office/NJC working party's report was eventually published on 31st July 1990 and there was relief in many quarters over its final conclusion "that there are cogent arguments for continuing with the current method of pay determination within the fire service". This however was coupled to two recommendations for increasing flexibility: one for the NJC to re-examine offering whole-time firefighters separate contracts on a voluntary basis to undertake retained duties; and the other that the NJC should consider means of encouraging more flexible use of overtime, following which the FBU should consider modifying their overtime ban. These recommendations were the subject of much serious debate at the close of 1990 amid speculation that any Government endorsement of the continuation of the pay formula would be dependent upon the FBU's attitude to the recommendations for greater flexibility. The employers had in 1989 proposed a limited facility whereby whole-time firefighters could undertake retained duties on a secondary basis but a FBU conference had unanimously rejected this.

Following a request from the FBU, a review of FBU and NAFO membership amongst officer ranks was conducted in 1987 and in consequence it was agreed that from January 1988 the representation on the NJC's officers' committee should no longer be eight seats each, but would in future be nine for the FBU as against seven for NAFO. In line with the resolution carried at the LACSAB "Lords" conference on employer strategy in April 1988, it was agreed in January 1989 that the employers' side of the NJC for chief and assistant chief fire officers should become part of the employers' organisation which governed the membership of the main fire brigades NJC and that the employers' membership for chief fire officers and for fire officers would be identical.

POLICE

The issue of the police London allowance was again pursued to arbitration following staff side claims for increases in 1986 and 1987 which the official side opposed because of acceptable manning levels. The allowance had been introduced because of undermanning in London and was additional to London weighting. The official side's view was upheld by the Police Arbitreation Tribunal (PAT) who decided there should be no increases in 1986 or 1987.

Early in 1988 after months of examination of many aspects of police pay and conditions, the official side of the PNB drew up a package of outline proposals covering pay, allowances and other service conditions as the basis for negotiations with the staff side in the context of the 1988 pay settlement. The official side were conscious that the staff side would strongly oppose many of their proposals for change and intimated they wanted to pursue their outline proposals as a package across the five PNB standing committees. They had however to accept the staff side's view that negotiations could not begin until full and detailed proposals were tabled on each of the issues in the relevant committee. The official side were at pains to point out they were not suggesting any change in the general principle enunciated by Edmund-Davies relating police pay to movements elsewhere; but they were concerned to examine the effects of using the underlying average earnings index. They believed police officers reaped a double benefit from receipt of their own annual increments and from the reflection of other workers' incremental credit included in the earnings indices, and that this could be rectified by the adjustment of certain salary points.

It was the official side's proposals on rent allowance which were most likely to be challenged strongly by the staff side – but changes were necessary in the light of the introduction of the community charge in place of domestic rates. The official side proposed that the rates element of rent allowances should be deleted on the introduction of the community charge; payment of compensatory grant should cease for new entrants; and in future the remaining allowance should be updated by reference to the retail price index. As expected the staff side argued strongly against any change which they reckoned to be a substantial worsening of their conditions, and that the purpose of the community charge was the same as rates – to raise revenue by local taxation for local purposes. Not surprisingly there was no resolution by negotiation and the submissions of both sides were heard by the PAT on 3rd February 1989.

In making their case at arbitration the official side were conscious that in 1984 the arbitrators decided that a case had not been established for modifying the rent allowance system, expressing the view that any review of the system should take place in the context of a complete reappraisal of the overall package of police pay and allowances. So the official side stressed that there had been a review of all police pay, allowances and conditions over the past year. Their submissions detailed "the case for change", contrasting the current situation with the vastly different position on police housing when the rent allowance was first introduced in 1919.

Given the complexities of the police rent allowance system, it was no great surprise when it became known just before Easter 1989 that the PAB award was correspondingly complex, presenting the PNB with much work and discussion within the broad framework of the award. The effect of the award was that –

(1) The existing rent allowance system would go and be replaced by a standard housing allowance in each force;

(2) Officers and their spouses would not be reimbursed their community charge, but the cost of existing payments for domestic rates would be built into the base of the new housing allowance so that the new cash base would be the same as the existing allowance;

(3) Those in provided housing would get the allowance but would pay an independently assessed rent;

(4) The standard allowance would be updated by reference to an index of housing costs;

(5) Compensatory grant would be phased out, but an equivalent amount of the new allowance would become pensionable; and

(6) Senior ranks would continue to receive higher allowances.

With operative dates for the new system of 1st April 1989 for Scotland and 1st April 1990 in England and Wales there was pressure to get the system up and running, yet it was equally essential that it was built on firm foundations. There was some disappointment at Belgrave Square that the official side's objectives had been only partially achieved, but nevertheless the award marked an important breakthrough because the standard housing allowance for each force would make it easier to portray the true value of police pay to the outside world.

Long and complex negotiations on implementing the arbitration award on rent allowances failed to reach agreement and the LACSAB Board were told at their January 1990 meeting that this had resulted in a return to the arbitrators who awarded:

(1) in favour of the official side on the basis for updating the new housing allowance for the future; and

(2) in favour of the staff side on the position of officers in housing provided by the police authority.

But the Home Secretary made it clear he would not accept agreement on this basis and he sought (a) rates to be removed from the kitty; (b) those in provided housing to be prevented from access to right to buy; and (c) the loss of tax reimbursement not to be balanced by pensionability. An agreement on such a basis within the PNB was clearly impracticable given the terms of the original arbitration award. A period of intense political activity ensued with intense lobbying of Ministers and MPs by the police staff associations, as a result of which a few concessions were made by ministers. The staff associations' campaign reached its climax in May 1990 when the Home Secretary's address at the Police Federation conference was heard in complete silence, but this did not deter Ministers from pursuing their objectives. After considerable delay the draft regulations on housing allowance were debated by Parliament in a late night sitting in June 1990. LGE of October 1990 pithily commented – "A comfortable Government majority of 292 to 191 disguised the flavour of the debate".

During this period 1987 to 1991 police pay agreements continued to be determined in accordance with the Edmund-Davies formula which linked them with average earnings generally. The rise in police pay increases reflected those elsewhere: for example, the police increase from September 1989 was 9.25% and that from September 1990 was 9.75%.

PROBATION AND MAGISTRATES COURTS STAFFS

Negotiations in the JNC for the probation service in 1987 were prolonged and difficult as reform of the salary structure was tackled in the light of a report of the review working group convened as part of the 1986 agreement. Ultimately a package was agreed after a ballot of probation officers, consisting of a general 5% increase from 1st July 1987 and a further 2% plus restructuring from 1st February 1988.

The 1989 settlement for probation officers was reached only after the employers' offer was the subject of a ballot of NAPO members who voted 468 to 102 in favour of it. This increased all salary points and excess rates by 8.6% and also included several important structural changes proposed by the employers. On this occasion probation ancillary staffs fared slightly better with a 8.8% increase on all grades in line with the APT&C settlement.

As 1990 drew to a close, probation pay for 1990 remained unresolved because of a dispute over unsocial hours. After some talk of a ballot on industrial action there was a reference to arbitration by the unions.

There was an important development in the determination of the pay of chief and deputy probation officers when their 1990 pay scheme introduced performance related pay (PRP) as one element. It was hoped this would make a significant contribution to the management of the probation service in the longer term. Kinsley Lord Management Consultants were engaged to work with LACSAB, the Home Office and the Society of Chief Officers of Probation to develop a programme of support to help local management take the scheme forward.

The dispute in 1988 over the pay of 8,000 magistrates' courts staffs attracted significant press coverage. The negotiations for this group had over the years tended to be in the slipstream of those for APT&C staffs, but great difficulties arose from 1986 onwards as the new Crown Prosecution Service enticed many courts clerks, lawyers who advise magistrates in court on magisterial law, despite very strong representations from the employers about the waste of public resources as one public service siphoned off the best staff from another. By 1988 losses to the courts service were causing delays in court sittings. The employers were prepared to improve the pay for qualified court clerks, but the officers' side pressed for more pay for all staff even although the recruitment/retention problems did not extend to them. The employers sought to make the best possible tactical move conscious of the crucial concurrent NALGO ballot on 1988 APT&C pay, but inevitably there was no agreement and a reference to arbitration. The employers' position at arbitration was not entirely helped when, just beforehand, one of their constituents, the Central Council of Magistrates' Courts Committees, unanimously supported a resolution which accepted the officers' side case. LGE of April 1989 suggested "there was comfort for all in the award" - 5.4% for most staff, 7% for court clerks, and a minimum grade for lawyers broadly related to their counterparts in the Crown Prosecution Service. But problems continued into 1989 for the senior staff of the service, justices' clerks, who remained unhappy about a 5.4% offer for 1988.

In the 1989 pay negotiations for magistrates courts staffs, the major difficulty, not for the first time, was in finding common ground in the management side between the magistrates' and the local authority representatives. The eventual outcome was 9.5% for court clerks; 8.6% for other court staff; and for justices' clerks a complicated restructuring exercise which added 10.7% to the paybill in a full year. All courts groups got 9.0% increases in their 1990 agreements.

TEACHERS

With the demise of the Burnham committee, a new employers' body was set up to represent the interests of local education authorities (LEAs) as employers of teachers, namely the National Employers' Organisation - Schoolteachers (NEOST) to be serviced by LACSAB. The principle objects of NEOST were (1) to secure the largest possible measure of co-operation between LEAs on pay and service conditions issues; and (2) to provide the employers' side of any national joint body which might be established to consider and determine such issues. This was a much smaller body than the management panel of the old Burnham primary and secondary committee. At their inaugural meeting in August 1987 they endorsed a draft of a constitution for a national joint council to negotiate teachers' pay and conditions to put to the Secretary of State.

In the meantime the Government announced the membership of the Interim Advisory Committee (IAC) on teachers' pay and conditions established under the Teachers' Pay and Conditions Act 1987 and which would be chaired by Lord Chilver. The first task of the IAC as it began work in September 1987 was to agree pay levels from 1st April 1988 to recommend to the Secretary of State after seeking views from employers and unions. Their remit from the Government was no major structural changes and a cost envelope of £300m (or 4.4%). NEOST submitted their views to the IAC after a meeting on 25th November and extensive consultations with authorities, pointing out - inter alia - that the IAC now had the employers' normal and unenviable responsibility of reconciling the irreconcilable. The IAC eventually reported on 19th April 1988 amid many reports from Government-appointed bodies on pay in the public sector. The LACSAB verdict in LGE of June 1988 was favourable - "Lord Chilver and his colleagues have done well.... no major issues have been dodged....an adroit use of recommendations, hints and reminders to keep most of the constituents happy....Generally the employers have much to be pleased about". Kenneth Baker, the Secretary of State, accepted the IAC recommendations which included a 7.5% increase in London weighting from 1st July 1987; a 4.235% increase on all salaries from 1st April 1988; and increases in incentive allowances from the same date. The IAC also came to the conclusion that national rates of pay should continue, provided LEAs had sufficient flexibility in applying them. The IAC package was estimated as costing £332m (4.75%), £32m above the Government's financial limit, and the Government refused to meet their share of this excess despite much employer protestation.

For the 1989 pay round the IAC were given a tighter timetable and a financial ceiling of £385m (just under 5%) which had to cover teacher shortage problems and to recognise additional responsibilities falling on heads and deputies with the onset of local financial management, quite apart from trying to improve teachers' morale. The NEOST evidence to the IAC stressed the importance of keeping within the financial guidelines and suggested the IAC should concentrate on reinforcing flexibility within the existing framework. The IAC completed their task and, when the Secretary of State, Kenneth Baker, published their report in February 1989, he indicated he accepted the recommendations. These were, from 1st April 1989, a 6% increase to the main scale; a 7% increase in the value of incentive allowances (together with a further 9,500 allowances); a 7.5% increase in the spot salaries of heads and deputies; and from 1st July 1988 a 5.6% increase in London weighting. The overall cost was £470m (6.4%) and again as in 1988 the Government refused to meet their share of the additional £85m over the financial limit they had set. LGE of April 1989 commented on what the IAC did not say, as they made no direct recommendations on special measures to deal with shortages of subject teachers, merely concluding that such measures should be flexible and local. It was nevertheless recognised that the IAC had in several of their recommendations added to local flexibility as desired by the employers.

In the autumn of 1989 the terms of reference of the IAC's review of teachers' pay as at 1st April 1990 were announced with a £600m cash limit – i.e. between 7.5% and 8% of the national salary bill. NEOST in their submissions to the IAC urged them again to keep within the cash limit set by the Government; to develop the national framework to give greater local discretion to meet the recognised variations in the recruitment and retention of teachers; to increase all salaries by no less than 7% and London area allowances by 8.8%; and to introduce salary ranges for heads and deputy heads. The outcome was that the Government accepted the recommendations of the IAC on a staged basis. A general increase of 7% on all scales and 8% on incentive allowances from 1st April 1990 was followed by some "topping up" on 1st January 1991 which eventually gave average increases of 8.3% on the main scale; 10.4% for heads and deputies; and 17% on incentive allowances B to E. The overall cost was stated to be 7.9% for the financial year 1990/1991 and 9.3% in a full year.

At the meeting of the LACSAB Board in October 1990 the LACSAB secretary reported that the IAC had already been given their terms of reference for 1991 by the Secretary of State, John MacGregor. The most important feature was that, unlike previous years, they were not given a specific cash limit. They were told instead that their recommendations taken as a whole should fall within the inter-quartile range of the annual percentage movements in the pay of non-manual employees outside the public sector. At that time the mid-point of the inter-quartile range was 8.7% and likely to rise and such figures did not appear to sit at all well with the Government's proposal that the inflation element in the RSG settlement for the following year should be 7.1%.

In April 1990 the Education Secretary announced new proposals on machinery for teachers' pay and conditions which would restore negotiating rights between unions and the local authority employers. But NEOST had reservations on several aspects, especially the Government's extensive override powers. In the summer of 1990 the Secretary of State said he was dropping those proposals and canvassed three possibilities – (a) a joint negotiating body to make recommendations to the Secretary of State, which would have to reach agreement by a specific deadline, and its negotiations could take place within the inter-quartile range of private sector settlements; (b) a pay review option, "something like the IAC . . . and possibly linked with a non-strike agreement", working within a cash envelope; or (c) allowing local negotiations at LEA or school level, thus extending the scope of local flexibility – but it was not clear what would be left of the national framework or control of expenditure.

NEOST when they met on 19th July 1990 quickly rejected the third option of local negotiations as they felt the risk of leap-frogging settlements was too great. The second option was not likely to find favour with the teacher unions, so the employers agreed to explore further the first option.

After further thought the Government decided that 1991 should be the last year in which the IAC advised the Education Secretary on schoolteachers' pay and conditions. It was agreed that from 1992 onwards there would be a return to a modified form of collective bargaining. The details were then put in the School Teachers' Pay and Conditions Bill in November 1990. There would be a return to direct negotiations between the employers and the unions, but the DES would not be involved as members of the negotiating body. Negotiations would however be subject to a timetable. If this was not met the Secretary of State would seek advice on pay and conditions from an independent body along the lines of the IAC. Any agreement reached in the negotiating body on pay, duties and working time would be subject to the approval of the Secretary of State with any rejection by him needing Parliamentary consent. Although not part of the formal arrangements, the Secretary of State let it be known that he would not normally reject any pay agreement which fell within the inter-quartile range of pay settlements in the private sector. More controversially the arrangements included a facility for individual LEAs to opt out of national agreements and to make their own arrangements, subject to the approval of the Secretary of State for the first year only. Opting-out LEAs would be required only to consult with the unions locally - not to negotiate. It remained to be seen whether the new arrangements would be effective and would overcome some of the problems associated with the former Burnham committee.

Fred Jarvis, who had been general secretary of the NUT for 15 years and who had served the union full-time for 33 years, retired in September 1989. Fred's period in teachers' pay negotiations had been far from easy as his tenure of office had coincided with a harsh climate and the eventual demise of the Burnham committee apparatus. As LGE of October 1989 put it - "the employers will miss his unfailing courtesy and wit".

FURTHER EDUCATION

After nearly 18 months' frustrating stalemate on the 1987 further education pay talks, the eventual breakthrough to a negotiated settlement early in 1989 was sudden, bringing to an end the apparently interminable dispute. The lecturers finally realised that the employers would not drop the conditions of service strings despite industrial action, and that they had little alternative but to negotiate an agreement covering conditions as well as pay. The key to the settlement lay in extending the pay offer to two years. It was nevertheless a very long negotiation on 7th and 8th January 1989, with the outline package hammered out by 3.30am on 8th January and most of the final details tied up by 8.00pm that day. The NJC for lecturers in further

Children listening to the librarian in a mobile library.

education subsequently ratified the deal on 2nd February. The main features were (a) a two-year pay deal providing an overall increase of 16.9%; (b) the introduction of a system for averaging hours; (c) consolidation of maximum teaching hours for new appointments equal to or higher than existing levels; (d) more flexible application of salary scales; (e) improved service conditions for part-time staff; and (f) commitment in principle to the introduction of staff development and appraisal, with an extra working week available each year for this. It was the hope of the employers that the application locally of this complex package would have a profound effect on the cost effectiveness of the service over the next decade, although it was realised that, under the Education Bill then in progress, polytechnics and other institutions of higher education were due to be transferred out of local government in April 1989. An employer's commentary with detailed advice was issued by LACSAB to all education authorities. To back this up a series of five regional meetings was held in April 1989 to provide a forum for authorities to raise any issues relating to the agreement.

There were many difficulties in implementing the agreement on averaging of hours – with NATFHE pressing locally for restrictive arrangements felt to be contrary to the spirit and letter of the national agreement – and LEAs wanted these sorted out first before making any deal on further education pay from 1st April 1989. The lecturers claimed a flat rate increase of £3,400 (20% of average salary) in late January 1989 and the employers consulted authorities between then and Easter. A detailed offer was put to the unions on 7th April, the main components being a 5.3% increase on all salary points from 1st April 1989 and the whole deal conditional upon clarification of the previous year's agreement on "averaging" of teaching hours. A period of considerable uncertainty ensued stemming from several factors: one of these was the setting-up in April 1989 of new negotiating machinery outside the LACSAB umbrella to deal with the pay and conditions of staffs of polytechnics and higher education colleges, lecturers having been in scope of the JNC for further education until then. Another factor was the change of leadership of NATFHE where Peter Dawson, general secretary for ten years, was challenged, being eventually toppled and succeeded by Geoff Woolf. When negotiations resumed in September 1989 the employers offered to raise their original offer to reflect other pay movements that summer. But negotiations broke down on the key productivity issue of averaging, with NATFHE calling a one-day strike and a complete ban on any averaging of hours, support for which was however uneven and patchy. After extensive negotiations over two days in December the employers presented a substantially improved offer in an attempt to forestall an escalation of industrial action and damage to the further education service. This offer raised the increase on all scales from 5.3% to 8.0%, now to operate from 1st September 1989; introduced a £700 non-consolidated lump sum; proposed further talks on principals' pay and conditions; and provided clarification of the existing text of the "averaging" agreement. But NATFHE rejected this improved offer despite growing evidence of dissatisfaction among their members with this stance.

Fresh proposals emerged late on 1st March 1990 after many hours of conciliation talks under the auspices of ACAS. The main changes from the employers' December offer were increases of 8.5% from 1st April 1989 rising to 9.0% from 1st April 1990, replacing the 8.0% offer and £700 unconsolidated lump sums; and the employers' proposals on "averaging" of class context hours revised by reducing the weekly and termly limits. The unions balloted their members on this. They voted by a narrow margin to accept the improved offer arising from the ACAS talks, and settlement was finally reached on this basis at the meeting of the NJC on 5th April 1990. Two longer-term aspects of the agreement were the new pay review date to be 1st September 1990 and the scrapping of the system of pay rates being based on the grading of courses.

A quick settlement occurred in the NJC in June 1990 providing increases in all rates of 9.15% from 1st September 1990 – in very sharp contrast to the protracted wrangling of previous years.

Much of the time of the LACSAB education section in this period was taken up with examining the continuous flood of Government proposals and legislation on education reform, commenting on all the employment aspects, and – in conjunction with the LACSAB advisory division – providing much guidance on these to LEAs.

STAFFING AND PEOPLE

David Thomas clearly had a remit to effect organisational change and lost little time in tackling this. As he took over as LACSAB secretary on 10th September 1987 a new senior management group of the secretary and four under secretaries was established, which meant that LACSAB would operate without a deputy secretary for the first time for many years. Ken Clark and Geoff Roberts continued as under secretaries; Charles Nolda, who would co-ordinate negotiating activities, and Tim Rothwell, who would lead on the advisory function and take over superannuation work, joined them as under secretaries on promotion.

Ken Clark retired in April 1988, having joined LACSAB in 1973 as assistant secretary and been promoted under secretary in 1978: in latter years he had been responsible for negotiations for new towns, development agencies and airports and for the Board's internal administration. Charles Nolda and Tim Rothwell then took over his negotiating and internal administrative functions respectively.

Further changes then took place on 1st January 1989 on Geoff Kelly's retirement after a stint of 23 years at Belgrave Square: he came in 1965 as LACSAB were brought into teachers' pay and had also handled residential staffs, chief executives, chief officers and police before taking over in 1974 as assistant secretary for the APT&C group. Charles Nolda then took over direct charge of negotiations for APT&C, manual and craft workers, while Derek Lodge moved over from assistant secretary, manual and craft workers, to take over negotiations for chief executives, chief officers, new towns and development agencies, as well as leading in all advisory work on job evaluation and grading matters. Marcia Barton and Gordon Thomson continued as assistant secretaries for the Home Office and research/information groups respectively.

All these changes reduced the management team from ten to eight and at the same time provided scope for developing the responsibilities of senior staff below management team level.

In his report to the LACSAB Board meeting in January 1989 the secretary commented on the changing patterns of work within the LACSAB secretariat arising from the employers' strategy debate and financial reviews. He also reported that his revised management structure had become fully effective from 1st January 1989.

On top of all the uncertainties facing LACSAB staff in this period, the LACSAB Board added yet another dimension when at their meeting in October 1988 they decided to look at the possibility of unlocking the property assets at 41 and 38 Belgrave Square. This decision seemed difficult to reconcile with the fact of the long lease for 41 Belgrave Square extending to the year 2043 at a fixed rent of £400 per annum and with total LACSAB office costs coming out at just over £8 per square foot. Fortunately the LACSAB Board quickly followed professional advice in January 1989 against pursuing alternative office accommodation.

Ceri Thomas, who had been editor of LGM for many years and had done much to improve it, left LACSAB in the summer of 1987 after a period on secondment to Templeton College, Oxford. Helen Pott, perhaps the best-known person in the provincial employers' network, retired in August 1988: Helen (who never let anyone remain in ignorance of where whitleyism began in local government) had been appointed secretary to Stanley Eaton, North Western provincial employers' secretary, in 1953, succeeding him in that job some 20 years later. It was a great shock to learn of the death in October 1989 of Alun Gronow, secretary of the AMA: prior to his time at the AMA, Alun had served at LACSAB between 1978 and 1981, first as assistant secretary and then as under secretary, dealing mainly with teacher pay negotiations. Laurence Welsh, editor of LGE from 1975 to 1983 died in December 1989 at the age of 96: he had been in local government all his working life (with the former London County Council) and, prior to being LGE editor, had been associated with it and its predecessor, "News Summary", as a contributor and production journalist. Derek Bass, LACSAB assistant secretary from 1950 until his ill-health retirement in 1973, died in November 1990. 1990 also saw the deaths both of Lord Morris, first chairman of the LGTB and before that of the Local Government Examinations Board, and then of Lord Ponsonby, who had been LGTB chairman since 1981.

LACSAB lost a most distinguished and effective chairman when Councillor Tony Prendergast retired in October 1989 after six and a half years in which he had guided LACSAB through a period of great change as the emphasis shifted significantly away from the traditional joint bargaining responsibilities. Tony Prendergast was chairman of the JNCs for both chief executives and chief officers and had served on the employers' side of the manual workers' NJC. His open-mindedness and shrewd common sense earned him the respect of members from all shades of political opinion and of trade union leaders. His departure was caused by the decision of his local authority, Westminster City Council, to withdraw from the AMA, whom he represented on the LACSAB Board.

Councillor Sid Dennett, South Western provincial employers and APT&C employers, was appointed chairman of LACSAB to succeed Tony Prendergast in October 1989, having previously been LACSAB vice-chairman for many years since 1973. Councillor John Toft, ACC and manual workers' employers, was subsequently appointed LACSAB vice-chairman to succeed Sid Dennett.

LACSAB lost the services of a valuable and experienced senior officer in

February 1990 when Marcia Barton accepted an appointment to the newly-created post of general secretary of the Association of Chief Police Officers (ACPO). Marcia had joined LACSAB in 1970 and had become widely known especially during her spell on the APT&C section. In April 1986 she was promoted assistant secretary in charge of the Home Office section covering the police and fire services and magistrates' courts staffs. Mike Cann was appointed assistant secretary in charge of the Home Office section to succeed Marcia Barton, and at the same time Mike Walker was also appointed assistant secretary, in his case to fill the vacancy as head of the education section.

In his report for the LACSAB Board meeting on 22nd October 1990, the secretary, David Thomas, was able to report that staff at all levels were co-operating in the significant amount of work involved in ensuring that the merger with the LGTB and the formation of the new LGMB would go ahead smoothly. Although staff representatives were being consulted on all the staffing implications, some uncertainty and apprehension remained. The decisions to transfer all staff to the new Board and to defer questions of office location had obviously helped. He was pleased to inform the Board that members of the LACSAB management team had been appointed to senior posts with LGMB as follows (Michael Clarke, LGTB, having been appointed chief executive):-

Charles Nolda - Director of Negotiations
Tim Rothwell - Director of Human Resources
Gordon Thomson - Head of Employment & Survey Research
Mike Cann - Assistant Employers' Secretary (Home Office)
Mike Walker - Assistant Employers' Secretary (Education)

An important decision of the new LGMB was that in future the Director of Negotiations (Charles Nolda) should be designated as employers' and joint secretary to inhibit the trade unions from seeking to get beyond and behind the LGMB's senior paid negotiator. At the same time the Director of Human Resourse Issues (Tim Rothwell) was designated secretary to the UK Steering Committee (UKSC) on superannuation. Both appointments taking effect from 1st April 1991 were being drawn to the attention of the bodies concerned with an assurance that the LGMB would continue to provide the full range of services hitherto provided by LACSAB. This demonstrated the important fact that, although LACSAB might be ceasing to exist as a separate entity, its work and the services it had provided to local government over many years would continue.

Derek Lodge, assistant secretary in charge of negotiations for chief executives, chief officers, new towns and development agencies and responsible for advisory work on job evaluation, resigned towards the end of 1990 to take an appointment with Hay Management Consultants. Derek, who joined LACSAB in 1974, will best be remembered for his stint in charge of manual workers' negotiations - especially his part in the marathon exercise in the mid-1980s. Geoff Roberts requested early retirement as from April 1991 but was offered a part-time appointment with the new LGMB. Geoff, who also joined the LACSAB staff in 1974, in his case as assistant secretary with promotion in 1978 to under secretary with overall responsibility for the Board's research and information services, did much to enhance LACSAB's reputation in the development of manpower and salary information for local government.

This book, having included brief pen-pictures of former LACSAB secretaries who have had much influence on its destiny, would be incomplete without a similar note on David Thomas, LACSAB secretary since 1987. David's distinguished career had spanned a wide variety of posts in local government and its national bodies; his great absorbing interest had been in the development of personnel management in local government; and it seemed entirely appropriate that he should be appointed LACSAB secretary in 1987 and to be at the helm as LACSAB then faced a period of extensive change. Having established an agenda for dynamic change to face the different tasks ahead in the 1990s through the LACSAB strategy debate he had initiated, he must have been disappointed not to have been able to see it through to full fruition when a review body recommended the cessation of LACSAB's separate existence and its merger with the LGTB (ironically after the review body with the actual remit to look at LACSAB had seen a healthy future for the Board).

David Thomas had joined the staff of Surrey County Council (a popular training ground for future LACSAB officers) on leaving school and served there for many years before spending six years at LACSAB in the 1960s (on APT&C and very much involved in the major restructuring of 1966). He worked for a short spell at the LGTB before returning to a senior personnel post with the Surrey County Council where he eventually became chief personnel officer. It was at this stage that he was very active in forming the Society of Chief Personnel Officers (SOCPO) becoming its founder president in 1975. He then went to the AMA as under secretary for manpower matters before rejoining LACSAB on his appointment as deputy secretary in 1981. This background was acknowledged as ideal by the headhunter appointed by the LACSAB Board to advise them on a successor for Brian Rusbridge in 1987. Like his earlier chief, Sir Reginald Griffiths, who he much admired, David was always keenly interested in the chemistry of any meeting as well as the issues, recognising always the importance of the human dimension. He was always keen to participate in the influencing of people and events, and it seemed to many a pity that his experience should be lost to local government and industrial relations when he decided to retire after 40 years' service in local government upon the merger of LACSAB and the LGTB on 1st April 1991.

CONCLUSION

Although this last (but not final) chapter comes to an end as LACSAB loses its separate identity, in many ways there is no actual conclusion as the work in all its spheres of activities on behalf of all local authorities up and down the country continues unabated, albeit as from 1st April 1991 under the auspices of the new Local Government Management Board.

FOOTNOTE

This book has been more than an historical record of one organisation. True it has traced the activities of LACSAB over more than 40 years and shown the key role it has played. There can be little doubt either that LACSAB developed a personality of its own over that period and was held in some esteem, not just in local government but also in the wider world of industrial relations. But this commentary on LACSAB's work has of necessity been set in the context of developments in personnel management and industrial relations elsewhere and the changes that have taken place in the social and economic life of the nation. We hope therefore that the book will be seen not only as a record of the past, but also as a reminder of the importance of local authorities and their staffs working together in the interests of local government and the public it serves.

The book has been completed during a time of great change. Local government is facing many challenges and is experimenting with new ways of ensuring that effective services can be delivered to the public. LACSAB itself is about to merge with the Local Government Training Board to form the new Local Government Management Board – thus bringing together in one organisation oversight of the total approach to human resource issues in what is still one of the largest sectors of employment.

Traditional approaches to management, pay determination and industrial relations are being questioned. But change is not an unknown phenomenon in local government. The chapters of this book illustrate very well the tremendous changes that have taken place within LACSAB and its sphere of influence over the years.

After initiating and following through the Employers' Strategy debate in 1987/88, and having responded in a positive way to the outcome of the financial review a year later, those close to LACSAB were perhaps entitled to expect a period of stability. But before the dust had settled the more significant reorganisation, which was to see the end of LACSAB as a separate entity, was being pushed through. At one key meeting to discuss this, Douglas Wynn, then one of the Vice-Chairmen of the APT&C Employers, slipped a piece of paper across the table to me with this quote on it –

> "We trained hard, but it seemed that every time we were beginning to form up into teams, we would be reorganised. I was to learn later in life that we tend to meet any situation by reorganisation, and a wonderful method it can be for creating the illusion of progress, while producing confusion, inefficiency and demoralisation."
>
> [Caius Petronius AD66]

There is a simple undeniable logic in local government having a single national organisation to oversee its approach to management and human resource policies. Most of the initial apprehension about the merger was caused, not by doubts about the main objective, but by a perception that it had more to do with a redistribution of power between the existing organisations involved. The new Management Board provides a unique opportunity for local government to work together. It is essential that sectional interests should take second place to the corporate needs of local government. Given their misgivings it is a tribute to all the members and officers associated with LACSAB that they have worked so hard to ensure that the new organisation is a success and can make genuine improvements in the service provided to local authorities without, one hopes, sacrificing the best of what has gone before.

Undoubtedly further changes in organisation and approach will be necessary in all aspects of local government, but the *way* we do things needs to be distinguished from the *principles* that should guide our approach.

If LACSAB has had a guiding principle over the years, it has been to observe the better features of Whitleyism. That expression has been defined and redefined over the years but, in LACSAB's Employers' Strategy Debate, Whitleyism was accepted as meaning that, as far as possible, employers and employees should seek to reach joint agreement on pay and other conditions of service; that the complexity of modern day employment structures makes it necessary for representatives of employers to negotiate with representatives of the employees; that collective bargaining should be conducted within an agreed framework at national, regional and local level; that there needs to be a "long stop" arrangement for conciliation or arbitration; and that both parties should take responsibility for seeking to resolve problems peacefully by negotiation and for honouring agreements.

Regard for those principles - however implemented - is one of the responsibilities handed by LACSAB to the Local Government Management Board. Those principles become even more important when set in the context of a more strategic approach to human resource management in local government.

I salute everyone associated with LACSAB over the past 43 years and wish those concerned with the new Management Board every success.

David Thomas
January 1991.

INDEX

(Incorporating Glossary of Abbreviations and Acronyms)